eTPU Programming Made Easy

*Introduction to the Freescale
Enhanced Time Processor Unit*

by

Munir Bannoura & Margaret Frances

AMT Publishing

eTPU Programming Made Easy

Introduction to the Freescale
Enhanced Time Processor Unit

Published
by
AMT Publishing
Farmington Hills, Michigan
www.amtpublishing.com

First Edition

Printed in the United States of America
ISBN 0-9762973-1-0

About the Authors

Munir Bannoura graduated in 1974 with a bachelor's degree of science. He immediately joined Burroughs Corporation as product engineer, working for the corporation in both Michigan and Scotland. In 1978, he became Professor of Electrical Engineering at the National Institute of Electricity and Electronics in Algeria. He joined Motorola Technical Training Operations in 1984 as a customer trainer and course developer. He travels all over the world to train customers on Freescale Semiconductor's advanced microprocessor and microcontroller product lines. Munir has written a book with Amy Dyson on how to microcode the Time Processor Unit titled "TPU Microcoding for Beginners" and a second book with Richard Soja titled "MPC5554 Revealed". Munir lives in Farmington Hills, Michigan, with his wife Sharlene.

Margaret Frances received her master's degree in computer science from the University of Minnesota in 1996. Since that time she has served as project manager and business analyst in software development in various industries including telecommunications and security. Margaret came to understand and appreciate the eTPU after joining her brother Andy Klumpp at ASH WARE Inc., as a contractor in 2003. In that capacity she helped to write the eTPU programming course, which is offered jointly by Freescale Semiconductor and ASH WARE. It was through that project that she and Munir met, after which Munir asked her to co-author this book. Margaret lives in Leeds, England, with her husband Bryan Frances and their two children, Julia and Alec.

Acknowledgements

The authors would like to thank Freescale Semiconductor for endorsing this book, with a special thanks to Bob Smith for his support. Some of the materials in Chapter 1, including figures and tables, came from an eTPU presentation written by Mike Pauwells and Jeff Loeliger.

Thanks to Richard Soja for his superb editing of this book as well as for his chapter on channel hardware details. We also like to thank the eTPU designer, Celso Brites, for his help by answering frequent questions while the book is being written.

Thanks to Ming Li for his help with the angle clock lab and Salim Momin for allowing us to use his host interface application notes written by Ming Li as an appendix.

Thanks to Walter Banks of Byte Craft Limited for allowing us to include the eTPU_C Compiler with the book. Thanks to Kirk Zurell, also from Byte Craft Limited, for his chapter on the installation and use of the eTPU_C Compiler.

Many of the examples in Part I of this book were written by Andy Klumpp of ASH WARE Inc. Thanks also to him for allowing us to include a training version of the eTPU Stand-Alone Simulator with the book.

Many thanks to Matthew Conklin for his art work and imagination in creating the book cover.

Dedication

To my wife Sharlene for being so understanding and not asking me to take her out to dinner or to a movie during my busy time writing this book. To my parents and my children, Daniel and Christopher, my brothers and sisters and their families. Thanks to my son Christopher and his darling wife Marisol for the work and help on the AMT Publishing website.

~ Munir

To Andy, for taking a chance in the first place; Munir, for asking me to write this book, and Sharlene and Marisol, for providing energy to do so; my parents Sue and Allan, who have always believed in me; Gabrielle, for more than twenty years of glorious friendship; and my children Julia and Alec, who didn't give a damn about this project. And most especially for Bryan, who makes everything wonderful.

~ Margaret

Preface

Those who are familiar with Freescale Semiconductor's Time Processor Unit (TPU) and TPU microcoding will have little difficulty coming to understand the workings of the Enhanced Time Processor Unit (eTPU) and how to code it. While there are of course functional, hardware, and memory enhancements in the eTPU over the TPU, and therefore new things to learn, it is also true that sophisticated compilation and simulation tools are available for this new timer system, allowing the coder to safely forget (if he or she wishes!) many of the complexities of the internal machinery of this engine. In particular, rather than laboriously writing assembly-level microcode, the coder can program the eTPU in "C."

If you are already familiar with the TPU, you may wish to concentrate first on coming up to speed with the eTPU's 32-channels and dual-action-unit hardware, its 13 channel modes, increased memory, and shared parameter RAM (SPRAM), its shared code memory (SCM), and of course its new angle clock hardware. With these topics behind you, you can move with facility into the new world of programming the eTPU using the old standby, "C."

But if you are unfamiliar with the TPU altogether, then you will need to learn the eTPU from scratch. Fortunately your task is easier than it would have been in learning the TPU 15 years ago, when it first arrived on the scene. With the eTPU, much is hidden from you primarily because the newer tools allow you to concentrate on algorithm construction and implementation rather than the language used to do these things.

This book has been written with both audiences in mind. Part I dives (almost) immediately into eTPU programming itself. Introducing eTPU concepts on an as-needed basis, Part I provides a problem-based approach to learning to code the eTPU. You will gradually come to learn the eTPU as you go. Part II provides a complete and detailed explanation of all aspects of the eTPU. Readers who want a full understanding of the eTPU itself before learning to program it, or who wish to gain quick insight into certain portions of the eTPU, can consult the second part of this book first or in tandem with Part I. In short, we hope that this dual-part approach will cater to almost all backgrounds (understanding "C" is a pre-requisite) and all learning styles—peruse the book in the order in which it makes the most sense to you.

The book is organized as follows, with chapters one through six constituting Part I and chapters seven through twelve constituting Part II:

Chapter 1. Introduction to the eTPU offers an overview of the eTPU and provides a basic comparison between the previous TPU implemented on the M68000 and MPC500.

Chapter 2. Understanding Channel Hardware introduces basic concepts of channel operation and provides simple program examples written in the "C" language using the Byte Craft Limited eTPU_C Compiler and the ASH WARE eTPU Stand-Alone Simulator.

Chapter 3. Programming Channel Hardware provides a moderately detailed discussion of channel match and transition events.

Chapter 4. Handling Events covers how and when a channel request service from the eTPU engine. It briefly discusses the entry table and eTPU code threads.

Chapter 5. Moving to Two Action Units introduces the eTPU's dual-action unit and explains how a channel can handle two matches and two captures.

Chapter 6. Moving to Multiple Channels introduces the concept of inter-channel communication through linking. It also addresses function assignment to channels with real-time function examples that can be tested with the tools provided in this book.

Chapter 7. Host Interface introduces the host interface which allows for the configuration of the eTPU engine. Step-by-step instructions are provided to download, configure global registers, initialize the channel and function, and start channel operation.

Chapter 8. Engine Architecture and Programming Model provides a detailed description of the eTPU engine architecture and programming model, including a description of each engine register and its operation. The arithmetic unit (ALU), the multiply-divide unit (MDU), and the internal buses are also covered in detail. The chapter also shows examples of how to access these resources with the arithmetic unit microoperation.

Chapter 9. Channel Hardware and Modes is the most hardware-intensive chapter, showing details of channel resources and how to configure a channel with one of the 13 different modes available. After reading this chapter, you will understand and appreciate the power and the flexibility of the eTPU channels.

Chapter 10. Clocking and Angle Clock introduces the eTPU angle clock hardware and the shared time and counter bus (STAC) clocking and operation. It includes a real-world example using the angle clock to control engine operation with simple code snippets.

Chapter 11. Threads and the Entry Table offers an in-depth description of threads and how the eTPU's two entry table encoding schemes are used for thread execution.

Chapter 12. The Scheduler describes the eTPU scheduler, service requests handling, and prioritization of channels. It also covers in detail how to calculate and analyze channel worst case latency service time.

Appendix A. Byte Craft Limited's eTPU_C Compiler describes how to install and use Byte Craft Limited's eTPU_C Compiler, a demonstration version of which accompanies this book. The appendix goes into some detail on the standard header files distributed with the compiler.

Appendix B. ASH WARE's eTPU Stand-Alone Simulator covers the installation and use of ASH WARE Inc.'s eTPU Stand-Alone Simulator, a demonstration version of which also accompanies this book.

Appendix C. Installing and Running the Labs does exactly as its name suggests.

Appendix D. Freescale Semiconductor's RAppID describes Freescale Semiconductor's RAppID. A demonstration version of this software also is included with this book.

Appendix E. eTPU Programming Application Note offers design information that will help programmers writer superior eTPU functions that avoid common pitfalls.

Appendix F. Host Interface Application Note shows how to build the host interface to access eTPU functions and provides detailed code examples.

Appendix G. Microinstruction Formats discusses the eTPU microinstruction formats and provides detailed information about ALU/MDU and flow control microinstructions.

Appendix H. Registers Glossary provides detailed information on all eTPU registers and register fields, as well as the instruction fields used to program them.

Appendix I. General Glossary is a dictionary of eTPU-specific terms.

About the Tools

This book includes a CDROM that contains software you need to complete a small programing project. The software comprises a demonstration version of the eTPU_C Compiler from Byte Craft Limited, a training version of ASH WARE's eTPU Stand-Alone Simulator, sample files so you can rapidly gain confidence using the tools, and the RAppID code initialization tool from Freescale Semiconductor.

Byte Craft Limited has provided written permission to AMT Publishing to distribute a training version of the eTPU_C Compiler and its user manual. The eTPU_C Compiler runs under MSDOS (or an MSDOS window under Windows®). Byte Craft can be reached at www.bytecraft.com.

ASH WARE Inc. has provided written permission to AMT Publishing to distribute a training version of the eTPU Stand-Alone Simulator and its user manual. This training version includes all features but is limited in the number of functions and the total number of instructions that it can load. The eTPU Stand-Alone Simulator runs on Windows® XP, 2000, NT 4.0, 98, 95 and ME. A fully functional version of the eTPU Stand-Alone Simulator may be purchased directly from ASH WARE, which can be reached at www.ashware.com.

Offering a quick and easy way to generate host code, the RAppID code initialization tool from Freescale Semiconductor is also included with this book.

For Further Information

To order more books or for book updates, contact AMT Publishing at www.amtpublishing.com.

For information about ordering the eTPU_C Compiler or other Byte Craft Limited products, contact Byte Craft Limited at www.bytecraft.com or 519-888-6911. The *eTPU_C Compiler User's Manual* is also available directly from Byte Craft Limited.

For information about ordering the eTPU Stand-Alone Simulator or other ASH WARE products, contact ASH WARE at www.ashware.com or 503-533-0271.

Further information about RAppID Code Generation Tools, can be obtained from Freescale Semiconductor at www.freescalesemiconductor.com.

The *eTPU Reference Manual* is available directly from Freescale Semiconductor.

Two eTPU application notes have been included with this book. Other applications notes are being planned. Details about upcoming and revised application notes can be obtained by contacting Freescale Semiconductor directly.

Information on eTPU programming courses as well as training courses on eTPU-based microcontrollers can be obtained from Freescale Semiconductor. Click on the Support link at www.freescale.com.

A public resource Web site for all parties interested in the eTPU and eTPU programming is maintained by the eTPU community and available at www.etpu.com.

Byte Craft Limited also maintains a web page with frequently asked questions (FAQs) which can be a valuable resource for eTPU users. This page can be found at www.byte-craft.com/public/etpuc/downloads/etpuc_faq.chm.

Table of Contents

Appendices

Part I

CHAPTER 1 *Introduction to the eTPU*

What Is the eTPU?

In order to answer this question adequately, we need to answer a prior question: what is the TPU, on which the eTPU is founded?

Microcontrollers have been called "the gadget collectors of the semiconductor world."[1] Packed with peripherals—serial and parallel input and output ports, memory management units, timers, interrupt controllers, flash, to name just a few—microcontrollers, at least through the 1980s, were overworking their CPU. Timers, in particular, were egregious CPU hogs. Some applications could use more than 70% of available CPU bandwidth to perform time management tasks. In fact, the number-one constraint of microcontrollers had been their inability to effectively perform high-speed timing tasks. The Time Processor Unit (TPU), introduced in 1989, was designed to solve this problem by offloading timing tasks from the CPU.

Found on MPC500, M68300 and M68HC16 microcontroller families, the TPU is an intelligent, semi-autonomous co-processor. A key feature of the TPU is a RISC-like engine that is tightly coupled to a set of I/O hardware timing channels. Since the TPU engine services all channel events, it can execute high-speed and complex timing tasks with little or no CPU intervention. The TPU operates in parallel with the host CPU, processing instructions and real-time input events, performing output waveform generation, and accessing

1. Amy Dyson and Munir Bannoura, "TPU Microcoding for Beginners," p.1.

shared data without host intervention. For timing tasks themselves, service latency is reduced because the TPU is optimized to interface with channel hardware and timer registers.

The TPU, one of the most successful peripheral devices ever put on a microntroller, is now available in triplicate on some chips. The same device controls automobile and airplane engines, transmissions, printers, induction motors, robots, and so on. By 2006, the TPU will run on a majority of the world's engines. Despite these successes, the TPU has had some limitations. These limitations have been addressed with the introduction of the Enhanced Time Processor Unit (eTPU), an improved and expanded version of the TPU. Available in 2004 on Freescale Semiconductor's MPC5500 and MCF5232 microcontroller lines, the eTPU is slated for inclusion on many additional lines.

What's New in the eTPU?

In the years since the TPU was first introduced, programmers have found certain challenges in microcoding the TPU, an activity that required fairly extensive proficiency in assembly programming. Additionally, as the TPU market expanded, the need for a faster and larger processor became clear. The eTPU resolves a number of these issues, as described in Table 1.1.

TPU Challenge	*eTPU Response*
Some timing requirements could not be met by the TPU.	*Introduced double-action channel hardware; increased time-base width from 16 to 24 bit; doubled number of channels from 16 to 32.*
Interface requirements were becoming more complex.	*More flexible parameter RAM; increased parameter RAM from 256 bytes up to 8Kbytes.*

Note: In the MPC5554 Implementation the shared code memory is 16K and the shared parameter RAM is 3K.

TPU Challenge	*eTPU Response*
Microengine too simple for complex applications.	*Added multiply/divide, logical and boolean operations; added angle clock hardware (for automotive and motion control applications); increased code memory from 8 Kbytes to a maximum of 64Kbytes.*
Code development was awkward and complicated.	*Provided "C" language compiler; introduced new higher-level tools for automatic code generation and improved structured programming.*

Table 1.1 eTPU Answers the Call

Introduction to eTPU Engine Hardware and Memory

Figure 1.1 shows the basic block diagram of an eTPU. (Note that because the MPC5500 family is initially targeted for automotive powertrain applications that require a large number of timing channels, some of the Freescale Semiconductor MPC5500 microcontroller implementations have two eTPUs.)

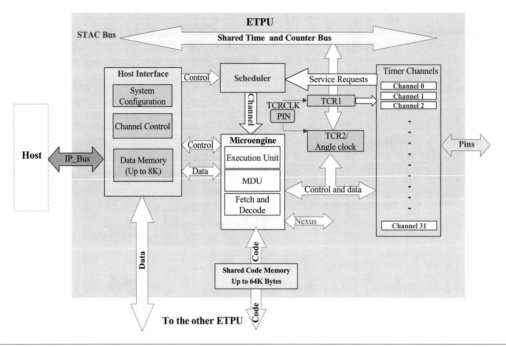

Figure 1.1 High-Level eTPU Engine Block Diagram

In brief:

- The host interface contains a set of global registers for system configuration. It also includes a set of control and status registers for initialization and channel status reporting.

- Thirty-two independent, orthogonal channels, each of which may implement a particular eTPU function. Each eTPU channel is general purpose and can run any eTPU function. (Although channel 0 behaves like any other channel, when angle mode is selected it connects to angle logic and offers additional capabilities which will be covered in *Chapter 10. Clocking and Angle Clock*.)

- A hardware scheduler assigns a service time-slot to each waiting channel, ensuring that all requests are acknowledged and serviced in a precisely controlled manner.

- The execution unit executes instructions to access parameter RAM; to configure channel hardware; to read timer values; and to perform arithmetic operations such as multiply, multiply and accumulate, and divide. It is also capable of performing logical operations and conditional branches based on a large number of flag settings. The parallelism of the architecture allows many operations to be performed in the same instruction cycle.

- Two timer count registers (**TCR1** and **TCR2**) provide two time bases and may be shared by all microengine channels. There are multiple options available for clocking the two counters: An external pin, **TCRCLK**, allows an external clock signal to clock either or both counters or to gate the internal clock to TCR2. The system clock prescaled by a programmable value can also be used to increment the counters. For applications that require a common time base shared between all timers in a multi-timer system implementation, an eTPU engine can provide angle or time information to all other timers on the MPC5500 family on the shared time and counter (STAC) bus.

- Triple-access parameter RAM (from 2.5K to 3K, expandable to 8K, bytes) is shared by the microengine(s) and the host CPU. This allows the CPU to access, control, and communicate with each eTPU channel. In a two-engine implementation, parameter passing between the two eTPUs provides a convenient communication mechanism without having to involve the host.

- Current MPC5500 microcontrollers contain a range of 10K to 16K (expandable to 64K) bytes of shared code memory (SCM) implemented as read/write memory for host CPU accesses, and read-only (instruction fetch) memory for the eTPU(s). This allows application software to copy eTPU functions developed for a particular application from flash memory to the SCM upon system start-up. When at least one eTPU is enabled, the SCM becomes an eTPU resource and no longer accessible to the host CPU. Any attempt by the host to access the SCM while the eTPU is enabled causes a machine check exception.

Introduction to Channel Hardware

The timer channel hardware handles match and transition events according to control information programmed by the microengine. Match and transition events are the building blocks for all eTPU functions. You'll use them to create waveforms, measure frequency, etc.

Figure 1.2 shows a (very) high-level schematic of the eTPU's channel hardware. In broad terms, each channel contains two match registers, two capture registers, and an input/output signal. (Each channel pin is programmed to be either input or output; in some MPC5500 family derivatives, a channel's input and output signal paths may be routed to separate pins, which allows that channel to perform simultaneous input and output functions.) Match registers are used to establish a certain time at which some action, such as generating an output pin edge, is to be taken. Capture registers are used to save the time at which the signal changes on the input pin (i.e., a transition) and/or the time at which a match occurs. The output pin can be programmed to transition on the basis of some input event (a certain time reached on one of the two time bases, or a certain change on the input pin).

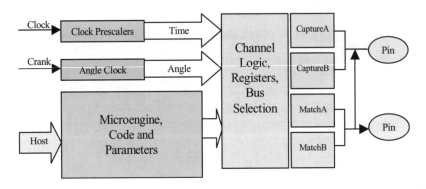

Figure 1.2 eTPU Channel, Conceptual Diagram

Having two match registers and two capture registers allows each channel to run double-action operations. Double-action support allows a channel to capture two transitions when configured for an input function, or to generate two match events when configured for output function, before that channel's eTPU function code has to respond. For example, we may want to know the exact times that the input pin transitions from high to low and then from low to high. With two capture registers, the channel hardware can remember both transition times. After the occurrence of the second transition, a service request can be signaled to the scheduler which in turn informs the eTPU engine that the channel should be serviced to handle both transitions. As another example, two matches can be scheduled on a given channel to drive the pin to one level on the first match and drive it to the opposite level on the second match, both before the eTPU function code has to respond.

Channel timing is derived from one or two timer count registers, **TCR1** and **TCR2**, both of which are available to all channels on the engine. Application software chooses the clock rate of the **TCRs** by programming certain control registers, while eTPU code determines for a given channel which time base to use for matches and which to use for captures (note that one time base may be used for matches and the other time base for captures). For example, **TCR1** can be used to provide time information, and **TCR2** can be used to provide angle information for the channels.

How Does the eTPU Work?

Briefly, each of the eTPU channels may be assigned a function, such as PWM, upon system initialization. (Note that a single function may be assigned to multiple channels. Further, a given channel might not be assigned any function to run.) Also upon system initialization, the software assigns a priority level to each utilized channel. The priority scheme gives frequent service to high-priority channels and lesser service time to low-priority channels. The channels contend with one another to be serviced; the scheduler determines which channel is to be serviced next, and passes that channel number to the microengine. The microengine services each request by executing a discrete (programmer-defined) portion of that channel's function, and then moves on to handle the next service request (which could be from the same channel or a different one) as specified by the scheduler. The eTPU implements a non-preemptive strategy in executing each service request: no other channel may pre-empt the servicing of a particular request.[2]

Application designers may program the eTPU to execute a wide range of simple and complex I/O timing tasks to meet their specific needs. For example, channels can be programmed to output pulses that are referenced to permutations of angle and time domains. Channels may be also used to count and measure complex input events. Input and output events can be made dependent on each other if desired.

Because of the vast number of applications that will be using the eTPU, Freescale Semiconductor will have a library of eTPU functions available for download by customers free of charge. The library will satisfy the requirements of some, though not all, of these applications. The eTPU_C Compiler from Byte Craft Limited (www.bytecraft.com) and the eTPU Stand-Alone Simulator from ASH WARE Inc. (www.ashware.com) are powerful tools that allow system designers to quickly develop application-specific eTPU functions in a high-level language. Lab exercises, which are provided with most chapters in the book, use these compilation and simulation tools. For the reader's convenience, this book is equipped with a CDROM that contains demonstration versions of these two tools, allowing the reader to start developing code immediately. For additional information on installing and using these tools, refer to appendices A through D.

---

2. Note that the host can force the current thread execution to end immediately by setting the force end (**FEND**) bit in the eTPU engine configuration register (**ETPUECR**).

CHAPTER 2

Understanding Channel Hardware

As mentioned earlier, each channel's pin can be configured as an input or output signal. The input signal is typically applied to the channel pin either from a sensor that monitors the occurrence of asynchronous events such as crank shaft tooth signals or from a slotted encoder that allows application software to determine angular or motor position. When the pin is configured as an output, its action is controlled by scheduling synchronous events to occur in the future. Typically, these events are output transitions that may be one-shot pulses or continuous pulses that can be used to control a particular target application such as Servo motors, a switch, stepper motors, sparks, fuel injectors, etc.

Because the eTPU channel is 100% programmable, it can be used to perform relatively simple timing tasks or extremely complex ones, in order to meet application requirements. In Part I of this book, we begin our discussion with simple examples and slowly progress to more complex, real application examples. This chapter provides a code-centric introduction to channel hardware concepts. The four examples provided in this chapter gradually introduce the reader to the concepts required to effectively control the output pin and read the input pin.

Toggling a Pin

The eTPU "C" code in Example 2.1 toggles an output pin.

```
#include <etpuc.h>

#pragma entryaddr 0x00;          // Set entry table base address,
                                 // a concept discussed in chapter 7
#pragma ETPU_function TogglePin; // TogglePin function declaration

void TogglePin () {              // Start of TogglePin function definition
    if (hsr == 3) {              // If a call from the CPU (i.e., a host
                                 // service request) of a particular type
                                 // (in this case, 3) arrives, then....
        pin = pin_high;          // Force the output pin high
        pin = pin_low;           // Force the output pin low
    }

    else {}                      // Handle any errors and unsupported
                                 // service requests
}

void main (void) {}              // The "C" language requires a main function
                                 // but eTPU code will not use it
```

Example 2.1 Code to Toggle a Pin

This code is complete and fully functional (assuming the etpuc.h header file is included).[1]
It executes on the eTPU and generates the waveform shown in Figure 2.1.

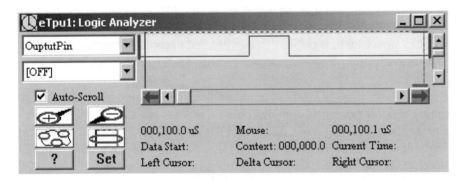

Figure 2.1 Our First Pulse

The logic analyzer window in Figure 2.1 is from ASH WARE's eTPU Stand-Alone Simulator. It shows an output pin going up and then back down, and that's it. As you might

---

1. The etpuc.h header file, written by Walter Banks from Byte Craft Limited and included with the eTPU_C
   Compiler, provides a series of defines that translate low-level register names and values to human-readable
   names and values. Two other header files are also included with the eTPU_C Compiler: etpuc_common.h
   and etpuc_util.h. See *Appendix A. Byte Craft Limited's eTPU_C Compiler* for details on using these
   header files and/or creating your own.

imagine, these two pin transitions correspond, respectively, to `pin = pin_high` and `pin= pin_low`.

Unfortunately, there is a severe limitation to the above code and waveform, which is that the pin movements occur at indeterminate times. To correct this problem, we will need to introduce the concept of eTPU time.

Introducing the eTPU Concept of Time

In the eTPU, time is represented as a 24-bit number. The eTPU engine contains two registers that serve as counters, or time bases: timer count register 1 (**TCR1**) and time counter register 2 (**TCR2**). Either of these two counters can be used as a time base for a channel to schedule an event in the future (among other things). For instance, to set a pin high 100 counter "ticks" in the future, based on **TCR1**, you would do the following:

1. Read the current time from **TCR1**;
2. Add 100 to this value;
3. Schedule the pin to go high at 100 **TCR1** ticks from current time.

This description is fairly imprecise; to make it more rigorous we need to introduce a couple of additional registers. First is the **Match** register. Each channel (remember that there are 32 channels in an eTPU engine) has two **Match** registers, **MatchA** and **MatchB**. A match register allows for some action to occur at a specific time (namely, the match time). A match register contains a match value, against which the **TCR** value is continuously compared. As soon as the **TCR** increments to the value in the **Match** register, a match occurs, resulting in some event or events (whatever has been programmed to occur as a result of a match).[2]

Next we need to introduce the event register temporary, or **ERT**. **ERT_A** and **ERT_B** are engine-wide (*not* merely channel-wide) registers that are implemented to ensure correct, coherent operation between the microengine and the channel hardware. The eTPU code is effectively asynchronous to the channel hardware and the **ERT** registers provide the syn-

---

2.Things are in fact a bit more complicated than this. Whether a match occurs and/or is actually recognized depends on a complex series of conditions related to a number of other registers (**IPAC**, **MEF**, **MRLE**, **MRL_A**, **MRL_B**, **TDL**, and **MTD**). The details of this are fleshed out in *Chapter 9. Channel Hardware and Modes.*

chronization needed to pass time values between the code executed by the microengine and the channel hardware. The **ERT** registers serve multiple purposes: in this case we need to use an **ERT** register because it's the only register from which a write can be made to the **Match** register. More precisely, **MatchA** may be populated only with contents of **ERT_A**; and **MatchB** with **ERT_B**.

The code we will write must support the facts that the contents of the **Match** register will be measured against the time base (either **TCR1** or **TCR2**) and the **Match** register will be loaded with the contents of the corresponding **ERT** register. See Figure 2.2.

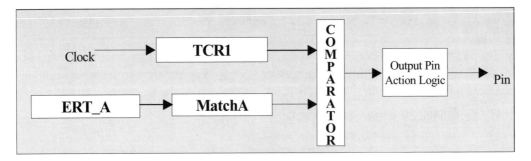

Figure 2.2 Setting Up for a Match

The sequence of events to set the pin high at a specific future time is as follows:

1. Get an initial count (**TCR1** current value in this case);

2. Calculate the desired future count against which the future action will be scheduled, and place the result into the **ERT_A** register;

3. Select the time base to use **TCR1** (as opposed to **TCR2**) for matches and to match on "equal to."[3] There is a single instruction that allows us to do these three things at once, although here we're not interested in captures. The instruction refers to an action unit; action units are discussed in *Chapter 5. Moving to Two Action Units*;

4. Configure the output pin action logic to set the output pin high when a match is detected by the comparator;[4]

---

3. The comparator is configurable for match on "greater or equal" or "equal only," See *Chapter 8. Engine Architecture and Programming Model* for details on comparator options.

4. The output pin can be programmed in a number of ways. It can be programmed to move at some scheduled time, as a result of a certain event, or immediately. It can be set high, low, or to toggle. See *Chapter 8. Engine Architecture and Programming Model* for more information.

5. Write the **ERT_A** register's contents into the **MatchA** register (an action that automatically enables match recognition event handling). This is done by setting to 0 an instruction field called **ERW_A**, which you can think of as being short for "ERT_A write." The important thing to remember is that two things are happening when **ERW_A** is set to 0: a write and an enable, the latter of which follows automatically as a result of the former.

See Example 2.2 for the code itself.

```
#include <etpuc.h>

#pragma entryaddr 0x00;

#pragma ETPU_function ScheduledPinToggle;

void ScheduledPinToggle () {
    int24 CurrentCount;
    if (hsr == 3) {                      // If a host service request of 3
                                         // arrives, then...
        CurrentCount = tcr1;             // Save off the current "time"
        erta = CurrentCount + 0x100;     // Add 0x100 to that current "time" and
                                         // place the results into ERT_A
        act_unitA = Mtcr1_Ctcr1_eq;      // For action unit A, use TCR1 for both
                                         // matches and captures and to match when
                                         // TCR1 exactly equals the value in the
                                         // MatchA register
        opacA = match_high;              // Program the output pin action control
                                         // to force  the pin to high when a match
                                         // occurs
        erwA = 0;                        // Write the contents of ERT_A into
                                         // MatchA, thereby enabling match
                                         // handling
    }

    else {}
}

void main (void) { }
```

Example 2.2 Code to Schedule a Pin Toggle

The resulting waveform is displayed in Figure 2.3.

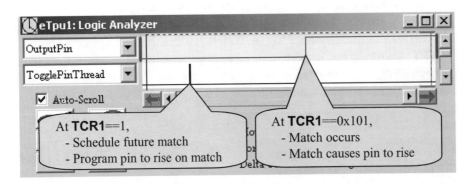

Figure 2.3 Scheduled Pin Toggle

This example causes a match at an absolute time—namely, the current **TCR1** time plus 100 ticks—but in most real-time applications, relative time is used. That is, events are typically scheduled at some future time relative to another event, which could be another match event or a transition event on the input pin. Let's now move to examples of the latter.

Reading an Input Pin

We've now built rudimentary programs that control the output pin. What about the input pin? The input pin state, which is the state of the pin state input register (**PSTI**), is controlled by some external logic and cannot be directly read by the eTPU. Instead, it is tested using the "C" if construct. So we might write the following program to test the state of the input pin:

```
#include <etpuc.h>

#pragma entryaddr 0x00;

#pragma ETPU_function ReadPin;

int InputPinState, CurrentTime;

void ReadPin() {

  if (hsr == 1) {                   // If host service request of 1, then...
      if (psti == 1)                // If the current input pin is high, then...
          InputPinState = 1;        // Set InputPinState to 1
      else
          InputPinState = 0;        // Otherwise, set InputPinState to 0
      CurrentTime = tcr1;           // Save off the current "time"
  }

  else {}
}

void main (void) { }
```

Example 2.3 Code to Test the State of the Input Pin

Suppose that the state, over time, of the input pin is as shown in Figure 2.4.

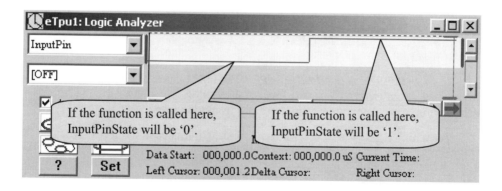

Figure 2.4 Testing the State of the Input Pin

While this function would store the input pin state and the **TCR1** count at which the pin state was read, it has a real limitation: we cannot determine exactly when a pin transition occurs. The program *could* be extended to wait for a transition and then store the time when it occurs using a polling loop, but this would take too much time and possibly starve other channels. Fortunately, there is a better way: we can use eTPU hardware to detect transitions automatically and record the time at which each transition occurs. This automatic transition detection is able to occur in part because of the presence of yet another kind of register: the **Capture** register. In direct analogy with the **Match** registers, each eTPU channel has two **Capture** registers, **CaptureA** and **CaptureB**. A **Capture** register does just what its name suggests: it captures the time at which some event has occurred.

The program needs to specify which kind of transition to detect (pin going high, going low, or toggling) and which **TCR** to use for the capture of the time at which that event occurred. We don't have to specify that a capture should occur; the capture occurs automatically by the hardware by virtue of a detected transition. See Figure 2.5.

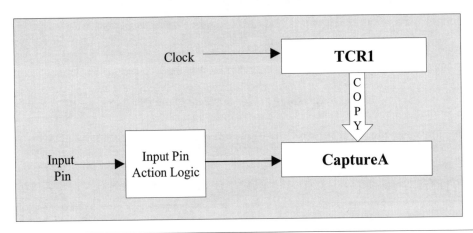

Figure 2.5 Preparing to Capture an Input Pin Transition

The steps for preparing detection of the input pin transition are:

1. Select which time base to use for the capture (in this case we'll use **TCR1**);[5]

2. Select the type of transition to detect (in this case we'll detect a falling edge).[6]

---

5. Again, the instruction that is used to do this actually specifies multiple things: the time base to be used for matches, whether to match on "greater or equal" or "equal only," and the time base to be used for captures. In this example we're not interested in matches and don't set up for them so the matching aspects of this instruction are not important. See *Chapter 8. Engine Architecture and Programming Model* for information on comparator options.

6. In analogy with the output pin, detection of the input pin transition can also be programmed in a number of ways. For instance, it can be set to detect a rising edge, a falling edge, or either edge. See *Chapter 8. Engine Architecture and Programming Model* for information on input pin options.

See Example 2.4 for the code that does this.

```
#include <etpuc.h>

#pragma entryaddr 0x00;

#pragma ETPU_function DetectPinTransition;

void DetectPinTransition() {

    if (hsr == 7) {                     // If host service request of 7, then...
        act_unitA = Mtcr1_Ctcr1_eq;     // For action unit A, use TCR1 for both
                                        // matches and captures and to match when
                                        // TCR1 exactly equals the value in the
                                        // MatchA register
        ipacA = high_low;               // Program the input action control to de-
                                        // tect a falling edge (i.e., high-to-low)
    }

    else {}
}

void main (void) { }
```

Example 2.4 Code that Sets Up for Pin Transition Detection

Suppose that the input pin transitions from low to high and then to low again, as shown in Figure 2.6.

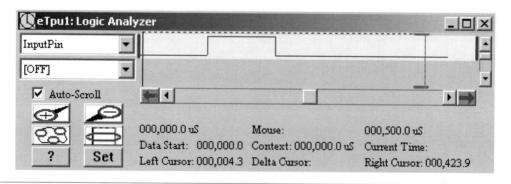

Figure 2.6 Transition Detection

With the code written in Example 2.4, pin transition detection occurs automatically, and autonomously, by eTPU channel hardware. The time at which the falling transition occurs is saved into the **Capture** register. The code we've written doesn't read the **Capture** register; we'll be doing this in the next chapter.

Lab 2

This lab will familiarize you with some of the features of the eTPU_C Compiler and eTPU Stand-Alone Simulator. You will also write your first eTPU function, albeit a small one. This lab, like all labs, assumes that you have installed both the Compiler and the Simulator (see appendices A and B).

Open the Lab 2 project by double-clicking on the file called Lab2.ETpuSimProject, which is located at <installation location>\Code Examples and Labs\Lab2. The eTPU Stand-Alone Simulator will open with four windows displayed. These windows are four of the many windows available in the Simulator. Let's look at each of these four in turn.

The logic analyzer (see Figure 2.7) has been set up to show an input pin and an output pin and two cursors (the two vertical lines). You can also see a bunch of timing information (lower middle and right) and a variety of control buttons (lower left).

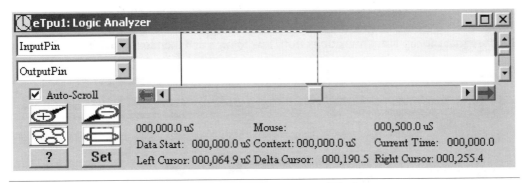

Figure 2.7 The Logic Analyzer Window

The execution unit registers window (see Figure 2.8) shows the contents of the execution unit's registers throughout the run. Recall from *Chapter 1. Introduction to the eTPU* that the execution unit executes instructions to access parameter RAM; to configure channel hardware; to read timer values; and to perform arithmetic operations such as multiply, multiply and accumulate, divide signed, and unsigned. It is also capable of performing logical operations and conditional branches based on a large number of flag settings. This window shows the contents of the registers that are in the execution unit. For this lab, we're going to concentrate on the contents of the **TCR1**, shown highlighted below.

Chapter 2. Understanding Channel Hardware

Figure 2.8 The Exaction Unit Registers Window

The channel window (see Figure 2.9) has been set up to show the values of the channel's various registers, latches, and flags throughout the run. For this lab, we're going to concentrate on the contents of the **CaptureA** register, shown highlighted below.

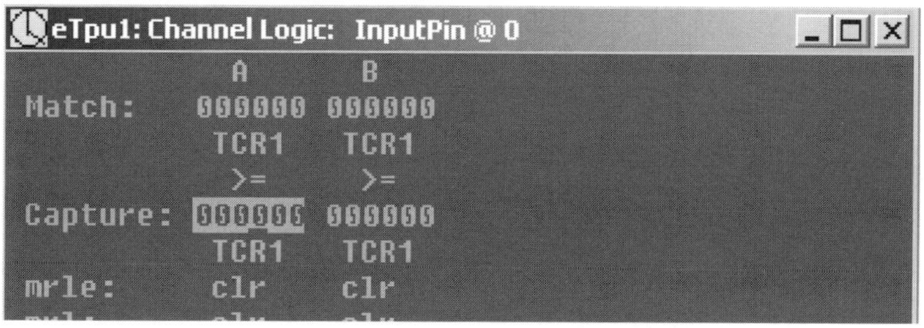

Figure 2.9 The Channel Window

Finally, the source code window (see Figure 2.10) displays the source code written for this lab (later you will be modifying this source code).

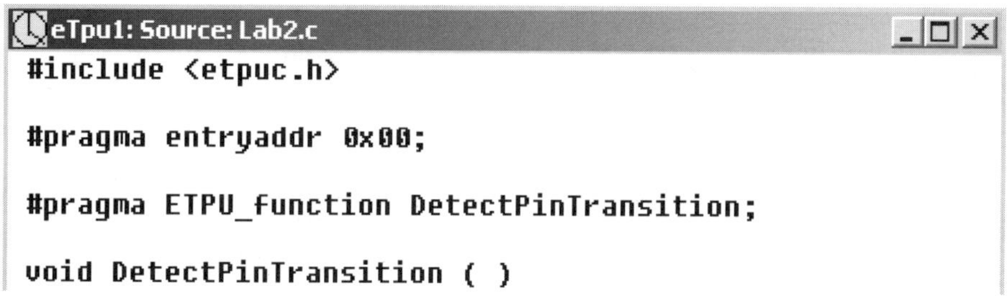

Figure 2.10 The Source Code Window

Okay, now we can get started.

1. Put the cursor in the right side of the logic analyzer window and right-click the mouse button. You should see a waveform like the one found below.

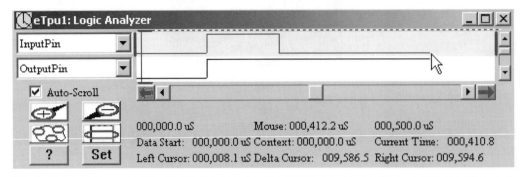

Figure 2.11 The Initial Pin Transition

2. Right-click in various parts of the to see how the run is affected. The mouse time shows the cursor position. In Figure 2.11, the mouse is at 412.2 µs. The current time is 410.8 µs, which is the time up to which the execution was run. (So the mouse was moved a bit to the right after the right-click occurred.)

3. The left and right cursors are blue (left) and green (right) vertical lines. In Figure 2.11, the left cursor is selected, as indicated by the two horizontal lines at the top and bottom of that cursor. Ensure that the logic analyzer is the active window and left-click to the left of the left cursor. The left cursor moves accordingly. Press the right arrow button. The left cursor moves to the rising edge, and the timing information changes accordingly. Select the right cursor, by clicking **Ctrl+right arrow**, and move it to the rising edge. The logical analyzer should look like Figure 2.12.

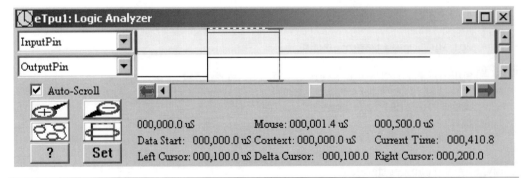

Figure 2.12 Moving the Cursors to the Rising and Falling Edges

4. Right-click in various locations in the logic analyzer. Note how the **TCR1** value changes when you do so. For instance, when the current time in the logic analyzer is 410.8 μs, the value in **TCR1** is hexadecimal 00503D as shown in Figure 2.13.

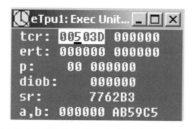

Figure 2.13 TCR1 During the Run

5. Now notice that the value of the selected **Capture** register is hexidecimal 002710 (see Figure 2.14) (assuming that the execution has been taken beyond the input pin's falling edge).

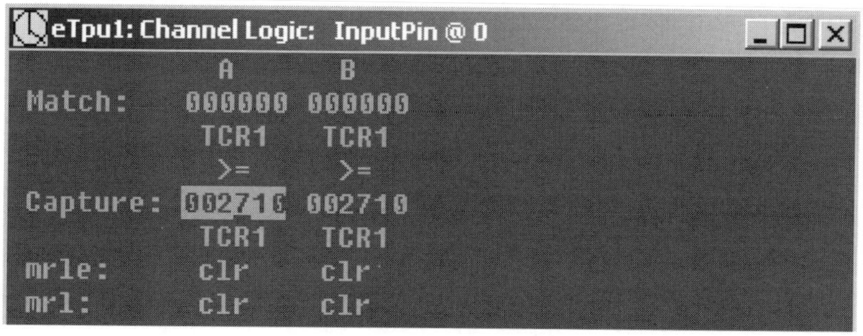

Figure 2.14 The Capture Register During the Run

6. We had written our function so that a falling edge on the input pin movement is detected. Does the **Capture** register reflect that edge?

7. We can check by moving the run exactly to the point of the falling edge and then seeing what the value of **TCR1** at that point is. Ensure that the right cursor is on the falling edge, as shown in Figure 2.12 above). Using the mouse, drag and drop the time associated with the right cursor into the current time field. You will see that the run regresses to the point of that falling edge, the capture register empties, and the current value of **TCR1** changes.

8. Suppose we want to detect both the rising and the falling edges of the input pin. Open Lab2.c in the eTPU_C Compiler (see *Appendix C. Installing and Running the Labs*) and change the code so that both edges are detected. (Hint: the setting

of the **IPAC_A** register needs to change. Find the options for this register in the etpuc.h file located with the eTPU_C compiler in the CD that accompanies this book.)

9. Compile the new code (see *Appendix C. Installing and Running the Labs* for instructions) and re-load the new source into the Simulator (there are variety of ways to re-load source code into the Simulator, the most transparent of which is to use the **Files/Executable, Fast** menu).

10. Right-click in various locations in the logic analyzer, including before the rising edge, between the rising and falling edges, and after the falling edge, notice the contents of the **CaptureA** register after each click.

11. Modify the source code again, this time to detect only the rising edge on the input pin and to produce an output pin edge as a result of the detected input pin edge. (Hint: change the input pin action control_A (**IPAC_A**) setting and add a line of code that sets the output pin action control_A (**OPAC_A**) register; again use the etpuc.h file as a guide.) When run in the Simulator, the code you produce should generate an output waveform that looks like Figure 2.15.

> **Note:** By default, an eTPU channel has an input signal and an output signal with only one pad or pin assigned to it. To have an input pad and an output pad connect to the same channel, the host application software at initialization time must assign a second pin (such as one of the enhanced modular I/O timer system pins) to that channel.

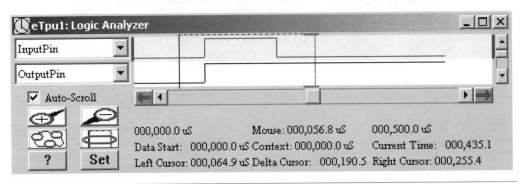

Figure 2.15   Waveform Produced from Input Pin Edge Detection

CHAPTER 3

Programming Channel Hardware

This chapter, which provides a moderately detailed discussion of matches and transitions, elaborates the examples from Chapter 2. Nevertheless, a simplified model (i.e., a single action unit) is presented; inter-action-unit manipulation is discussed in *Chapter 5. Moving to Two Action Units*.

Simplifying the Model (Temporarily)

Each channel in an eTPU contains two action units, action unit A and action unit B (see Figure 3.1). Each action unit contains its own transition detection and match circuitry: Action unit A contains a match register (**MatchA**), a match recognition latch (**MRL_A**) a capture register (**CaptureA**) and a transition detection latch (**TDL_A**); likewise, action unit B contains a match register (**MatchB**), a match recognition latch (**MRL_B**) a transition detection latch (**TDL_B**), and a capture register (**CaptureB**). The two action units share an input signal and an output signal. Programmable interconnected enabling/disabling logic allows the two action units to cooperate in detection and/or generation of two edges. The programmable channel "mode," discussed in *Chapter 9. Channel Hardware and Modes*, governs this cross-action-unit logic. In this chapter, we discuss a single-action-unit taken in isolation, presenting a simplified model for ease of understanding.

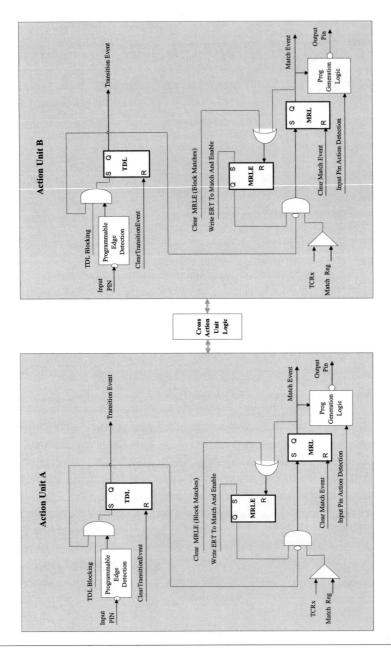

Figure 3.1 Dual Action Units

Setting up for a Match

A match occurs when the value of one of the two engine time bases, **TCR1** or **TCR2** (whichever one has been specified by the programmer)[1], is equal to the value that has been written to the **Match** register. But there is more to it than that, because a match can occur without being recognized. And in order for follow-on activity to take place as a result of a match, that match must be recognized. By default, match recognition is disabled; the programmer must specifically enable match recognition. Writing a value to a **Match** register automatically sets that action unit's match recognition latch enable (**MRLE**) flag, thereby enabling match recognition on that action unit. When a match does occur, the **MRLE** is automatically cleared, disabling further match recognitions against that same **Match** register.[2] In other words, subsequent match events will not occur until and unless a new match is scheduled by writing a new value to the **Match** register. Furthermore, pin transition detection sometimes blocks subsequent match recognition by preventing the **MRL** from being set in a case of a match. This occurs only in certain channel modes. The programmer can also specifically turn off the match recognition latch enable (**MRLE**) to block the **MRL** from being set when a match event occurs. Regardless of the reason that match recognition is disabled, writing a value to the **Match** register will set the **MRLE** thereby re-enabling match recognition.[3]

Specifying the Consequences of a Recognized Match

When a match occurs and is recognized (recognition is reflected in that action unit's match recognition latch (**MRL**) being set to 1), a variety of things can happen. Matches can be used to toggle the output pins; they can be used to determine when one of the two time base counters reaches a certain value; and they can provide transition detection windows. Each of these possibilities is discussed in turn below.

---

1. See "Capturing the Match or Transition Time" on page 31 for details on the two clock counters.
2. As a taste of things to come in *Chapter 9. Channel Hardware and Modes*, note that in some channel modes, a match occurring against one action unit's Match register disables matches on both action units' Match registers!
3. Provided that certain other conditions are met. Keep reading!

First, the programmer may specify that a recognized match should produce a pin toggle on the output pin for that action unit. The output pin action control (**OPAC**) register, which governs output pin behavior for a single action unit, can be programmed so that upon a match the pin goes high, goes low, or toggles (goes high if it's low or goes low if it's high).[4] See Figure 3.2 for a schematic of the output pin's being set to high upon match. The **OPAC** setting can be programmed at initialization and the initial value will "stick." If that output pin's behavior needs to be changed, **OPAC** can be re-written.

> **Note:** The **OPAC** register works in conjunction with the **PSC** and **PSCS**, registers. See *Chapter 12. Engine Architecture and Programming Model* for details.

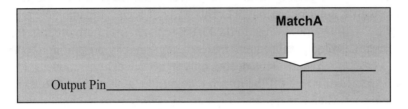

MatchA

Output Pin

Figure 3.2 Set Pin High on Match

Second, matches can be used to determine when one of the two time bases reaches a certain value. This is discussed further in "Capturing the Match or Transition Time" on page 31.

Third, matches can provide a window for input pin transition detection. Input pin transition detection logic is governed by the input pin action control (**IPAC**) register, which can be programmed in such a way that a match contributes to the input pin detection behavior. For instance, **IPAC** may be programmed so that a transition is detected (i.e., that action unit's transition detection latch (**TDL**) is set to 1) only if the input pin is high when a match occurs. Alternatively, it can be programmed so that the **TDL** is set to 1 only if the input pin is low when a match occurs. See Figure 3.3 for a schematic showing **TDL** being set only if the pin is high when a match occurs. You can see that when the first of the two matches occur, the input pin is low, so

> **Note:** The two **IPAC** options described in this paragraph do not really detect transitions in the usual sense. Rather, they sample the state of the input signal upon the occurrence of the match. So, for instance, consecutive matches with the pin high will produce the same result (**TDL** set to 1) upon the second match as does the second match in the example shown in Figure 3.3.

---

4. Input pin action can also control output pin behavior. This is also governed through an **OPAC** setting.

the **TDL** will not be set. When the second match occurs, however, the pin is high, and so **TDL** will be set. The transition is then known to have occurred during the window between the two matches. The two **IPAC** settings described in this paragraph are fairly expensive code-wise; the same transition detection logic can be implemented simply by setting up to capture the input pin transition time.

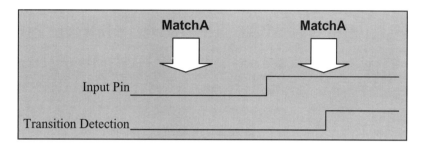

Figure 3.3 Detecting a High Input Pin on Match

Clearing the Match Recognition Latch

As noted above, a recognized match sets the **MRL** to 1. At that point the **MRL** must be cleared to 0 before any subsequent match can be recognized. This is done in eTPU code, after which recognition of a new future match is made possible (again, of course, provided that other conditions are met).

Setting Up for Transition Detection

A transition occurs when an input pin goes from low to high or high to low. But a pin can toggle without being detected (i.e., without that action unit's **TDL** being set to 1 as a result). Recall the input pin action control (**IPAC**) register, which is used to program input pin transition detection logic. As discussed above, this register can be programmed to sample the input state upon a match and respond accordingly, but it can also be programmed in such a way that matches have nothing whatsoever to do with the input pin detection logic. In particular, it can be programmed to detect a rising edge of the input pin, a falling edge, or either edge. These are the more typical settings for this register. Figure 3.4 shows an input pin transition being detected specifically as a result of a rising edge.

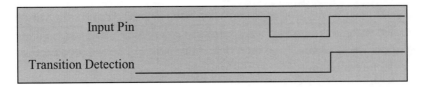

Figure 3.4 Detecting a Rising Edge

Specifying the Consequences of a Detected Transition

When a transition is detected, multiple follow-on events can take place. First, as mentioned in "Setting up for a Match" on page 27, in certain channel modes transition detection can disable match recognition by blocking the **MRL**. Second, a specific detected input pin transition can produce a specific output pin behavior (this is applicable only when the channel has been configured to control two pins). In particular, **OPAC** can be programmed so that the output pin is set to high, to low or to toggle upon the detection of an input pin transition. See Figure 3.5 shows the output pin going low upon a detected input pin edge.

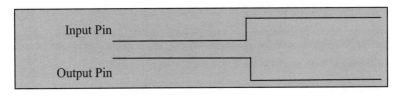

Figure 3.5 Setting Output Pin Low on Input Pin Transition Detection

Clearing the Transition Detection Latch

In direct analogy with matches and the **MRL**, detection of one transition disables detection of subsequent transitions of that same input pin until that action unit's **TDL** is cleared to 0. Clearing the **TDL** enables subsequent transitions to be detected (provided that the **IPAC** setting has the channel hardware detecting them).

Capturing the Match or Transition Time

Each action unit has a **Capture** register, which automatically "captures" the **TCR** value on a match recognition and on a transition detection. In other words, for example, if the **MRL** goes from 0 to 1, then the **Capture** register contains the match time. Likewise, if the **TDL** goes from 0 to 1, then the **Capture** register contains the transition time. If a match occurs but the **MRL** is already set to 1, the **Capture** value is left unchanged. Similarly, if a transition occurs but the **TDL** is already set to 1, the **Capture** value is left unchanged. In other words, a capture occurs as a result of a *change* from 0 to 1 of either the **MRL** or the **TDL**.

What happens when both the **MRL** and the **TDL** get set to 1 from 0? Since both detected transitions and recognized matches result in a capture, when both occur, one needs to take priority. Recall that when a transition is detected, the **MRL** for that action unit may be blocked, thereby disabling subsequent match recognition. In order to prevent the channel from missing a pin transition when measuring a long pulse, it is the transition that takes precedence over the match rather than vice versa. So when both a recognized match and detected transition occur, the **Capture** register will contain the transition time. If the recognized match occurs first, the detected transition will cause the **Capture** register to be overwritten; if the detected transition occurs first, the **Capture** register will not be overwritten as a result of a subsequent match.

The programmer cannot access the **Capture** register directly. Instead, the contents of the **Capture** register are made available by the microengine to the programmer via the (oddly named) event register temporary (**ERT**), which is read- (and write-) accessible by the programmer. The **ERT** is an engine register, so is shared by all channels on the engine. However, there are actually two **ERT**s, **ERT_A** and **ERT_B**, correspondingly, respectively, to action unit A and action unit B. For details on the transfer of the **Capture** into **ERT**, see *Chapter 11. The Scheduler.*

Setting the Time Base

There are two 24-bit timers for an eTPU engine that are available to all of the channels in that engine, timer count register 1 (**TCR1**) and timer count register 2 (**TCR2**).[5] These two timers, or counters, provide reference time bases for all match and input capture events.

---

5. In angle mode **TCR2** represents the angle.

When coding, you must specify the following three time-base issues for each action unit: whether **TCR1** or **TCR2** will be used to compare against the **Match** register; whether **TCR1** or **TCR2** will be copied into the **Capture** register on transition and match events (yes, this is a single question); and whether a match occurs when the chosen time base is greater-than-or-equal to the match time or only exactly equal to the match time.

Putting It All Together

Figure 3.6 depicts the basic operation of transitions and matches. If the channel is configured to be an input channel and a transition of the programmed edge is detected (where the transition is the type, such as rising or falling, etc., specified in the **IPAC** register), the **TDL** flag is set and the selected time base (either **TCR1** or **TCR2**) is captured into the **Capture** register. If the channel is configured to be an output channel, then when the selected time base (either **TCR1** or **TCR2**) equals the match register, the following follow-on activities result: the match recognition flag (**MRL**) is set, the time base (again, either **TCR1** or **TCR2**) is captured into the capture register, and the pin transitions according to the output pin action control (**OPAC**). Capturing the selected time base into the **Capture** register marks the exact time of the input or output event. Furthermore, the setting of **TDL** or **MRL** causes the channel to request service from the scheduler. When an input channel is eventually serviced, eTPU code must clear **TDL** to allow capturing of a subsequent edges. If the channel service was requested because of a match, eTPU code must clear **MRL** and write a new value in the match register to allow for subsequent matches.

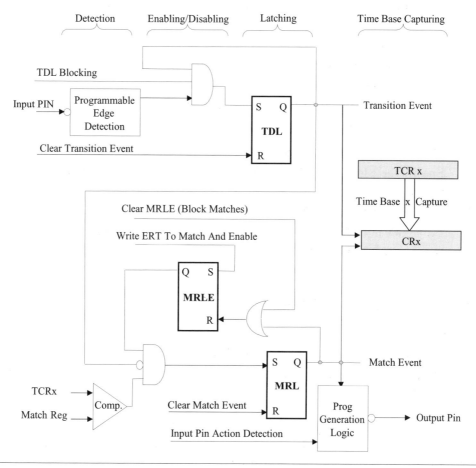

Figure 3.6 An Action Unit's Circuit Diagram

And Putting It into Practice

To get a feel for how this works in practice, we'll provide two complete programs, one that performs match recognition and the other that performs transition detection.

For matches, we first need to initialize the system and set up for the first match. This is done by the following sequence of steps:

1. Select a channel mode (channel modes are discussed in *Chapter 9. Channel Hardware and Modes*);

2. Set up the time base:

   a. Specify the action unit (action units are discussed in *Chapter 5. Moving to Two Action Units*);

   b. Specify **TCR1** or **TCR2** for match comparison;

   c. Specify **TCR1** or **TCR2** for capture;

   d. Specify equal or greater-than-or-equal for matches;

3. Specify the edge to be generated on match (this is optional depending on the application needs);

4. Put the match time into **ERT**;

5. Write **ERT** into the **Match** register thereby enabling matches by setting the **MRLE**;

6. Enable match and transition servicing (servicing events is discussed in *Chapter 4. Handling Events*).

Next, to generate each subsequent match we:

7. Put time at which next match will occur into the **ERT** register;

8. Clear the match event (i.e., clear the **MRL**);

9. Write the **ERT** register into the **Match** register thereby enabling matches by setting the **MRLE**.

See Example 3.1 for the actual code. The code after the first `if` statement (which is called once) does the initialization work. The code after the second `if` statement (which is called each time a match occurs) sets up for the subsequent match. The execution of each of these blocks of code is a thread. Threads are discussed in *Chapter 11. Threads and the Entry Table*.

```
#include <etpuc.h>

#pragma entryaddr 0x00;

#pragma ETPU_function MatchFunction;

void MatchFunction () {
    int24 LastCount, NextCount;

    if (hsr == 7) {
        pdcm = sm_st;                    // Set predefined channel mode to single
                                         // match, single transition
        act_unitA = Mtcr1_Ctcr1_eq;      // Use TCR1 for matches; match on equality
        opacA = match_toggle;            // Toggle the output pin on match
        LastCount = tcr1;                // Get current time
        erta = LastCount + 50;           // Determine when the match will occur and
                                         // put the result into ERT
        erwA = 0;                        // Copy ERT to the Match register, thereby
                                         // setting MRLE
        mtd = 0;                         // Enable match, transition event handling
    }

    else if (m1 == 1) {                  // If a match occurs ...
        LastCount = erta;                // ERT contains the match time
        NextCount = LastCount + 50;      // Calculate next match time
        erta = NextCount;                // Save the result to ERT
        mrlA = 0;                        // Clear the match recognition latch
        erwA = 0;                        // Copy ERT to the Match register, thereby
                                         // setting MRLE
    }

    else {}
}

void main (void) {}
```

Example 3.1 Programming a Series of Matches

The results can be seen in Figure 3.7.

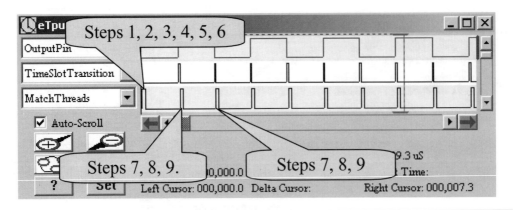

Figure 3.7 Match Recognition in Action

Notice that the toggling of the output pin occurs immediately upon each match. When the first match occurs the output pin goes high, and when the next match occurs, 50 **TCR1** ticks later, the output pin goes low, etc. The output duty cycle is exactly 50% (that is, high time equals low time), as expected.

Let's move to transitions. A similar pattern will emerge: we write initialization code and then code to detect each of the edges. To set up for edge detection, we perform the following initialization steps:

1. Select a channel mode (channel modes are discussed in *Chapter 9. Channel Hardware and Modes*).
2. Set up the time base:
    a. Specify the action unit (action units are discussed in detail in *Chapter 5. Moving to Two Action Units*);
    b. Specify **TCR1** or **TCR2** for match comparison.
    c. Specify **TCR1** or **TCR2** for capture.
    d. Specify equal or greater-than-or-equal for matches.
3. Specify the edge to detect (rising, falling, or either)
4. Enable match and transition servicing (servicing events is discussed in *Chapter 4. Handling Events*).

To detect each subsequent edge:

5. Save off the contents of the **ERT**, as this register contains the time of the detected edge. (Depending on the application needs, this step may be optional.)

6. Clear the transition event (i.e., clear the **TDL**).

See Example 3.2 for the code.

```
#include <etpuc.h>

#pragma entryaddr 0x00;

#pragma ETPU_function TransitionFunction;

void TransitionFunction () {
    int24 TransitionTime;

    if (hsr == 7) {
        pdcm = sm_st;                      // Set predefined channel mode to single
                                           // match, single transition
        act_unitA = Mtcr1_Ctcr1_eq;        // Use TCR1 for captures
        ipacA = any_trans;                 // Detect any input edge
        mtd = 0;                           // Enable match, transition event handling
    }

    else if (m2==1) {                      // If transition occurred...
        TransitionTime = erta;             // Save off captured transition time
        tdl = 0;                           // Clear transition detection latch
    }

    else {}
}

void main (void) {}
```

Example 3.2 Programming Ongoing Transition Detection

The result looks like Figure 3.8.

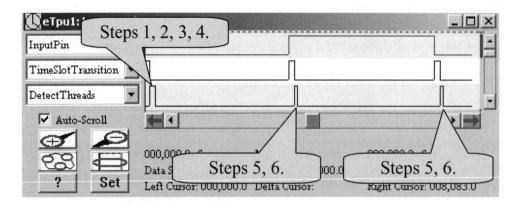

Figure 3.8 Transition Detection in Action

As pointed out earlier, the eTPU engine contains two action units rather than just one, but before we can move on to a discussion of each pair of action units and how they interact, we need to introduce the eTPU as an event-servicing system. This is the topic of the next chapter.

Lab 3

Open the Lab 3 project by double-clicking on the file called Lab3.ETpuSimProject, which is located at <installation location>\Code Examples and Labs\Lab3. The eTPU Stand-Alone Simulator will open with four windows displayed: the logic analyzer, the channel window, a source code window, and the execution unit registers window. The lab being run here is the same code as in Example 3.1: a repeating match function that produces an output pin edge each time a recognized match occurs.

1.   Run the simulation by pressing **F9** or by using the **Run/Go** menu (see Figure 3.9).

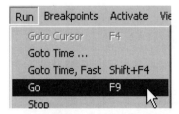

Figure 3.9 Running the Simulator

The logic analyzer display should look like Figure 3.10.

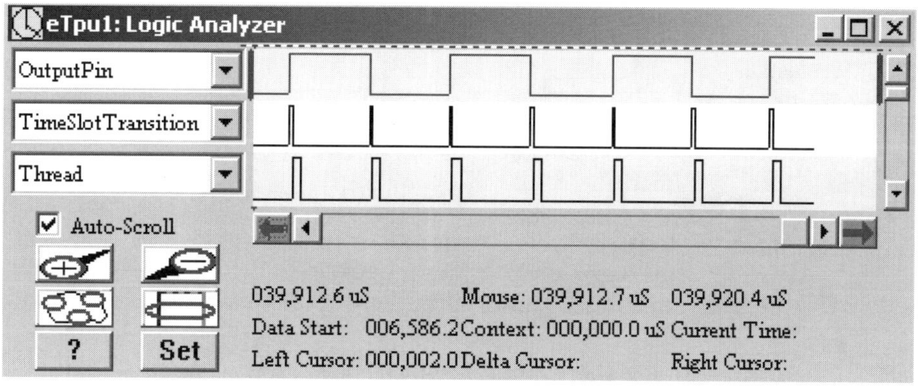

Figure 3.10 Logic Analyzer Running Lab 3

2. Click on the **Run\Go** menu again and when it opens (this may take a couple of seconds), click on **Stop**. Notice the values of the **MatchA** and **CaptureA** registers on the channel window and the **TCR1** and **ERT_A** registers on the execution unit registers window.

3. Click the zoom buttons in the lower left corner of the logic analyzer window.

4. Press **Ctrl+R** or use the **Run/Reset** menu options to reset the Simulator. Notice the values of the **MatchA** and **CaptureA** registers on the channel window and the **TCR1** and **ERT_A** registers on the execution unit registers window.

5. Press the **F8** key a few times, noticing the contents of the above-mentioned four registers as you do so.

6. Modify the Lab3.c file in an editor so that: **TCR2** is used for both matches and captures; a MatchCount variable keeps track of the number of matches that have occurred; and only seven matches are created. Compile and run until you produce a waveform that looks like Example 3.11. Be sure to clear the match events!

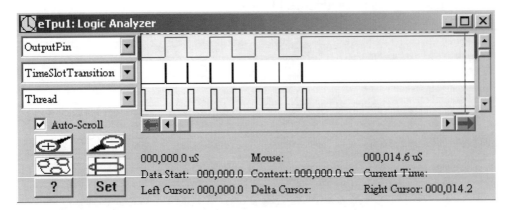

Figure 3.11 Six Matches, Each Producing an Output Pin Pulse

7.   Open the local variables window via the **View/Local Variables** menu options

8.   Reset if necessary, and then step through (**F8**) the execution, noting how the contents of the local variables window changes throughout the run as you do so (see Example 3.12).

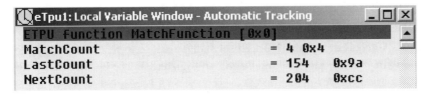

Figure 3.12 Noting the Contents of Variables Throughout the Run

CHAPTER 4

Handling Events

This chapter introduces the eTPU as an event-servicing device.

Events

So far we have discussed two types of events: matches and transitions. Altogether there are four types of eTPU events:

- Host service request (HSR): an event generated by the host processor;
- Link service request (LSR): an event generated when one channel calls on another channel to do something;
- Match: an event generated by a recognized match that was scheduled at some **TCR1** or **TCR2** count in a **MatchA** or **MatchB** register;
- Transition: an event generated when a channel has been programmed to detect a particular input signal edge and that edge occurs.

eTPU code executes *only* in response to one of these events.

For any given channel, event-response code is created within a special series of `if-else` statements, as follows:

```
#include <etpuc.h>

#pragma entryaddr 0x00;

#pragma ETPU_function MyEventSourcesFunc;

void MyEventSourcesFunc ( )
{
    if (hsr == 1) {
        ;                       // Code to handle host CPU service request
    }

    else if(lsr == 1) {
        ;                       // Code to handle service request
                                // from another channel
        lsr = 0;                // Clear link service request latch
    }

    else if(m1 == 1) {
        ;                       // Code to handle a MatchA or TransitionB event
        mrlA = 0;               // Clear MatchA event
        tdl = 0;                // Clear transition events
    }

    else {
        ;                       // Code to handle errors
    }
}

void main (void) { }
```

Example 4.1 Code Responds to Events

At run-time the relevant portions of this function are executed in response to an event of the specified kind. For instance, if a match occurs against the **MatchA** register (i.e., a MatchA event), the code following the third `if` statement is executed. (`m1` refers to a MatchA or TransitionB event, whereas `m2` refers to a MatchB or TransitionA event.) The execution of the portion of code following an `if` statement in an eTPU function is called a *thread*. A thread is a service routine that executes in response to a specific event or combination of events on a given channel.

Suppose a match event occurs on some channel and is serviced by a given thread. Necessarily, this event was recognized by the microengine because a certain bit in a certain register--in this case it would be that channel's match recognition latch A or B (**MRL_A** or **MRL_B**)--is set to 1. (It would have been set to 1 upon the occur-rence of the match event; a match against the **MatchA** register sets **MRL_A**; a match against the **MatchB** register sets **MRL_B**.) In order to prevent a given event from forevermore seeking servicing, the thread that services that event must in the end clear it. What this

Note: This latch clearing is typically done at the end of the thread as you may wish in the middle of the thread to test the latch that brought you into the thread.

means in the case of a match event is that the **MRL_A** (or **MRL_B**, as the case may be) must be cleared back to 0. Similarly, transition and link events must be cleared during that services them. You'll notice that Example 4.1 includes just such "clear" statements. Host service request events are automatically cleared by the eTPU itself, so no code is required to do so. If match, transition, and link service requests are not cleared in their respective threads, the channel will continue to request service for the earlier event after the thread ends. A situation such as this should be avoided to prevent starvation of other channels that are in need of service.

The Entry Table

While eTPU functions are written in C and have all the markings of a procedural language, execution of eTPU codes is, as stated, event-driven. When an event occurs, the microengine goes straight to the block of code that will service the resulting request. The microengine knows where to find the code to service a given event (or events) by using the *entry table*.[1] The entry table is a mapping of each event (or cluster of events) to a given line of code--namely, the line of code that starts the thread that will service the event(s). The entry table is a vector table residing in code memory that contains thread start addresses. The location of the entry table in code memory is specified both in eTPU and in host code, and the two specifications must match one another.

> **Note:** In all examples and labs in this book the entry table is specified at location 0x00 so as to work with the demonstration Simulator, which requires that the entry table start at this position. In the production Simulator there is no such restriction, although in general it is a good idea to place the entry table at the beginning of SCM in order to ensure as large a contiguous space as possible for program code.

In Figure 4.1, you can see that the first entry point in the MyEventSource portion of the entry table contains the start address of the block of code that handles a host service request of 1. Another entry point contains the start address of the block of code that handles a link service request. Yet another entry point contains the start address of the block of code that handles a MatchA or a TransitionB event. Finally, many of this function's entry points will contain the start address of block following the catch-all `else` clause at the end of the function (i.e., presumably this will be filled with error handling code).

---

1. The entry table is also sometimes referred to as the *event vector table*.

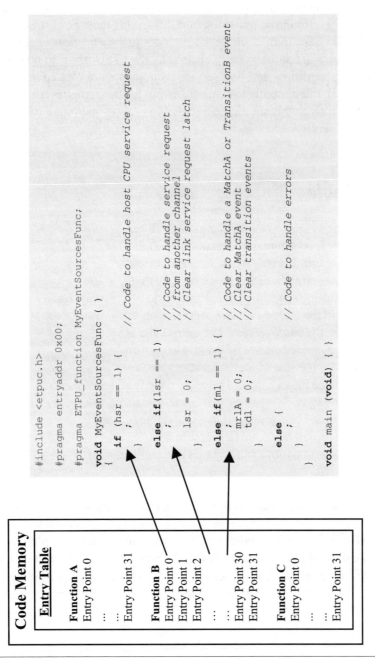

```
#include <etpuc.h>

#pragma entryaddr 0x00;

#pragma ETPU_function MyEventSourcesFunc;

void MyEventSourcesFunc ( )
{
    if (hsr == 1) {      // Code to handle host CPU service request
        ;
    }
    else if(lsr == 1) {  // Code to handle service request
        ;                //    from another channel
        lsr = 0;         // Clear link service request latch
    }
    else if(m1 == 1) {   // Code to handle a MatchA or TransitionB event
        ;                // Clear MatchA event
        mrlA = 0;        // Clear transition events
        tdl = 0;
    }
    else {
        ;                // Code to handle errors
    }
}

void main (void) { }
```

Code Memory

Entry Table

Function A
Entry Point 0
... ...
Entry Point 31

Function B
Entry Point 0
Entry Point 1
Entry Point 2
... ...
Entry Point 30
Entry Point 31

Function C
Entry Point 0
... ...
Entry Point 31

Figure 4.1 Mapping the Entry Table to an eTPU Function

The nature of the entry table is a bit more complex than just described. While it is true that a thread is executed only in response to an event (or combination of events), more goes into the decision of which thread to execute than mere event information. The states of two programmatically driven channel flags (**Flag0** and **Flag1**) contribute to the decision, as does the state of that channel's pin. These latter pieces of information (i.e., flag and pin states) are called, below and elsewhere in the literature, *channel conditions* or *conditions*.

As you can see in the left-hand side of Figure 4.1, for each function there are a total of 32 entry points in the entry table. However, there are many more than 32 possible event/condition combinations. How many are there? There are 1792. This number is obtained as follows. There are 7 types of HSRs, 2 LSR states, 2 MatchA states, 2 MatchB states, 2 TransitionA states, 2 TransitionB states, 4 **Flag** states, and 2 input pin states. 7*2*2*2*2*4*2= 1792. Since it would take far too much code memory to map 1792 entry points (and remember that would be 1792 for each function), some entries in the table must handle multiple event/condition combinations.

An entry table encoding scheme is the set of rules that: a) specify which event/condition combinations are recognized; and b) govern which event/condition combinations map to which rows in the physical entry table in code memory.[2] There are two flavors of encoding scheme available for the eTPU. Details of each are provided in *Chapter 11. Threads and the Entry Table*. At this stage you should take some time to study the two types of encoding schemes, provided in that chapter.

Both the compiler and the eTPU itself must be "told" which encoding scheme is to be used for each eTPU function defined. These specifications must match one another.

---

2. Throughout the literature, the entry table encoding scheme is also variously referred to as the *encoding scheme* and *channel condition encoding scheme*.

How does this all work? The programmer writing a function specifies which encoding scheme to use and then writes code for those event/condition combinations that are relevant to the function at hand. (A mandatory `else` clause at the end of each eTPU function "handles" any unused event/condition combinations and therefore often contains error-handling code.) The compiler creates, in code memory, the entry table for that function and all other functions. The eTPU is set in motion by the host. An event (such as an input pin edge) occurs. The microengine detects the event, sees which event/condition combination applies (depending on the event in question and the other channel conditions), finds that entry in that function's portion of the entry table, from it discovers the address of the thread to be executed (i.e., the entry point), and executes that thread. If appropriate, the event is cleared by the thread. The microengine either proceeds to service the next waiting service request or lies idle until the next service request occurs.

> **Note:** The use of the entry table results in faster context switch time because less execution time is needed to determine which thread should run. The if-else statements in the source code translate into encoded entry points (vectors) rather than a sequence of conditional instructions that would be generated by a conventional "C" compiler.

There are up to 32 possible entry points for each function, but will all functions actually specify code for each of the 32 possibilities? Probably not. In addition to an empty `else` clause to handle any unused event/condition combinations, a programmer may decide to handle multiple event/condition combinations within a single thread. For instance, the first four event/condition combinations in the standard encoding scheme all have to do with an **HSR** equal to 001, where the differences among the four depend on the **Flag0** and input pin states. If the latter two pieces of information are irrelevant, the programmer may write the following code (for instance).

```
#include <etpuc.h>

#pragma entryaddr 0x00;

#pragma ETPU_function AllStandardThreadsFunc, standard;

void FunctionA (void) {}
void FunctionB (void) {}

void AllStandardThreadsFunc()
{
   if (hsr == 1) {
     FunctionA();                              // Handle entry points 0,1,2,3
   }

   else if (( (lsr == 1) && !(m1 == 1) && (m2 == 1) && (flag0==0)) ||
            ( (lsr == 1) && (m1 == 1) && !(m2 == 1) && (flag0==1)) ) {
     FunctionB();                              // Handle entry points 28,31
   }

   else {
                                               // Handle all other entry points
   }
}

void main (void) {}
```

Example 4.2 Combining Event/Condition Combinations in Code

In Example 4.2, the standard encoding scheme is being used. The first thread handles entry points 0 through 3 from that function's portion of the entry table while the second thread handles entry points 28 and 31. The third thread (in this case an empty thread) handles all remaining entry points; in other words, if some *other* event/condition combination occurs (i.e., any of entry points 4 through 27, or 29-30), nothing happens. (In reality, each expected or unexpected event should be handled. For example, all unused entries should be terminated gracefully in case they are invoked unintentionally. Graceful termination of unused entries ensures that eTPU code will not cause system runaways.)

Beyond the Entry Table

With a maximum of 32 entry points but 1792 possible event/condition combinations, eTPU functions commonly require additional conditional logic to further narrow the event handler. The eTPU supports conditional logic on links, matches, and transitions but not for host service requests. So, for instance, you may need to supply conditional logic that differentiates between a MatchA and a TransitionB event, a differentiation that is not supported by the entry table itself. See Example 4.3 for an example.

```
#include <etpuc.h>

#pragma entryaddr 0x00;

#pragma ETPU_function ThreadConditionalsFunc;

void ThreadConditionalsFunc() {
   if (hsr == 1) {}

   else if (m1 == 1) {
     if (mrlA == 1)
       {
       // Handle MatchA
       mrlA = 0;
       }
     if (tdlB == 1) {
       // Handle TransitionB
       tdl = 0;
       }
   }

   else {}
}

void main (void) {}
```

Example 4.3   Internal Conditional Logic

The eTPU_C Compiler's "switch" construct requires three instructions regardless of the number of cases. See Example 4.4.

```
#pragma entryaddr 0x00;

#pragma ETPU_function SwitchFunc;

void SwitchFunc() {
int8 CurrentState;
   if(hsr == 1) {}

   else if (m1 == 1) {
     switch (CurrentState) {
       case 0:
         // Handle case 0
         break;
       case 1:
         // Handle case 1
         break;
     }
     mrlA = 0;
     tdl = 0;
   }

   else {}
}

void main (void) {}
```

Example 4.4   Internal Switch Logic

Gating Match and Transition Servicing

You'll notice that in virtually all host service request threads there is an instruction to enable match and transition event handling (`mtd = 0`). While the servicing of link and host requests cannot be blocked, that of matches and transitions can. In fact, after a hardware reset match and transition service requests are disabled or blocked until that default state is changed. For instance, if either event (match or capture) occurs it will set its corresponding flag (**MRL** or **TDL**) but no follow-on servicing occurs since service requests to the scheduler are blocked. The `mtd = 0` instruction is sticky and typically executed only during channel initialization. It enables the path of these requests to the scheduler until another command disables the path. Refer to Figure 4.2 which depicts the gating of all requests generated by **MRL_A/B** and **TDL_A/B**.

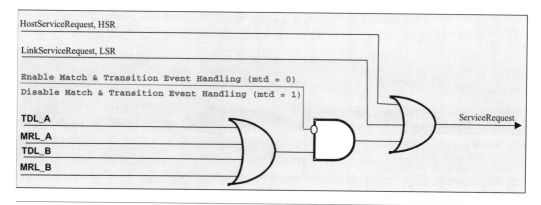

Figure 4.2 Gating Match and Transition Servicing

If an active match or transition service request is being blocked because such servicing has not yet been enabled or has been actively disabled, the request will immediately go through once match and transition servicing is enabled. Also, note that match and transition service disabling affects only servicing; it does not affect branch tests, entry table selection, or output pin action on the basis of **MRL** or **TDL**.

Lab 4

In this lab you will be focusing on event handling and what happens if:

- you don't enable match recognition

- you don't clear the flag associated with an event such as a transition, match or link
- you have events qualified by flag and pin states
- you get the order of the `if-else` statements wrong
- multiple service requests are pending on the same channel.

For this lab, you may want to take advantage of certain bugging facilities in the Simulator, such as breakpoints, stepping, and code coverage, each of which is described in *Appendix B. ASH WARE's eTPU Stand-Alone Simulator*. Now for the lab itself:

1. Complete the Lab4.c file so as to produce the rectangular waveform as shown in Figure 4.3. Set HighTime to 0x400 and LowTime to 0x100. As you write and debug the code, ensure the following

   a. Match recognition is enabled;

   b. The latches associated with match, transition, and link events are cleared in the thread that handles these events;

   c. The state of **Flag0** is used as one of the channel conditions;

   d. The order of the `if-else` statements is correct.

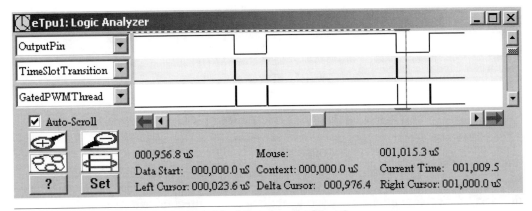

Figure 4.3 A Rectangular Waveform

2. Extra credit: Ensure that the execution has gone at least to 1,000 µs. Scroll to the top of the logic analyzer to reveal an InputPin. Scroll the execution to the right until you see the input pin go from low to high. Better than scrolling to the right, use the up arrow to select the input pin (the selected item is shown in red). Then use the cursors to move the execution exactly to the transition. See Figure 4.4.

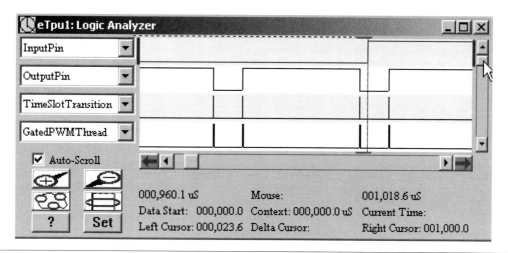

Figure 4.4 Input Pin Transition

Modify the lab so that the rectangle waveform ends as soon as the input pin transitions. Your waveform should look like Figure 4.5.

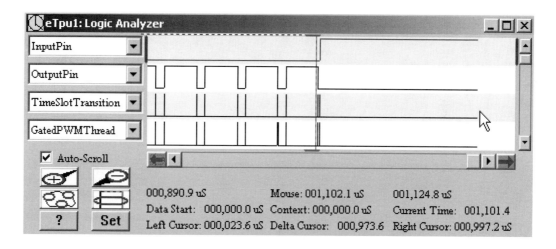

Figure 4.5 Stopping the Waveform Upon Pin Transition

CHAPTER 5

Moving to Two Action Units

This chapter explains how the eTPU's two action units can be used to produce efficient, rigorous, and powerful functions.

Dual Action Unit Power

Until now we have been working with a single action unit, but each eTPU channel contains two action units, and they can be programmed to interact in complex ways. Recall that each channel contains an input signal, an output signal, and two action units. These two action units, designated action unit A and action unit B, each contain one of each of the following registers: match, match recognition, transition detection, capture, input pin action control, and output pin action control. Whether a given register in this list belongs to action unit A or action unit B is indicated by appending an **A** or a **B** onto the register name (e.g., **MatchA**, **MRL_A**, **CaptureB**, **TDL_A**, etc.)[1] Likewise, whether a given match or transition event has occurred on action unit A or B is indicated by appending an A or B onto the event name (e.g., MatchA, TransitionB, etc.). See Figure 5.1 for block diagram.

---

1. You may find in other literature the use of **MRL1** rather than **MRL_A**, etc. The usage of letters rather than numerals is intended to reduce confusion between these action-unit-specific registers and twinned engine registers (e.g., **TCR1/2** and **ERT1/2**), not to mention channel-specific but non-action-unit-specific twinned registers such as **Flag1** and **Flag0**.

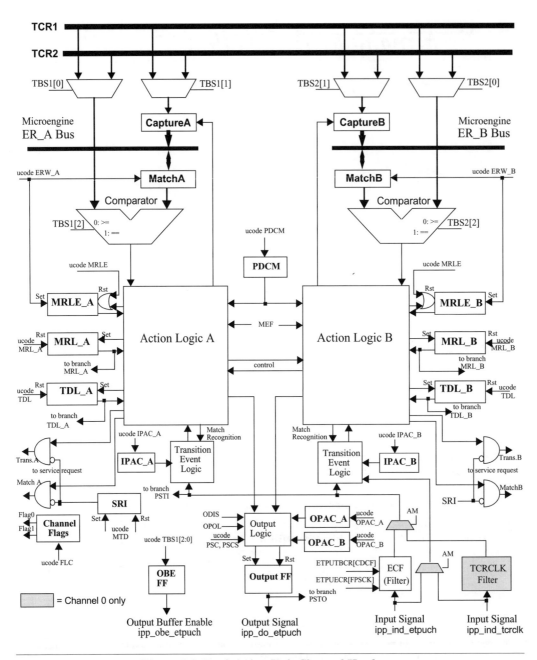

Figure 5.1 Dual-Action Unit Channel Hardware

The simplest story to tell about dual-action unit eTPU channel hardware is this: If a match occurs against the **MatchA** register (and **MRLE_A** is set), then **MRL_A** will be set and a capture will occur in **CaptureA**. Likewise, if a match occurs against the **MatchB** register (and **MRLE_B** is set), then **MRL_B** will be set and a capture will occur in **CaptureB**. If the channel's input pin transitions according to the **IPAC_A** setting, then **TDL_A** will be set and a capture will occur in **CaptureA**. If, after the **TDL_A** is set, the channel's input pin transitions according to the **IPAC_B** setting, then **TDL_B** will be set and a capture will occur in **CaptureB**. (In a given capture register, a detected transition time capture will replace a recognized match time capture, but not vice versa—so for instance when both **TDL_A** and **MRL_A** get set, and regardless of the order of their being set, **CaptureA** will contain the time that **TDL_A** was set.) When the **MRL_A** or **TDL_A** gets set, the channel's output pin will toggle (or not) according to the **OPAC_A** setting; likewise, when the **MRL_B** or **TDL_B** gets set, the channel's output pin will toggle (or not) according to the **OPAC_B** setting.

You can see that the simple story is far from simple, and we didn't even talk about service requests. Nevertheless, the channel's predefined channel mode (**PDCM**) setting, which is specified for a given function in its initialization thread, can complicate matters still further. The **PDCM** setting controls match and transition gating logic and determines which match and transition events result in service requests. See Figure 5.2.

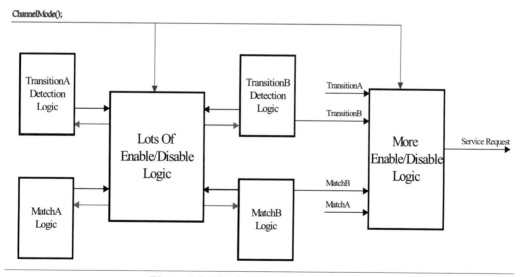

Figure 5.2 The Two Action Units Interact

There are five different activities that the **PDCM** setting controls: a) match and transition enabling and blocking; b) match recognition service request gating; c) transition detection service request gating; d) match recognition time capturing; and e) transition detection time capturing. While channel modes are necessarily referred to in the examples in this chapter, channel modes are explained in depth in *Chapter 9. Channel Hardware and Modes*.

Measuring an Input Pulse

Suppose we want to measure a pulse on an input signal. To show the power and flexibility of a dual-action unit channel, we'll provide an example that utilizes just a single action unit (functionally equivalent to a TPU3 function) and one that utilizes both action units.

Measuring an Input Pulse Using a Single Action Unit

Example 5.1 shows the code that measures an input pulse with a single action unit.

```
#include <etpuc.h>

#pragma entryaddr 0x00;

#pragma ETPU_function MeasurePulseOne, standard;

void MeasurePulseOne ( int24 PulseWidth ) {
static int24 RisingEdge;
int24 FallingEdge;
   if (hsr == 7) {
     pdcm = sm_st;                    // Use single match, single transition
                                      // channel mode
     act_unitA = Mtcr1_Ctcr1_eq;     // Use TCR1 for for captures
     ipacA = any_trans;              // Detect any input edge
     mtd = 0;                        // Enable match, transition event handling
   }

   else if (m2 == 1) {               // If transition occurred...
     if (pss == 1 ) {                // If pin sampled state is high...
       RisingEdge = erta;            // Set RisingEdge to transition time
     }
     else {                          // If pin sampled state is low
       FallingEdge = erta;           // Set RisingEdge to transition time
       PulseWidth = FallingEdge - RisingEdge;   // Calculate pulse width
     }
     tdl = 0;                        // Clear the transition detection latch
   }

   else {}                           // Error recovery code
}

void main (void) { }
```

Example 5.1 Code That Measures a Pulse Using a Single Action Unit

This function utilizes the function variable PulseWidth, a static local variable `Ris-ingEdge`, and a dynamic local variable `FallingEdge`.[2] The function consists of two threads (ignoring the error recovery thread): one initialization thread (called when an HSR of 7 is issued on the channel to which the function is assigned) and another thread that is called when a MatchB service request or a TransitionA service request is issued on the channel to which the function is assigned. Since the code doesn't set up for any matches, this second thread will be executed only when a TransitionA service request is issued. We use a single transition detection latch, **TDL_A**, to detect both rising and falling edges of the input pin. Each edge will capture the current time and cause a service request to be issued. When the second thread is entered, we need to test the latched state (pin sampled state) of the input pin to determine whether the thread was entered due to a rising or falling edge. If it is a rising edge, the edge time will be saved to `RisingEdge`. If it is a falling edge, the edge time will be compared with earlier-saved rising edge time, and the difference will be saved.

Figure 5.3 shows the pin pulses and servicing threads in action.

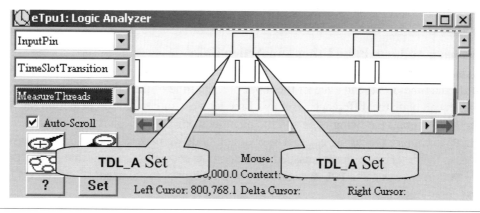

Figure 5.3 Measuring an Input Pulse Using a Single Action Unit

You can see that each input pin transition results in a thread, which is fairly inefficient. Furthermore, while this particular input waveform is sufficiently wide to allow each edge to be captured, if the pulse is too narrow, we may miss input pin edges, as shown in Figure 5.4.

---

2. See *Chapter 6. Moving to Multiple Channels* for the differences among the various kinds of eTPU variables.

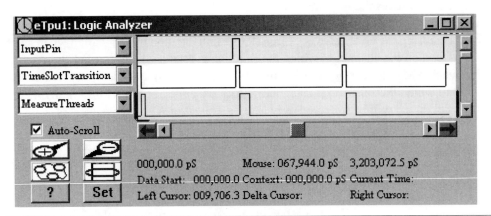

Figure 5.4 Missing Input Pin Edges Using a Single Action Unit

As shown in this figure, each rising edge is detected but the resulting thread does not occur soon enough to clear the **TDL_A** latch in order to allow the hardware to detect the falling edge. The falling edge is missed each time.

Measuring An Input Pulse Using Two Action Units

Let's implement this same functionality using two action units. Once again, we want to capture the time of a rising edge of the input pin, the time of the falling edge of the pin, and then calculate the difference. But this time let's use one transition detection latch (**TDL_A**) to capture the rising edge and the channel's other transition detection latch (**TDL_B**) to capture the falling edge. The channel mode we pick will be a double-transition mode, so that a service request is issued only upon the second transition (that is, on **TDL_B**, since **TLD_A** always gates **TDL_B** regardless of the channel mode used). Let's take a look at the code:

```
#include <etpuc.h>

#pragma entryaddr 0x00;

#pragma ETPU_function MeasurePulseTwo, standard;

void MeasurePulseTwo ( int24 PulseWidth ){
int24 RisingEdge, FallingEdge;
  if (hsr == 7) {
    pdcm = em_nb_dt;                // Use either match, non-blocking,
                                    // double transition channel mode

    act_unitA = Mtcr1_Ctcr1_eq;     // Use TCR1 for captures on action unit A
    act_unitB = Mtcr1_Ctcr1_eq;     // Use TCR1 for captures on action unit B;
                                    // it is important that the same clock (in
                                    // this case TCR1) is used for captures in
                                    // both action units

    ipacA = low_high;               // Detect a rising edge on action unit A
    ipacB = high_low;               // Detect a falling edge on action unit B
    mtd = 0;                        // Enable match, transition event handling
  }

  else if (m1 == 1) {               // If TransitionB occurred...
    RisingEdge = erta;              // Save off rising edge time
    FallingEdge = ertb;             // Save off falling edge time
    PulseWidth = FallingEdge - RisingEdge;  // Calculate pulse width
    tdl = 0;                        // Clear both transition events
  }

  else {}  // Error recovery code
}

void main (void) { }
```

Example 5.2 Code That Measures a Pulse Using Both Action Units

This function receives uses a function variable called PulseWidth and dynamic local variables called RisingEdge and FallingEdge.[3] The function consists of two threads (ignoring the error recovery thread): one initialization thread (called when an HSR of 7 is issued on the channel to which the function is assigned) and another thread that is called when a MatchA service request or a TransitionB service request is issued on the channel to which the function is assigned. Since the code doesn't set up for any matches, this second thread will be executed only when a TransitionB service request is issued.

Figure 5.5 shows the pin pulses and servicing threads in action.

---

3. See *Chapter 6. Moving to Multiple Channels* for the differences among the various kinds of eTPU variables.

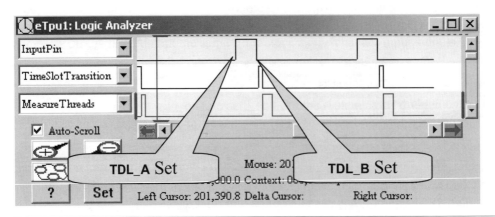

Figure 5.5 Measuring an Input Pulse Using Two Action Units

You can see how much more efficient this is--twice as efficient as using a single action unit. And it works regardless of the size of the pulse.

Programming a PWM

As a second example to show the power of dual-action unit channels, we'll program a PWM using first just a single action unit and then using two.

Programming a PWM Using a Single Action Unit

Once again this is equivalent to the PWM as written for the TPU3.

```
#include <etpuc.h>;

#pragma entryaddr 0x00;

#pragma ETPU_function PWMOne, alternate;

void PWMOne (unsigned int Period, unsigned int HighTime) {
   if (hsr == 3) {
      pdcm = sm_st;                  // Use single match, single transition
                                     // channel mode
      act_unitA = Mtcr1_Ctcr1_eq;    // Use TCR1 for matches; match on equality
      opacA = match_toggle;          // On MatchA, toggle output pin
      pin = pin_low;                 // Force the output pin low
      flag0 = 0;                     // Initialize Flag0
      erta = tcr1 + Period - HighTime;    // Set up match time
      erwA = 0;                      // Write ERT_A to MatchA and enable matches
      mtd = 0;                       // Enable match, transition event handling
   }

   else if ((m1 == 1) && (flag0 == 0)) {   // If MatchA with Flag0 cleared...
      flag0 = 1;                     // Set Flag0
      mrlA = 0;                      // Clear MatchA event
      erta = erta + HighTime;        // Set up next match time
      erwA = 0;                      // Write ERT_A to MatchA and enable matches
   }

   else if ((m1 == 1) && (flag0 == 1)) {   // If MatchA with Flag0 set...
      flag0 = 0;                     // Clear flag -0
      mrlA = 0;                      // Clear MatchA event
      erta = erta + Period - HighTime;    // Set up next match time
      erwA = 0;                      // Write ERT_A to MatchA and enable matches
   }

   else {}
}
void main (void) {}
```

Example 5.3 PWM Code Using A Single Action Unit

This function consists of three threads (ignoring the error recovery thread): one initialization thread (called when an HSR of 3 is issued on the channel to which the function is assigned); one thread that is called when either an **MRL_A** service request is issued on the channel to which the function is assigned and **Flag0** is high, and the third when an **MRL_A** service request is issued on the channel to which the function is assigned and **Flag0** is low. The second thread schedules the next falling edge, and the third thread schedules the next rising edge.

Figure 5.6 shows the matches and servicing threads in action.

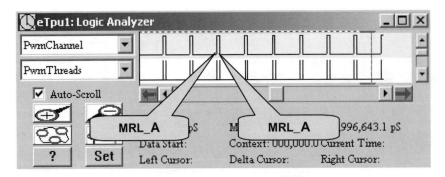

Figure 5.6 PWM Using a Single Action Unit

Once again servicing time is higher than it needs to be; a thread occurs with each match. We can cut the servicing time in half by utilizing both action units.

Programming a PWM Using Two Action Units

So let's program the PWM using the full dual-action power available in the eTPU. Our function will have two threads: an initialization thread that, among other things, programs a rising output pin edge to occur upon one match and a falling output pin edge upon another match; and a thread that executes when the second match occurs and schedules both the next rising edge the next falling edge. The channel mode we'll use issues a service request when a match occurs against **MRL_B**.

This function, utilizing both action units, requests servicing half as often as the previous function. The function can handle an initial low pulse as well, although that is true as the first PWM function as well. Midway through the run shown in Figure 5.7, the host has changed the hightime, keeping the period the same; the function responds gracefully.

```
#include <etpuc.h>

#pragma entryaddr 0x00;

#pragma ETPU_function PWMTwo;

void PWMTwo ( int24 Period, int24 HighTime ) {
    if (hsr == 7){
        pdcm = m2_st;                        // Use Match2, single transition mode
        act_unitA = Mtcr1_Ctcr1_ge;          // Use TCR1 for matches on action unit A
        act_unitB = Mtcr1_Ctcr1_ge;          // Use TCR1 for matches on action unit B
        opacA = match_high;                  // On MatchA, set pin high
        opacB = match_low;                   // On MatchB, set pin low
        pin = pin_low;                       // Initialize output pin
        erta = tcr1 + Period - HighTime;     // Calculate match time for
                                             // action unit A
        ertb = tcr1 + Period;                // Calculate match time for action unit B
        erwA = 0;                            // Write ERT_A to MatchA and enable matches
        erwB = 0;                            // Write ERT_B to MatchB and enable matches
        mtd = 0;                             // Enable match, transition event handling
    }

    else if (m2 == 1){                       // If MatchB occurs...
        erta = tcr1 + Period - HighTime;     // Calculate next match time for
                                             // action unit A
        ertb = tcr1 + Period;                // Calculate next match time for act. unit B
        erwA = 0;                            // Write ERT_A to MatchA and enable matches
        erwB = 0;                            // Write ERT_B to MatchB and enable matches
        mrlA = 0;                            // Clear MatchA event
        mrlB = 0;                            // Clear MatchB event
    }

    else {}  // Error recovery code ...
}
void main (void) {}
```

Example 5.4 PWM Code Using Both Action Units

Figure 5.7 shows the pin pulses and servicing threads in action.

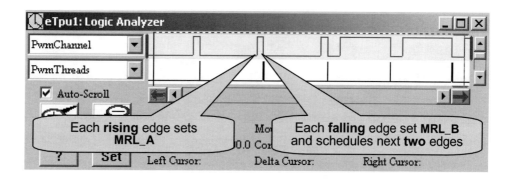

Figure 5.7 PWM in Action (Starting with a High Pulse)

We're now ready to move to a more a more complicated picture of the eTPU: multiple functions running on multiple channels, which is the topic of the next chapter.

Lab 5

Open the Lab 5 project in the Simulator. You will see the logic analyzer, a source code file, and a few other windows. This lab gets you familiar with the concept of using both action units.

1. A transmission rotation detector sends pulses that need to be measured. If the pulse width exceeds either of two timeout values, then a global error indicator needs to be set. Modify the Lab5.c file to set the global error indicator if the pulse width exceeds either of two maximums values, in terms of number of **TCR1** ticks, that are provided to the function in the form of two function variables. The channel mode has been provided for you. In this lab, three pulses are sent to the channel to which the function has been assigned. The first has a width of 15 μs (750 **TCR1** ticks), the second has a width of 30 μs (1500 **TCR1** ticks), and the third has a width of 40 μs (2000 **TCR1** ticks). (**TCR1** ticks once every 20 ns in this example.) Given the values of the function variables provided (in this case 0x700, or 1792, for the first function variable and 0x950, or 2384, for the second), the first two pulses should leave the error flag cleared while the third pulse should set it. Figure 5.8 shows the match and transition threads occurring on the channel to which the function has been assigned.

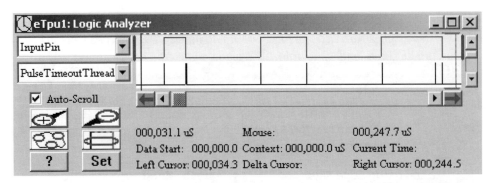

Figure 5.8 PulseTimeout

CHAPTER 6

Moving to Multiple Channels

This chapter describes various concepts associated with multi-channel programming. The details can be found in Part II in *Chapter 12. The Scheduler*.

Context

Until this juncture, a single function has been running on a single channel, monitoring a single input pin or toggling a single output pin. But eTPU code typically consists of multiple eTPU functions. Each function may be assigned to one or more channels. It is the role of the host CPU to tie a function to the appropriate channel(s). The compiler assigns sequential values to each function (e.g., PWM = 0, SPARK = 1, UART = 2, etc.), and the host writes each of these function values (e.g., 0, 1, 2, etc.) to the channel function select (**CFS**) field in the channel <x> configuration register (**ETPUCxCR**) of the channel(s) to which that function is to be assigned. Figure 6.1 shows how multiple channels may be assigned the same function (in this case PWM).

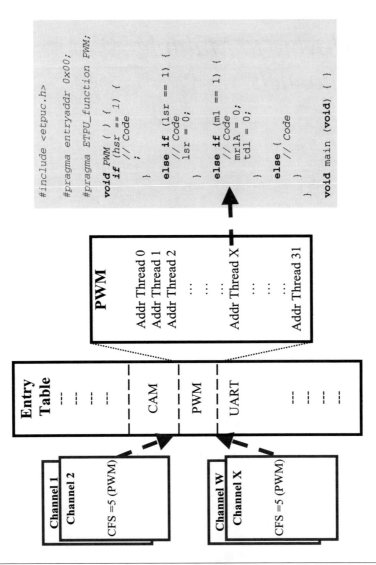

```
#include <etpuc.h>

#pragma entryaddr 0x00;

#pragma ETPU_function PWM;

void PWM ( ) {
    if (hsr == 1) {
        // Code
        ;
    }
    else if (lsr == 1) {
        // Code
        lsr = 0;
    }
    else if (m1 == 1) {
        // Code
        mr1A = 0;
        td1 = 0;
    }
    else {
        // Code
    }
}

void main (void) { }
```

Figure 6.1 Multiple Channels Executing the Same Function

An eTPU engine has 32 orthogonal channels. And of course each eTPU channel includes an input/output signal pair. During program execution of a given thread, the contents of the special engine-wide **CHAN** register determines which of the 32 channel input/output signal pairs is acted upon in that thread. This run-time **CHAN** specification helps to make up the thread's "context." The **CHAN** specification is transparent to the programmer and is automatically set at the beginning of the thread. Also immediately before the thread begins execution (a period of time known as a *time-slot transition*), the contents of the **CaptureA** and **CaptureB** registers of the channel to be serviced are loaded into the respective **ERT** registers.

How does this work in real life? Take the "real-life" description of event-handling from Chapter 4 and add channel-relevant details (the additions are italicized): The programmer writing a function specifies which type of entry table to use (standard or alternate) and then writes code for those event/condition combinations that are relevant to the function at hand. (Code in the mandatory `else` clause at the end of each eTPU function should handle any unused event/condition combinations.) *The CPU software assigns that function to a channel (or more).* The compiler creates, in code memory, the actual entry table for that function and all other functions. The eTPU is set in motion by the hose. An event (such as an input pin edge) occurs. The microengine detects the event, *determines the channel on which the event occurred, determines the function assigned to that channel,* sees which event/condition combination applies (depending on the event in question and the other channel conditions), finds that entry in that function's entry table, and from it determines the address of the thread to be executed (i.e., the entry point). *During the time-slot transition, the contents of the capture registers of the channel to be serviced are loaded into the respective* **ERT** *registers and the* **CHAN** *register is loaded with the new channel number.* The microengine then executes the thread at hand. If appropriate, the event is cleared by the thread, and the microengine either proceeds to service the next waiting service request or lies idle until the next service request occurs.

A thread's run-time context is made up of a variety of information, including (not exhaustively):

- The channel number in question (**CHAN** register);
- The function being run on that channel (**ETPUCxCR.CFS**);
- Match-recognition, transition-detection, and link indicators (used for conditional execution and clearing);
- The contents of the **ERT_A** and **ERT_B** registers;
- The state of the input pin upon thread entry;
- The *current* input pin state (this may be different from the state upon thread entry, namely if the pin toggles between the time of thread entry and the time that the pin is sampled within the thread);
- The current output pin state;
- Configuration of input pin transition detection (**IPAC_A** and **IPAC_B**);

- Configuration of output pin action control (**OPAC_A** and **OPAC_B**);
- Function variables;
- The semaphore lock state;
- Engine-register flags such as zero, carry, negative, and overflow (**Z, C, N, V**).

> **Note:** All of these items, except for the semaphore lock state and the engine register flags, constitute the context that is automatically restored on a context switch (time slot transition). Semaphores and engine register flags are not strictly part of channel context but rather are resources that are valid only during execution of a thread. These would have to be saved using eTPU code if needed.

All of the above should be familiar to you, with the exception of semaphores, engine-register flags, and function variables. Semaphores are discussed in *Chapter 12. The Scheduler*; and engine-register flags are discussed in *Chapter 8. Engine Architecture and Programming Model*. We'll move now to a discussion of function variables.

Function Variables

In standard "C" data scoping, all variables have scope. The possibilities include:

- Global: A single static copy common to all functions.
- Static local: A single static copy accessible to only that function, otherwise hidden.
- Dynamic local: The variable exists only during thread execution, then disappears.

The eTPU supports all of the above. In Example 6.1, you will see eponymously-named examples of each.

```
#include <etpuc.h>

#pragma entryaddr 0x00;

#pragma ETPU_function VariablesFunc;

int24 MyGlobalDelay;

void VariablesFunc () {
    int24         MyDynamicLocalDelay;
    static int24  MyStaticLocalDelay;

    if (hsr == 1) {
        MyGlobalDelay=5;
        MyDynamicLocalDelay=7;
        MyStaticLocalDelay=9;
    }

    else {}
}

void main (void) {}
```

Example 6.1 Standard "C" Variables Are Supported

Suppose you want to run a PWM function on multiple channels, but with each channel having a unique period and pulse width. For instance, you want to do the following:

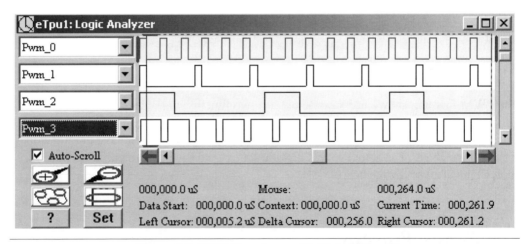

Figure 6.2 PWM Running on Multiple Channels

One way to do this would be to write separate functions for each channel, using, for instance, static local Period and PulseWidth variables unique for each. But this is wasteful, and the eTPU provides a better way: function variables.

```
#include <etpuc.h>

#pragma entryaddr 0x00;

#pragma ETPU_function PWM;

void PWM ( int24 Period, int24 HighTime ) {
   if (hsr == 7){
      pdcm = m2_st;                     // Use Match2, single transition mode
      act_unitA = Mtcr1_Ctcr1_ge;       // Use TCR1 for matches on action unit A
      act_unitB = Mtcr1_Ctcr1_ge;       // Use TCR1 for matches on action unit B
      opacA = match_high;               // On MatchA, set pin high
      opacB = match_low;                // On MatchB, set pin low
      pin = pin_low;                    // Initialize output pin
      erta = tcr1 + Period - HighTime;  // Calculate match time for
                                        // action unit A
      ertb = tcr1 + Period;             // Calculate match time for action unit B
      erwA = 0;                         // Write ERT_A to MatchA and enable matches
      erwB = 0;                         // Write ERT_B to MatchB and enable matches
      mtd = 0;                          // Enable match, transition event handling
   }

   else if (m2 == 1){                   // If MatchB occurs...
      erta = tcr1 + Period - HighTime;  // Calculate next match time for
                                        // action unit A
      ertb = tcr1 + Period;             // Calculate next match time for act. unit B
      erwA = 0;                         // Write ERT_A to MatchA and enable matches
      erwB = 0;                         // Write ERT_B to MatchB and enable matches
      mrlA = 0;                         // Clear MatchA event
      mrlB = 0;                         // Clear MatchB event
   }

   else {}  // Error recovery code ...
}

void main (void) {}
```

Example 6.2 PWM Code

The PWM function shown in Example 6.2 has two function variables, Period and HighTime. Each instance of this PWM function will have its own copy, or version, of these variables, and therefore each channel that runs this function can have unique values for these variables. The actual values that the Period and PulseWidth variables hold for each channel are set by the host.

Link Service Requests

A link service request may be used when one function needs to communicate with another function for the purpose of triggering a set of sequential events. For example, suppose we want to run a triggered pulse on multiple channels, as shown in Figure 6.3.

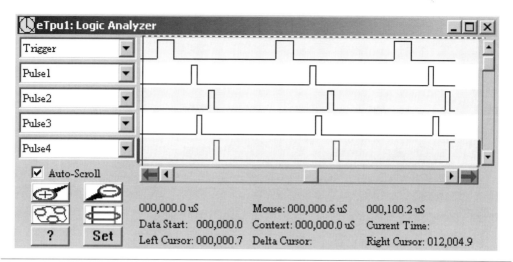

Figure 6.3 Triggered Pulse on Multiple Channels

Here, each time a trigger occurs, we want to set in motion a pulse in four other channels. In other words, we want the channels to communicate with each other directly without host intervention. This can be done by means of link service requests (LSRs), or links.

First we'll write a function that will execute when the trigger occurs. In this function, the trigger count will be saved off, and a link request will be issued to start the other channels that have been assigned the triggered pulse function.

```
#include <etpuc.h>

#pragma entryaddr 0x00;

#pragma ETPU_function PulseTrigger;

int24 TriggerCount;

void PulseTrigger( int24 PulseChan0, int24 PulseChan1,
        int24 PulseChan2, int24 PulseChan3 ) {
    if (hsr == 1) {
        act_unitA = Mtcr1_Ctcr1_ge;    // Use TCR1 for captures
        mtd = 0;                       // Enable match, transition event handling
        ipacA = high_low;              // Detect a falling edge
    }

    else if (m2 == 1) {               // If MatchB or TransitionA
        TriggerCount = erta;          // Save off the transition time
        link = PulseChan0;            // Link to pulse channel 0
        link = PulseChan1;            // Link to pulse channel 1
        link = PulseChan2;            // Link to pulse channel 2
        link = PulseChan3;            // Link to pulse channel 3
        tdl = 0;                      // Clear transition latches
    }

    else  {}
}
```

Example 6.3 PulseTrigger Code

The triggered pulse function we'll write is similar to the PWM, but in this case we have a link service request as one of the conditionals in the series of if-else statements and a reference to the global variable triggerCount. Again, a single function is written, to be assigned to the four different channels; the unique delay and pulse width for each channel are passed through as function variable values by the host.

```
#pragma ETPU_function DelayedPulse;

void DelayedPulse ( int24 Delay, int24 PulseWidth ) {
    if (hsr == 3) {
        pin = pin_low;               // Initialize output pin to low
        act_unitA = Mtcr1_Ctcr1_ge;  // For action unit use A TCR1 for
                                     // matches, greater-than-or-equal-to
        act_unitB = Mtcr1_Ctcr1_ge;  // For action unit use B TCR1 for
                                     // matches, greater-than-or-equal-to
        opacA = match_high;          // On MatchA set pin high
        opacB = match_low;           // On MatchB set pin low
        pdcm = m2_st;                // Use Match2, single transition channel mode
        mtd = 0;                     // Enable match, transition event handling
    }

    else if (lsr == 1) {             // If link service request...
        erta = TriggerCount + Delay; // Calculate next match time for action
                                     // unit A
        ertb = TriggerCount + Delay + PulseWidth;   // Calculate next match time
                                                    // for action unit B

        erwA = 0;                    // Write ERT_A to MatchA and enable
        erwB = 0;                    // Write ERT_B to MatchB and enable
        lsr = 0;                     // Clear link service request event
    }

    else if (m2 == 1) {              // If MatchB or TransitionA...
        mrlA = 0;                    // Clear MatchAevent
        mrlB = 0;                    // Clear MatchBevent
    }

    else  {}
}
```

Example 6.4 Delayed Pulse Code

Here the two functions PulseTrigger and Delayed Pulse are part of the same file. The entry table base address is specified just once, as is the inclusion of the header files.

If you run this example in the Simulator, you'll see that first each of the five host service request threads gets executed, one for each of the five channels. The channel running the TriggerPulse function is assigned a higher priority and so is run first, which in turn sets up the transition detection logic (to detect a falling edge) on that channel. When the falling input pin edge occurs on that channel, a link service request is issued to each of the four DelayedPulse channels. The link service thread of each of the DelayedPulse channels then gets executed, each of which sets up two future matches on the channel in question. Then, for each channel, when a match against **MatchB** occurs (which necessarily occurs after a match against **MatchA** because **MatchA** has been set to TriggerCount + Delay while **MatchB** has been set to TriggerCount + Delay + PulseWidth, both match events are cleared. If and when another falling edge on the PulseTrigger input pin occurs, the cycle starts over again.

The Scheduler

In the triggered pulse example above, four channels request service once the trigger occurs. How does the engine decide which channel to service first, which second, etc? It is the job of the scheduler to determine, when multiple channels require service, the order in which to respond to them. A detailed explanation of the scheduler is available in *Chapter 12. The Scheduler*. Here we'll provide a high-level description.

It is important that the rules employed by the scheduler are both fair and efficient. Channels that are running high-priority functions should get faster service, but not to the extent that a lower-priority channel's service requests are never handled. Remember that when a channel gets serviced, it is a particular thread that is executed. The time during which any particular thread executes is called a "time slot." Each time slot is assigned a priority—high, middle, or low. There are more high-level time slots than middle, and more middle-level time slots than low. This ensures that higher-priority channels are serviced more often than lower-priority channels. Further, a round-robin algorithm is employed to ensure that multiple channels of the same priority get serviced in turn. In short, we have two priority schemes—the primary one ranking inter-priority-level requests and the secondary one handling intra-priority-level requests—working simultaneously to ensure both fairness and efficiency.

Channel Disabling

As mentioned earlier, a channel may be assigned (by the host) a priority of high, middle, or low. The priority level of a channel is used by the scheduler to assign threads to time slot transitions. In addition to these three available priorities, a channel may have its priority set to null! This effectively disables the channel. In fact, out of reset, all eTPU channels are disabled.

It is possible to change the channel priority level (even setting it to null) in the middle of thread execution. If the host disables a channel while it is being serviced, the thread is not preempted and is allowed to complete. A pending service request that occurs before or while a channel is disabled remain pending, and ignored. If and when a channel becomes enabled (by receiving a priority level of high, middle, or low), any pending service requests for that channel enter the queue and are serviced according to the scheduling algorithms described above.

> **Note:** Each channel has a service status (**SS**) bit in the eTPU channel service status register (**ETPUCSSR**). This bit is set at time slot-transition and stays set until the thread ends. To avoid data coherency problems, if the host disables a channel it should then poll this bit to ensure that the channel service is completed before attempting to access channel resources.

Putting It All Together

At this stage we're ready to put everything together. Take the "real-life" description of multi-channel execution from earlier in this chapter and add scheduling details (the additions are italicized): The programmer writing a function specifies which type of entry table to use (standard or alternate) and then writes code for those event/condition combinations that are relevant to the function at hand. (A mandatory empty else clause at the end of each eTPU function should handles any unused event/condition combinations.) The programmer assigns that function to a channel (or more). The compiler creates, in code memory, the actual entry table for that function and all other functions. The eTPU is set in motion by the host. An event occurs. *A service request is issued. The scheduler receives the service request and determines which request is to be serviced next, according to the algorithms mentioned above. When it is time to service the request in question,* the microengine determines the channel on which the event occurred, determines the function assigned to that channel, sees which event/condition combination applies (depending on the event in question and the other channel conditions), finds that entry in that function's entry table, from it discovers the address of the thread to be executed (i.e., the entry point). During the time-slot transition, the contents of the capture registers of the channel to be serviced are loaded into the respective **ERT** registers. The request is serviced and, if appropriate, the event is cleared by the thread. The microengine either proceeds to service the next waiting service request (from that channel or another one) or lies idle until the next service request occurs.

Lab 6

This lab utilizes links and function variables in a function that runs on multiple channels. In order for you to solve this lab, you will need to become familiar with the way that the Simulator simulates instructions from the host. The Simulator makes use of what is known as a script commands file to simulate host instructions. Open the Lab6.ETpuCommand file in a text editor to see the following (see Figure 6.4):

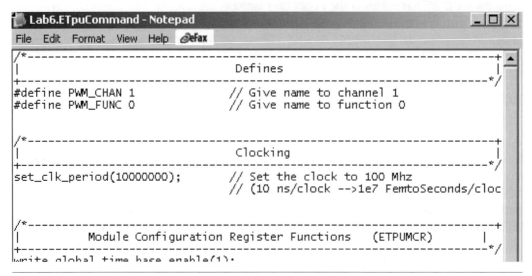

Figure 6.4 Script Commands File

Take a careful look at this file. You can use it as a template for eTPU simulations that you want to perform. Refer to *Appendix H. Registers Glossary* as well as the help files in the Simulator to determine what the options are for various of the engine registers named in this file and what the syntax is for those options. For the purposes of this lab, you will want to pay special attention to those instructions that configure PWM_CHAN and PWM_FUNC.

Now open Lab6.Vector, also in a text editor, to see the following (see Figure 6.5).

```
Lab6.vector - Notepad                                    _ □ ×
File  Edit  Format  View  Help  @eFax
// Assign the channels logical names
node InputPin           ch0.in
node PwmChannel         ch1.out
node tcrclk             |tcrclk

// Threads stuff ..
node TimeSlotTransition ThreadsTst
node Idle               ThreadsIdle
node Active             ThreadsGroupA
node PwmThreads         ThreadsGroupB

// Create two single node groups
// (Multiple node groups are possible)
```

Figure 6.5 Vector File

Test vector files are the Simulator's representation of the external interface to the eTPU. The thread instructions in this particular file provide logical names for thread information that is captured in the Simulator (given the right configuration). The last set of instructions implement a waveform on channel 0's input pin. The first set of instructions provide logical names for the channels' input and output pins. Here, the output pin for channel 1 is given the name *PwmChannel*. Once this vector file is loaded into the Simulator, we can use the drop-down lister on the left to choose to display *PwmChannel* instead of *ch1.out* in the logic analyzer. See Figure 6.6.

Figure 6.6 Displaying an Output Pin's Alternate Name

Let's now move to the lab itself.

1. Open and run Lab6.ETpuSimProject in the Simulator. You'll see a standard PWM function.

2. Modify the Lab6.c file to trigger the start of the PWM from a pulse. You will create a trigger function that will use the waveform that is already established (by means of the vector file) on channel 0's input pin. The trigger itself should occur

upon the second pulse on the input pin. A global variable should hold the time of the falling edge of the second pulse, which should gate the start of the LowTime of the PWM. The LinkToChannel instructions should call, respectively, channel numbers 1, 2, 3, and 4 directly, rather than using function variables for the channel number as was done in Example 6.3. The PWM function must be modified to be gated from the link request.

3.   Using any text editor, modify the Lab6.ETpuCommand file to run the PWM function on channels 1, 2, 3, and 4, and to run the Trigger function on channel 0. Use function number 0 for the Trigger function and function number 1 for the PWM function (assuming that the `#pragma ETPU_function Trigger` occurs before `#pragma ETPU_function PWM` in the source code file). Use the standard entry table encoding scheme for all channels. Set each channel's base address as indicated in Table 6.1. Set the priority of the trigger channel to 3 (high) and that of the PWM channels to 1 (low). Set the period, and high-time of the PWM on each of the four channels as indicated in Table 6.1.

Channel	RAM Base Address	Period	High-Time
0	0x300	--	--
1	0x350	0x100	0x010
2	0x400	0x160	0x035
3	0x450	0x120	0x075
4	0x500	0x080	0x005

Table 6.1 Period and High-Time for Multi-Channel, Triggered PWM

To import a revised script commands file into the Simulator, use the Files/Primary Script, Fast menu option (or Ctrl+P). See Figure 6.7.

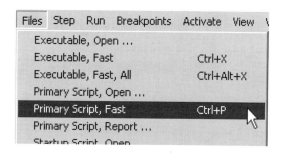

Figure 6.7 Loading a Modified Script Commands File

4. If desired, modify the Lab6.vector file, using any text editor, to provide logical names for the additional channels used.

To import the revised vector file into the Simulator, use the Files/Vector, Fast menu option (or Ctrl+V). See Figure 6.8.

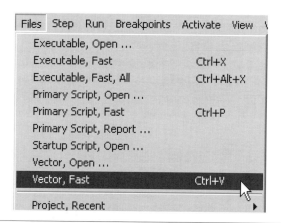

Figure 6.8 Loading a Modified Vector File

To display the additional channels, you can just enlarge the logic analyzer and then select the desired channels to display as in Figure 6.6.

The resulting waveforms should look like Figure 6.9. You can see that the time between the falling edge of the input pin's second pulse and the rising edge of PWM_1's first pulse is 4.8 ms;[1] this corresponds to 240 **TCR1** ticks, which is what is expected (0x100 - 0x010).

(Given the clocking and time base configuration instructions in the script commands file for this lab, **TCR1** ticks once every 20 ns.)

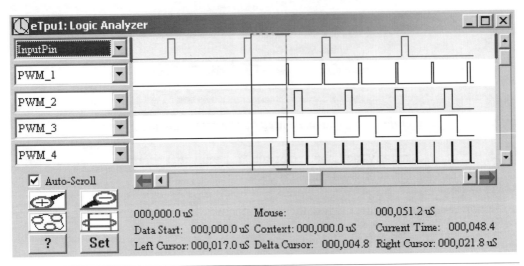

Figure 6.9 Multi-Channel, Triggered PWM in Action

As you change, compile, run, and debug your code, you may wish to keep track of the global variable TriggerTime as well as the function and local variables. See *Appendix B. ASH WARE's eTPU Stand-Alone Simulator* for information on opening and properly utilizing windows in the Simulator that provide views of these types of variables.

---

1. A small bug in the version of the Simulator included with this book drops the input pin edge 20 ns early, so each of the delta times in this lab is actually wide by 20 ns. This problem is scheduled to be fixed in a subsequent version of the Simulator.

Part II

CHAPTER 7 *Host Interface*

Introduction to the Host Interface

The host interface is made up of several registers that enable application software to set up the appropriate microengine and channel configurations as needed by the target application. Also provided is a set of local registers that allow complete control of each channel. There are a certain number of steps that are required by software to globally configure the microengine and locally configure and initialize each channel. The global and local configuration steps are provided at the end of this chapter. In dual eTPU implementations, the host interface is one contiguous memory mapped space that is utilized by both microengines.

Engine Configuration Registers

eTPU Module Configuration Register

The eTPU module configuration register (**ETPUMCR**), shown in Figure 7.1, is used for global configuration and error status reporting. A two-engine implementation will utilize a single **ETPUMCR**.

0	1	2	3	4	5	6	7	8	9	10	11	12	13	14	15
R 0	0	0	0	MGE_A	MGE_B	ILF_A	ILF_B	0	0	0	SCMSIZE				
W GEC															

16	17	18	19	20	21	22	23	24	25	26	27	28	29	30	31
R 0	0	0	0	0	SCM MISF	SCM	0	0	VIS	0	0	0	0	0	GTBE
W						MISEN									

Figure 7.1 eTPU Module Configuration Register (ETPUMCR)

Below is a brief description of each field in this register. These descriptions assume a dual-engine implementation. (In the case of a single-engine implementation, the **MGE_B** and **ILF_B** fields are not used, and the **GEC** field is utilized solely for the sake of the single engine.)

- **Global Exception Clear (GEC)**
  This bit reports a global error condition or conditions generated by either eTPU_A or eTPU_B. When set, this bit indicates that an illegal instruction or global eTPU code exception condition was encountered by one of the two microengines. This bit is also set when the multiple input signature calculator (**MISC**) error is reported in the SCM. To clear this bit, the exception handler must write a logic 1 to it. All error flags reported in the **ETPUMCR** will automatically be cleared when the **GEC** bit is cleared.

- **Microcode Global Exception A/B (MGE_A, MGE_B)**
  Each eTPU engine has its own **MGE** bit for error reporting. The bit is set by eTPU code to indicate that an unusual condition, such the loss of an expected input signal, has occurred during execution in the respective engine. The eTPU engine can report this status to allow host software to take control of the situation.

- **Illegal Instruction Flags A/B (ILF_A, ILF_B)**
  These flags indicate that eTPU_A or eTPU_B, respectively, encountered an illegal instruction during program execution.

- **Shared Code Memory Size (SCMSIZE)**
  Recall from Chapter 1 that the eTPU contains shared code memory (SCM) implemented as read/write memory for host CPU accesses, and read-only (instruction fetch) memory for the eTPU(s). The MPC5500 family will eventually have many derivatives, each of which may have a different shared code memory size. After reset, the application software will need to know the shared code memory size

available in a particular implementation for proper initialization and loading. This information is held in the read-only **SCMSIZE** field.

- **Shared Code Memory Multiple Input Signature Flag (SCMMISF)**
  The eTPU utilizes a multiple input signature calculator (MISC) in order to provide indication of data corruption of the SCM. The MISC reads each SCM address and generates a 32-bit, data-dependent signature. The calculated signature is compared with the original signature value in the eTPU MISC compare register (**ETPUMISCCMPR**). The **ETPUMISCCMPR** is global to both engines and contains the original 32-bit signature value written by software when the SCM is first loaded with eTPU code. If the two signatures do not compare, a global exception is reported to the host CPU by setting the **SCMMISF** bit in the **ETPUMCR**. This procedure is repeated continuously if the multiple input signature is enabled.

- **Visibility (VIS)**
  Application software must write the **VIS** bit with a logic 1 in order to load the SCM with eTPU functions. When set, the **VIS** bit allows software (or the DMA) to access the SCM. After the eTPU functions have been loaded into the SCM, this bit must be cleared in order to allow the microengine to read the SCM. As long as the **VIS** bit is set, the microengine will stay in the halted state and will not be able to run.

  > **Note:** The **VIS** bit may be written only when the eTPU engine is stopped. After reset, the eTPU is running. To stop it, set the **MDIS** bit in the eTPU engine configuration register (**ETPUECR**). In a dual-eTPU systems, both engines must be stopped before **VIS** can be written.

- **Global Time Base Enable (GTBE)**
  Setting this bit will simultaneously enable the time bases of both eTPU engines. This bit is also mirrored in the enhanced modular I/O system timer module configuration register (**EMIOSMCR**) to provide time base synchronization between all three timer modules in the MPC5500 family, if applicable.[1]

eTPU Engine Configuration Register

Each eTPU engine has a configuration register (**ETPUECR**) containing configuration and status fields that are programmed independently. These fields allow the software to set up the filter mode for the input signals and to control eTPU engine operation. Figure 7.2 shows the register format.

---

1. Note that some MPC5500 family derivatives include two eTPU engines and a modular I/O timer system (eMIOS).

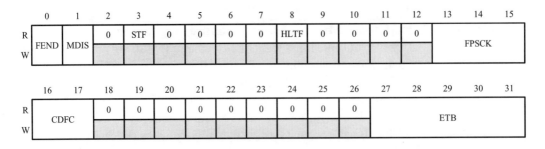

Figure 7.2 Engine Configuration Register (ETPUECR)

Below is a brief description of each field in this register.

- **Force End (FEND)**
  Setting this control bit ends the current thread being executed by the eTPU engine. Typically, this bit should be set only when the engine reports a global error such as illegal instruction or SCM multiple input signature error. After forcing the thread to end, software should take the appropriate action to handle the global error condition.

- **Module Disable Bit (MDIS) and Stop Flag (STF)**
  Assertion of the **MDIS** bit causes the eTPU engine clocks to stop. **TCR1** and **TCR2** cease to increment, and input sampling stops. However, the BIU continues to run and the host can

  > **Note:** In dual-eTPU systems, since each eTPU has its own engine configuration register, application software can choose to run one and stop the other.

  access SPRAM and certain registers normally (see below for the exceptions). If **MDIS** is asserted while a thread is being executed, the microengine will stop after that thread completes. An engine asserts its **STF** to indicate that it has stopped. Since thread execution time is unknown, the host should poll the **STF** after the assertion of the **MDIS** bit to ensure thread execution has ended. After **MDIS** is set, and even before **STF** is asserted, data read from the channel configuration and control registers are not meaningful and a write is ineffective and produces a bus error. Also in this situation, a write to a time-base register is ineffective and produces a bus error (although a read from a time-base register is unaffected). The application software may need to disable the eTPU engine for one or more of the following reasons:

  a. To load the shared code memory (SCM);

    b.   To reduce power consumption by shutting down system clocks when the engine is idle;

    c.   An illegal instruction error is reported in the **ETPUMCR**;

    d.   A multiple input signature error is reported in the **ETPUMCR**.

- **Filter Prescaler Clock Control (FPSCK[0:2])**
  When the channel is configured as input, the input signal passes through a programmable input filter to eliminate any signal duration that is less than the expected input signal period. The **FPSCK** field controls prescaling of the clock from 2 to 256. Filtering can be controlled independently by each engine, but all input digital filters in a given engine have the same clock prescaling.

- **Channel Digital Filter Control (CDFC[0:1])**
  These bits select a digital filtering mode for the channels when configured as inputs to improve noise immunity. The eTPU has three digital filtering modes that provide programmable trade off between signal latency and noise immunity. Table 7.1 provides details on these three modes.

CDFC	*Digital Filter Selected*
0 0	Two-sample mode: This mode uses the filter clock (i.e., the system clock divided by (2, 4, 8,.., 256)) as a sampling clock (selected by **FPSCK** field in **ETPUECR**). When two consecutive samples agree with each other, the input signal state is set. This is the default reset state.
0 1	Three-sample mode: When three consecutive samples agree with each other, the input signal state is set. (This mode is similar to the TPU2/3 two-sample mode.)
1 0	Reserved.
1 1	Continuous mode: The signal needs to be stable for the whole filter clock period. This mode compares all the values at the rate of system clock divided by two, between two consecutive filter clock pulses. The signal needs to be continuously stable for the entire period. If all the values agree with each other, the input signal state is updated.

Table 7.1 Channel Digital Filter Control Selection

- **Entry Table Base (ETB[0:4])**
  The shared code memory (SCM) is accessible by both the host CPU and the eTPU. It is mapped in the host at memory locations 0xC3FD_0000 to 0xC3FD_3FFF[2] while the eTPU maps it starting at address 0x0000. The 5-bit **ETB** field, which is

  Note: The host CPU views SCM memory as byte addressable, while the eTPU views the SCM as 32-bit addressable.

programmed by the host, indicates the starting location of the entry table for the eTPU functions in SCM. If **ETB** is written with a 0 by the host, the entry table will be placed at location 0xC3FD_0000 (i.e., offset of 0x000) as viewed by the host and therefore will be seen by the eTPU at address 0x000. If **ETB** is written with a 1 by the host, the entry table will be at placed at location 0xC3FD_0800 (i.e., offset of 0x800) as viewed by the host and therefore will be seen by the eTPU at address 0x200. Table 7.2 shows multiple address offset options.

ETB	*Entry Table Base Address (host addressing)*	*Entry Table Base Address (eTPU code addressing)*
00000	0x000	0x000
00001	0x800	0x200
00010	0x1000	0x400
...	...	...
11110	0xF000	0x3C00
11111	0xF800	0x3E00

Table 7.2 Entry Table Base Address Options

TCR1 and TCR2 Clocking

Each eTPU engine has two timer counter registers, designated as **TCR1** and **TCR2**. The formats for each of these registers is as shown in figures 7.3 and 7.4.

---

2. Note these addresses are applicable to the MPC5554 implementation and could be and probably will be different on the ColdFire implementations.

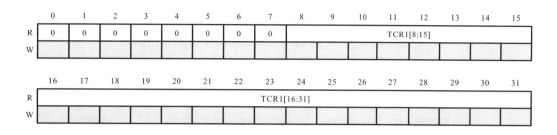

Figure 7.3 eTPU Time Base 1 (TCR1) Visibility Register (ETPUTB1R)

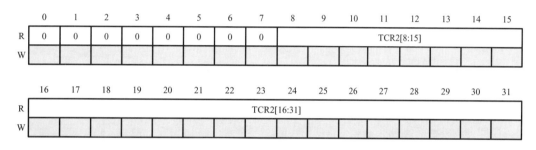

Figure 7.4 eTPU Time Base 2 (TCR2) Visibility Register (ETPUTB2R)

Both counters are 24-bit time base counters which are shared by all 32 channels for matches and captures. **TCR1** and **TCR2** clocking is controlled by the eTPU time-base control register (**ETPUTBCR**), which provides multiple options to select the clock source for each counter.

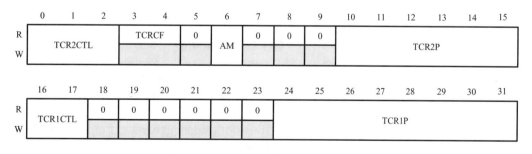

Figure 7.5 eTPU Time Base Configuration Register (ETPUTBCR)

TCR1 operation and clock selection of **TCR1** is controlled by the **TCR1CTL** field and is as shown in Figure 7.6. There are two choices available to clock **TCR1**:

- Externally clocked by the **TCRCLK** input, after the digital filter;
- Driven from the system clock divided by 2.
- "No clock" for TCR1.
  This works in either normal or angle mode.
  This option may be selected for the purpose
  of debug and development.

> **Note:** The "no clock" option
> (**TCR1CTL** =11) is useful only
> during debug and development.
> When TCR1 is in client mode,
> TCR1 clock selection is void.

A third clocking option is also available from the STAC bus. For STAC bus operation refer to *Chapter 10. Clocking and Angle Clock.* Any clock source selected by **TCR1CTL** is prescaled by a factor of 1 to 256 as defined by the **TCR1P** bit field in the **ETPUTBCR**.

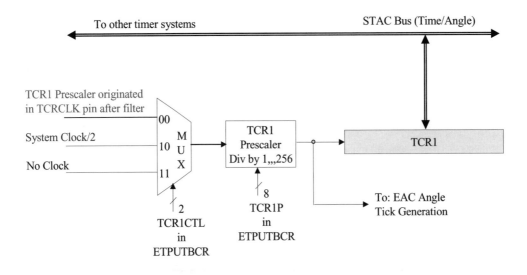

Figure 7.6 TCR1 Clock Selection

TCR2 clocking is controlled by the **TCR2CTL** field in the **ETPUTBCR** and has numerous choices of clock selection to meet certain requirements, as shown in Table 7.3.

For angle-based engine control applications, the tooth signal generated from the flywheel may be applied to **TCRCLK** input pin as the clock source to increment **TCR2**. The input signal edge is software programmable which allows incrementing **TCR2** on rising, falling, or both transitions. In angle mode, the type of edge detection on the input channel must match that of **TCRCLK** (only channel 0 is used for this mode).

TCR2CTL	TCR2 Clock
000	Gated DIV8 clock (system clock /8). When the external **TCRCLK** signal is low, the DIV8 clock is blocked, preventing it from incrementing **TCR2**. When the external **TCRCLK** signal is high, **TCR2** is incremented at the frequency of the system clock divided by 8.
001	Rise transition on **TCRCLK** signal increments **TCR2**.
010	Fall transition on **TCRCLK** signal increments **TCR2**.
011	Rise or fall transition on **TCRCLK** signal increments **TCR2**.
100	DIV8 clock (system clock/8)
110	No edge detection
111	No clock. This is similar to **TCR1CTL**=11, except that it should not be used in angle mode.

Table 7.3 TCR2CTL Clock Source

The **TCRCLK** digital filter can be programmed to use either the system clock divided by 2 or the same filter clock of the channels as controlled by the **TCRCF** field in **ETPUTBCR**. Another **TCRCLK** filter option is referred to as the *digital integrator*. The digital integrator mode uses a 2-bit up/down counter. In this mode, the 2-bit counter counts up to 3 when the input signal is a valid logic 1 and counts down to 0 when the input signal is a valid logic 0. For example, if the counter is at a count of 2 and the input signal changes to from 1 to 0, the counter will start to count down. In other words, if the 2-bit counter = 3 the input signal is assumed to be a logic 1, but if the counter = 0 the input signal is assumed to be a logic 0. In these two states, if there is no change on **TCRCLK** input the counter remains frozen at its current value.

TCRCF	Filter Input	Filter Mode
00	System clock divided by 2.	Two-sample
01	Filter clock of the channels.	Two-sample
10	System clock divided by 2.	Integration
11	Filter clock of the channels.	Integration

Table 7.4 TCRCLK FIlter Clock/Mode

When system clock divided by 2 is selected, the synchronizer and the digital filter are guaranteed to pass pulses that are wider than four system clocks (two filter clocks). Otherwise the **TCRCLK** is filtered with the same filter clock as the channel input signals.

Gated Mode

This mode increments **TCR2** with the rate derived from the system clock divided by 8. The **TCRCLK** pin signal is used to gate this count, enabling pulse accumulator operations.

Internally Clocked Modes

In these modes, **TCR2** is driven by the internal clock, with a count rate of the system clock divided by 8. All clock sources pass through a prescaler. In addition, the **TCR2** time base can be originated from the EAC, which is a hardware angle clock and angle counter. Figure 7.7 shows the diagram for **TCR2** clock control.

Angle Clock Mode

TCR1 or **TCR2** may be used to drive the shared timer and counter (STAC) bus when the appropriate **TCR** is selected as a server. As a server in angle mode, **TCR2** bus usually provides time or angle information to other timers channels via the STAC bus. For more information on STAC bus operation refer to *Chapter 10. Clocking and Angle Clock.*

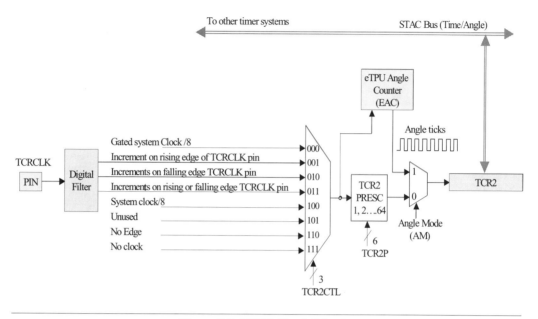

Figure 7.7 TCR2 Clock Selection

Other Options

If in angle mode, **TCR2CTL** = 110 selects "no edge" for **TCRCLK** detection by the eTPU angle clock (EAC). In this selection **TCR2** will still be incremented by the tick generator, and can be kept running by the eTPU code asserting insert physical tooth (IPH). This is useful when the **TCRCLK** signal becomes unreliable. In such cases, the eTPU code can use the CAM signal instead of the crank signal to calculate engine angular position.

The **TCRCLK** input signal detection by channel 0 is independent of this and selected by **IPAC_A/B**, so it can keep on monitoring the tooth signal even with **TCR2CTL** = 110.

> **Note:** The No Clock option is useful only during debug and development. When No Clock option is selected, (TCR2CTL=111) TCR2 should not be used in Angle Mode.

Channel Configuration and Status Registers

Channel configuration and status registers allow application software (and in some cases the eDMA as well) to initialize, control, and exchange messages and handshakes with the eTPU.

eTPU Channel x Configuration Register

The eTPU channel x configuration register (**ETPUCxCR**) holds configuration information for a given channel.

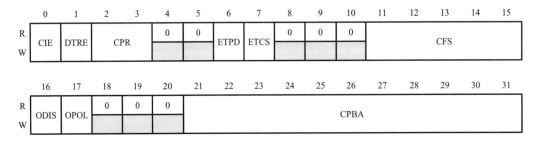

Figure 7.8 eTPU Channel x Configuration Register (ETPUCxCR)

A full explanation of each field is described below.

- **Channel Interrupt Enable (CIE)**
  Setting this bit enables interrupts for the channel See the description of the **CIS** bit in the **ETPUCxSCR** register, below, for further information.

- **Channel Data Transfer Request Enable (DTRE)**
  Setting this bit enables data transfer requests for the channel. See the description of the **DTRS** bit in the **ETPUCxSCR** register, below, for further information.

- **Channel Priority (CPR)**
  This 2-bit field assigns a priority level of low (01), middle (10) or high (11) to a channel. After reset, these 2 bits are cleared, thereby disabling the channel and preventing it from issuing service requests. This field should be the last field written during channel initialization. Software may write 0 to this bit field to disable an active channel. Writing a 0 to the priority bit field while the channel is executing will not preempt the current thread, but the channel becomes inactive thereafter.

- **Entry Table Pin Direction (ETPD)**
  This bit selects which channel signal, input (**ETPD** = 0) or output (**ETPD** = 1), is used in entry point selection. The **ETPD** value has to be compatible with the function chosen for the channel, selected in the field **CFS**.

- **Entry Table Condition Select (ETCS)**
  The **ETCS** field selects either a standard or an alternate entry point encoding scheme and must be compatible with the encoding scheme used by the function assigned to that channel. The entry point table itself is internal to the microengine. Software should write the bit value that is provided by the developer of the eTPU coded function.

- **Channel Function Select (CFS)**
  A function is a set of routines written to produce an output signal or detect the occurrence of an input signal. The signals may be simple pulses or quite complex pulse trains that are synchronized to either a time base, such as an RS232 protocol to receive at a particular baud rate, or a positional based system such as monitoring the angular position of a rotating engine crankshaft or electric motor. There can be up to 32 different timing functions loaded into SCM. The 5-bit **CFS** field, known as a *function code*, indicates which one of the 32 functions is assigned to the channel. The function code can be any value between 0x0 to 0x1F and are assigned by increasing number from 0, based on the order in which the source code is compiled. Multiple channels can be assigned the same function.

- **Output Disable (ODIS) and Output Polarity (OPOL)**
  Input signals to the eTPU channels driven from the enhanced modular I/O timer system (eMIOS) channels 8-11 and 20-23 may be used to disable the outputs on groups of eight eTPU_A and eTPU_B channels. The signal routing is fixed and is as shown in Table 7.5. For example, eMIOS input channel 11 may disable eTPU_A channels 0 to 7. These signals may be used by the eTPU channels to provide an emergency shut down upon the detection of a specific event on one of the eMIOS channels. Each eTPU channel has a control bit (**ODIS**) which allows the channel to accept or ignore the eMIOS signal routed to its group. If the **ODIS** bit is set the channel will drive its output pin to the opposite polarity of the **OPOL** bit when the eMIOS input asserts.

eMIOS Channel	eTPU Engine	Channels
11	A	0 to 7
10		8 to 15
9		16 to 23
8		24 to 31
20	B	0 to 7
21		8 to 15
22		16 to 23
23		24 to 31

Table 7.5 EMIOS Output Disable Signal to eTPU Channel Assignments

- **Channel Parameter Base Address (CPBA)**
  The **CPBA** field allows variable numbers of parameters to be assigned to each channel, (unlike the TPU which has the same number of parameters assigned to each channel). Each channel has its own **CPBA** that specifies the start address of that channel's portion of parameter RAM. This base address may be from 0 to 4K bytes in steps of 8 bytes. The parameter RAM address as seen by the host begins at 0xC3FC_8000 and ends at 0xC3FC_9BFF.

  > **Note:** Recall from that in dual eTPU implementations, the parameter RAM is shared by the two eTPU engines as well as the host CPU. Since parameters are accessible to both eTPUs, channel communication and message passing between the two engines are allowed directly without host or eDMA intervention.

  The host can access the parameter RAM as bytes, halfwords, and words, while the eTPU engines accesses can be upper 8 bits, lower 24 bits, or all 32 bit word.

eTPU Channel x Status Control Register

The eTPU channel x status control register (**ETPUCxSCR**) holds run-time status information for a given channel.

	0	1	2	3	4	5	6	7	8	9	10	11	12	13	14	15
R	CIS	CIOS	0	0	0	0	0	0	DTRS	DTROS	0	0	0	0	0	0
W	CIC	CIOC							DTRC	DTROC						

	16	17	18	19	20	21	22	23	24	25	26	27	28	29	30	31
R	IPS	OPS	OBE	0	0	0	0	0	0	0	0	0	0	0	FM	
W																

Figure 7.9 eTPU Channel x Status Control Register (ETPUCxSCR)

A full explanation of each field is described below.

- **Channel Interrupt Status (CIS)**
  The eTPU channel requests a CPU interrupt by setting the **CIS** bit. The CPU will acknowledge the channel request if the **ETPUCxCR.CIE** bit is set. Software should write a logic 1 to a set **CIS** bit to clear it. Writing 0 has no effect. Some texts may specify use of a **CIC** bit to clear the **CIS** bit, but they are at one and the same location.

- **Channel Interrupt Overflow Status (CIOS)**
  If a channel requests a second interrupt while the **CIS** is still set, an overflow status is indicated by setting the **CIOS** bit. When software eventually acknowledges the interrupt request, it should poll this bit to find out if an overflow condition occurred. Software should write a logic 1 to **CIOS** bit to clear it. Writing 0 has no effect. Some texts may specify use of a **CIOC** bit to clear the **CIOS** bit, but they are at one and the same location.

- **Data Transfer Request Status (DTRS)**
  Some eTPU channels have eDMA channels assigned to them and they may request a data transfer instead of interrupting the host CPU. The eTPU channel may signal an eDMA transfer request by setting the **DTRS** bit instead of asserting an interrupt request to the host. The eDMA will acknowledge the channel request if the **ETPUCxCR.DTRE** bit is set. After the DMA transfers the data requested by the channel, the DMA engine automatically clears this bit. (In the MPC5554 implementation, only 21 DMA channels are assigned to eTPU A and B combined.)

- **DMA Transfer Overflow Status (DTROS)**
  If a channel requests a second DMA transfer while the **DTRS** bit is still set, an overflow status is indicated by setting the **DTROS** bit. When the host CPU eventu-

ally acknowledges the channel interrupt request, software can test this bit to find out if an overflow condition occurred. Software should write a logic 1 to **DTROS** bit to clear it. Writing 0 has no effect. Some texts may specify use of a **DTROC** bit to clear the **DTROS** bit, but they are at one and the same location.

- **Input Pin State (IPS) and Output Pin State (OPS)**
  Software may read the **IPS** bit to determine the current state of the input signal. This bit indicates the state of the filtered signal at the input pad. The **OPS** is a status bit that indicates the logic level driven to the output pad. As stated earlier, a channel's input and output signals may be connected to the same pad or to two different pads.

- **Function Mode (FM)**
  The function mode may be used to specify up to four different operating modes of a function. Software can set and clear these bits as specified in the documentation for the selected eTPU function. If used, the function mode bits are tested by eTPU code to determine the mode selected within a function.

eTPU Channel x Host Service Request Register

The eTPU channel x host service request register (**ETPUCxHSRR**) is used by the host to issue service requests to the channel.

	0	1	2	3	4	5	6	7	8	9	10	11	12	13	14	15
R	0	0	0	0	0	0	0	0	0	0	0	0	0	0	0	0
W																

	16	17	18	19	20	21	22	23	24	25	26	27	28	29	30	31
R	0	0	0	0	0	0	0	0	0	0	0	0	0		HSR	
W																

Figure 7.10 eTPU Channel x Host Service Request Register (ETPUCxHSRR)

- **Host Service Request (HSR)**
  Host software writes a non-zero value to this 3-bit field to issue a host service request (**HSR**) to the channel. When the channel is serviced by the eTPU engine, these bits are automatically cleared to provide a handshaking mechanism between the host and the eTPU. To prevent overwriting of this field for an unserviced request, the host should write a non-zero value to this field only if the value is currently 0. Writing 0 to this field when the field contains a non-zero value will with-

draw any pending host service requests. If the HSR field is written with 0 during thread execution, the thread continues execution and will not be preempted.

eTPU Initialization Sequence Example

There are a certain number of steps required by software to globally configure the microengines and locally configure and initialize each channel. This eTPU configuration sequence example assumes an MPC5554 MCU derivative is used and is starting from a power-on reset. After configuring the eTPU module, the channel is configured and the function is initialized to execute a PWM.

Module Configuration

1. If the SCM MISC function is needed, write the calculated 32 bit signature value generated by the compiler from SCM array into the **ETPUMISCCMPR** register.
2. Set the **MDIS** bits in **ETPUECR_A/B** to stop both eTPU engines.
3. Set the **VIS** bit in the **ETPUMCR** to make the SCM visible to the host, clear all global exceptions, and enable the MISC function if desired. This step must occur after the previous one, because the **VIS** bit can be set only when both engines are stopped.
4. Copy the object code of eTPU functions into SCM from on-chip flash.
5. Clear the **VIS** bit to enable the SCM interface to the eTPU engines.
6. Clear the **MDIS** bits in both engines to enable system clock to the eTPUs.
7. Write the **ETPUECR** to select the filter clock prescaler (**FPSCK**), the digital filtering mode (**CDFC**), and the base address for the entry table (**ETB**).
8. Write global variables, if any, to the parameter RAM.
9. Write the **ETPUTBCR** to select the clock sources of **TCR1** and **TCR2** prescalers, select the digital filter mode, **TCRCLK** pin filtering and enable angle mode (**AM**), if required.
10. If STAC operation is required, write to the eTPU stack configuration register (**ETPUSTACR**) to select the desired server and clients on each module. *For additional information on STAC bus operation see chapter 10, Clocking and Angle Clock.*

   • Note: The ETPUSTACR is also known as ETPU Red Line Configuration Register (ETPUREDCR).

Channel Configuration

1. Write the **ETPUCxCR** to assign one of 32 functions (**CFS**), select the parameter base starting address for the channel (**CPBA**), and enable interrupts to the host or DMA transfer requests (**CIE**).

   > **Note:** If re-initializing a currently enabled channel, first turn off the channel by clearing its channel priority bit field.

2. If the assigned eTPU function uses a function mode, then write the appropriate function mode (**ETPUCxSCR.FM**).

Function Initialization

1. Write pertinent parameters for configured channels to parameter RAM.

2. Enable the global time base (**ETPUMCR.GTBE**) to enable time bases. Setting this bit in an MPC5554 implementation will enable time bases in both engines and the eMIOS timer system.

3. Issue a host service request to initialize the active channels by writing the **ETPUCxHSRR**.

4. Assign a low, middle, or high priority (**CPR**) in the **ETPUCxCR** of the channel that has been assigned that function. Once the channel has been assigned a priority, it becomes active and can request service from the scheduler.

5. If software needs to issue a multiple back-to-back host service requests, it should monitor the **HSR** field until the eTPU engine signals completion of function initialization. The host sets the **HSR** bits and the eTPU clears them only when the request is serviced.

Lab 7

This labs gives you additional practice in modifying host and channel configuration information by means of the Simulator's script commands file.

1. Open Lab7.ETpuCommand in a text editor and make the following modifications.[3]

---

3. Changing the entry table base address is not one of the requested changes only because the demonstration version of the Simulator requires that the **ETB** be set to 0x00.

a. Set the clock to 120 Mhz;

b. Set the **TCR2** to system clock/8 (you will be capturing **TCR2** rather than **TCR1** in both action units);

c. Set the **TCR2** prescaler to 2;

d. Set the channel's entry table encoding scheme to alternate;

e. Set the channel's priority level to low;

f. Send a host request of 3 to the channel.

2. Modify the Lab7.c file to accommodate the above changes.

3. Compile, run, and debug your code until it runs as intended.

CHAPTER 8 — *Engine Architecture and Programming Model*

The eTPU Microengine Instruction Set

While eTPU functions will normally be written in the "C" language, which hides much of the complexity of the eTPU engine hardware, the system designer will nevertheless find the information provided in this chapter important during the design and implementation, especially the debugging, of their code. Our objective in this chapter is to give the reader a complete understanding of the eTPU microengine by describing the programming model (i.e., the register set that is accessible by the microengine eTPU code for data and operand manipulation) and some of the microoperations.

eTPU microinstructions have a fixed width 32 bits, and each is capable of executing multiple operations in parallel during one microcycle execution time (i.e., two system clocks).[1] There are four types of eTPU microinstructions:

1. SPRAM Operations
2. ALU/MDU Operations
3. Channel Configuration and Control Operations
4. Flow Control Operations

We discuss each of these in turn, below. But we first move to a discussion of the microengine itself.

---

1. A complete listing of all microinstruction formats is provided in *Appendix G. Microinstruction Formats.*

Engine Architecture

The eTPU microengine fetches and executes instructions from the shared code memory (SCM). It uses the shared parameter RAM (SPRAM) to communicate with the host CPU. In dual-engine implementations, the SPRAM may also be used to pass parameters between the two engines.

As with other microprocessors, the eTPU engine has two organizations, the hardware architecture and the software architecture. The eTPU software architecture is reflected in the programming model, which indicates what resources are available to the programmer. The block diagram shown in Figure 8.1 shows the engine hardware and its bus connections to the programming model, which is visible to the eTPU code. As shown in this figure, the eTPU microengine consists of two execution units: the arithmetic/logic unit (ALU) and the multiply/divide unit (MDU). The ALU executes typical add, subtract, compare, shift, and logical operations, while the MDU executes multiply, multiply-accumulate, and divide operations. To increase performance, the ALU and the MDU can execute and process operations in parallel. The inclusion of the MDU hardware and the availability of numerous registers in the eTPU programming model allow the microengine to perform complex calculations without CPU intervention.

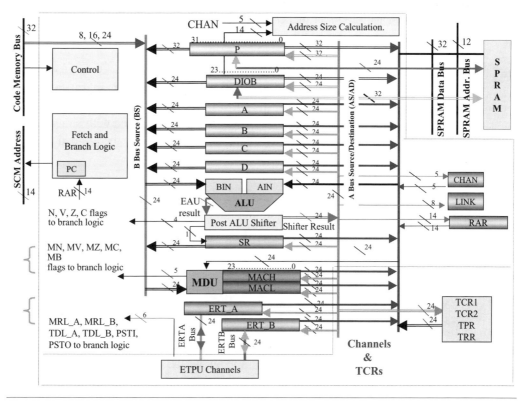

Figure 8.1 eTPU Execution Units

The eTPU microengine has a total of 18 registers. These registers are accessible only by eTPU code. Most of these registers are 24-bits wide and are used as general purpose, but there are some with a different width and serve as a special purpose. Each of these registers is described below:

- **Preload Register (P)**
  This is the only register that is 32 bits wide. It is typically used for reading and writing the SPRAM. When **P** is used as SPRAM source or destination, there are only 3 possibilities of access: all 32 bits, lower 24 bits, and upper 8 bits. During each time-slot transition, **P** is preloaded with either parameter 0 or parameter 2 of that channel's data, as determined by the preload parameter (**PP**) field in the entry point. **P** can also be used as a general-purpose scratch pad register and either a source or destination operand during arithmetic operations.

- **Data Input Output Buffer (DIOB)**
The **DIOB** is a 24-bit register that can be used as
a general purpose register. This register has
additional capability and may be used as an

  > Note: The **DIOB** and the **P** registers are the only two registers that have direct access to the SPRAM.

  SPRAM addressing register (described in the next section). As such, it can be
pre-decremented or post-incremented allowing for a stack operation in the
SPRAM. As with the **P** register, the **DIOB** is also preloaded during time-slot
transition. During each time-slot transition, **DIOB** is preloaded with either parameter 1 or parameter 3 of that channel's data, as determined by the preload parameter (**PP**) field in the entry point.

- **A, B, C, and D Registers**
These four 24-bit, general-purpose registers are used only in arithmetic operations
to hold intermediate results. They do not have any other special uses.

- **Multiply-Accumulate High and Low Registers (MACH and MACL)**
Both of the multiply-accumulate registers are 24-bit registers and are used mainly
by the MDU. They can also be used as source and destination in most arithmetic/
logic operations. More information about these registers are provided later in this
chapter in the section on MDU operations.

- **Shift Register (SR)**
The **SR** is a 24-bit register that can be used as source and destination register for
arithmetic and logical operations. The **SR** can be right shifted by 1 bit at time. A
concatenation of the ALU result and **SR** allows for a 48 bit shift right when both
are specified for a shift right operation.

- **Event Register Temporary A and B (ERT_A and ERT_B)**
These two registers are 24 bits wide and are the only two that have direct read and
write access to **MatchA** and **MatchB**, which is to say that the **ERT** registers are the
only mechanism for setting up for a match. During the time-slot transition, **ERT_A**
and **ERT_B** are loaded with a copy of **CaptureA** and **CaptureB** registers respectively. The value loaded into the **ERT** register indicates the exact time of the captured event (either a match or a transition). **ERT_A** and **ERT_B** can also be used as
general-purpose registers by the ALU.

- **Timer Count Registers 1 and 2 (TCR1 and TCR2)**
These 24-bit counters provide the time base for all 32 channels. A read operation
of **TCR1** or **TCR2** will get the current "time" (or count) in that register; a write
operation to each of these two registers will update their contents. For more information on these counters, refer to *Chapter 10. Clocking and Angle Clock.*

- **Tooth Program Register (TPR)**
This 16-bit register can be programmed by the eTPU code when the engine is

operating in angle clock mode. When the engine is not in angle clock mode, this is a general-purpose register. See to Chapter 10 for more information.

- **Tick Rate Register (TRR)**
  This 24-bit register contains angle tick integer and fractional period information when the engine is configured to be in angle clock mode. Refer to Chapter 10 for additional information. When the engine is not in angle clock mode, this register can be used as a general purpose register.

- **Return Address Register (RAR)**
  Although it can be used as source or destination in arithmetic operations, the main purpose of this 14-bit register is to hold the program counter (PC) value upon a subroutine call. On

  > **Note:** In the TPU, the **RAR** was not accessible and as a result subroutine nesting was not possible.

  return from the subroutine, this register is copied back into the program counter (PC). Being accessible to the eTPU code, this register allows for subroutine nesting by saving return addresses to parameter RAM. During time slot transition, this register is loaded with the value 0x3FFF. This register is 14 bits wide because that is all that is necessary to access any one-word location in the SCM (the SCM maximum size is 64K bytes and contains only eTPU coded instructions, and instructions are always 32-bit words).

- **Link Register (LINK)**
  This register is eight bits wide and is used to issue a link service request to any one of the 32 channels by holding the channel number in the five least significant bits of **LINK** register of the channel for which the link is being issued. In dual-engine implementations, the **LINK** register can specify a channel in either of the two engines. Engine selection is determined by the **LINK** register's two most significant bits. In a single engine eTPU, **LINK** is ignored when sent to the other engine (eTPU_B). Refer to Table 8.1 for engine service request selection.

Engine Selection	*Description*
00	This engine
01	Engine 1
10	Engine 2
11	The other engine[a]

a. In dual-engine implementations, the other engine option allows a function to run on either engine.

Table 8.1 Link Service Request Encoding

- **Channel Register (CHAN)**
  This register is five bits wide and is loaded with the channel number of the channel being dispatched for service upon a time-slot transition. Changing the value of this register allows the current channel to control the hardware of another channel.

The registers described above are connected to the internal buses of the eTPU engine as shown in Figure 8.1. Note that most registers can source either the A bus or the B bus during ALU operation, with the destination results always driven on the A bus. However, registers smaller than 24 bits wide can source only the A bus. Note that there is a third bus connection between the **P**/**DIOB** registers and the SPRAM bus.

Shared Parameter RAM Access Microoperations

As pointed out earlier, the SPRAM is data memory space that can be used for message passing between the eTPU and the host. Typically the CPU writes parameter information to SPRAM at initialization and during eTPU function execution. For example, for the PWM function, the CPU writes the period and the high time in channel parameters. For its part, the eTPU gives feedback to the CPU through SPRAM. For example, a channel executing period measurement function will write the period measured to a channel parameter.

The access to SPRAM is made by providing an address and a register to perform a data transfer. Only **P** and **DIOB** registers can exchange data with SPRAM since they are the only two with a bus connection to it. The **P**/**DIOB** (**P/D**) microinstruction field indicates whether **P** (0) or **DIOB** (1) is to be used for parameter exchange. The microengine always addresses SPRAM on 32-bit

Note: An 8-bit transfer will be upper bits. For example, **P[31:24]** = SPRAM[31:24]). A 24-bit transfer will be lower bits. For example, **DIOB[23:0]** = SPRAM[23:0]).

boundaries, whether for 8-, 24-, and 32-bit operand data accesses. While SPRAM data accesses are always 24 bits for **DIOB**, the microinstruction field register size (**RSIZ**) determines whether the data is 8, 24, or 32 bits wide for **P**. The direction of the data transfer is determined by the read write (**RW**) field in all addressing modes: **RW** = 0 indicates a read from the SPRAM while **RW** = 1 indicates a write to SPRAM.

SPRAM can be cleared using the zero (**ZRO**) microinstruction field. The size of the operand cleared may be 8, 24, or 32 bits depending on the **RSIZ** field specified in the instruction. The **ZRO** field also allows clearing of **P** and **DIOB** registers. In a **DIOB** clear operation, the size is always 24 bits regardless of the **RSIZ** field. For clearing **P**, the size can be 8, 24, or 32 bits depending on the **RSIZ** field specified.

The SPRAM is mapped to two locations in the host's memory space: normal and mirrored. In the address offset range 0x8000 to 0xBFFF, each SPRAM value appears as a normal 32-bit value. In the mirrored parameter signed extended (PSE) offset range 0xC000 to 0xFFFF, the SPRAM values operate as 24-bit signed values. When the SPE area is read by the host, the most significant bit of the operand is duplicated in the upper remaining bits, effectively sign extending the data to 32 bits regardless of the operand size. The parameter RAM sign extension reduces host overhead when there is a need to use signed arithmetic operations.

There are three SPRAM addressing modes: channel-relative, direct (absolute), and by_diob (indirect).

- **Channel-Relative Addressing Mode**
  This is the most commonly used RAM addressing mode. What makes this addressing mode very handy is the fact that the channel number for the channel about to be serviced is loaded into the channel register during the time-slot transition. The microcoded RAM subcommand: **ram   p <- prm1**. is a channel-relative example. It says to load parameter 1 of *whatever channel number is in the channel register*. This makes it a relative address, since the actual parameter 1 used is relative to the channel. In other words, you can run this function on any channel and this subcommand will get that channel's parameter 1. The maximum number of parameters that can be accessed in channel-relative addressing modes is 8 or 128, depending on the instruction format used. Note each channel has a its own 11-bit parameter base address (**CPBA**) in the eTPU channel x configuration register (**ETPUCxCR**). This pointer is used to specify which set of parameters are used by that channel. Because **CPBA** is an 11-bit pointer, a channel can select a set of parameters in any location in a 16K parameter RAM. Currently only 3K or 4K parameter memory is implemented. The address immediate (**AID**) microinstruction field is used for channel-relative addressing: **AID[0:2]** is used to select one of eight parameters and **AID[0:6]** is used to select one of 128 parameters.

  > **Note:** Although a channel can access a huge number of parameters, there may be side effects of actually doing so. For example, if one channel uses 128 parameters, other channels will most likely be using some of these parameters as well, a situation that could lead to data coherency problems.

- **Absolute Addressing**
  In absolute addressing, the address range is 256 parameters, addressed by (**AID[0:7]**). These parameters are located in SPRAM addresses from 0 to 255. The

SPRAM physical address can be specified as follows: **physical _address = AID[0:7].**

- **Indirect Addressing**

    Indirect addressing mode is available only through the use of the **DIOB** register. Since it is accessible only on a 32-bit boundary, the physical address in register **DIOB** are bits 13-2 and the least significant 2 bits are not used. An example of this addressing mode is as follows: **physical_address = DIOB[13:2].** This addressing mode is useful when a channel needs to use a pointer to another channel. For example, channel x writes an address to a parameter called `Address`. Channel y then loads `Address` into **DIOB** and uses indirect addressing mode to access the parameter. Indirect addressing mode can have post-increment or pre-decrement on **DIOB**, allowing stack operations. When post-increment/pre-decrement addressing is used, **DIOB** increments/decrements on a word (32 bit) boundary; **DIOB[0:1]** bits are never used. Since the SPRAM address range is a maximum of 4096^2 thirty-two bit words (16K bytes), **DIOB[14:23]** are not used in indirect addressing mode.

The Arithmetic Logic Unit

The ALU performs the usual arithmetic and logical operations (referred to as microoperations). The instruction to be performed is indicated by the ALU/MDU operation (**ALUOP**), ALU/MDU operation immediate (**ALUOP**I), or shift (**SHF**) instruction fields. Some microinstruction formats contain none of these three fields, in which case the ALU will perform an addition. The ALU is capable of performing addition and subtraction using the carry (**C**) flag as the carry-in; bitwise AND, OR, NOT, and XOR; and shift/rotate of 1, 2, 4, 8, and 16 bits. Subtraction, negation, increment, and decrement can be performed by using source inversion along with the **C** flag. The ALU's output goes directly to a 1-bit shifter, called the post-ALU shifter, so it is possible, for instance, to add and shift using only one microinstruction. For example, you may wish to multiply by 2 the result of an addition or a subtraction. A shift left will do this without any additional execution time. (And division by 2 is accomplished with a shift right.)

The ALU always performs 24-bit operations on its inputs, called A-source and B-source, and produces a 24-bit result (where 8- and 16-bit inputs are zero padded to 24 bits). Likewise, the 24-bit ALU output is always truncated to the destination register size.

---

2. Current eTPU SPRAM memory sizes are 2.5K, 3K and 4K bytes.

The ALU has its own condition code flags that are updated only when the programmer indicates an update operation. The following is a detailed explanation on when and how these flags are updated.

ALU Condition Code Flags

Condition code flags allow the microengine to make decisions based on the result of arithmetic or logical operations by using conditional branch subcommands. There are four such flags associated with the ALU: carry (**C**), negative (**N**), overflow (**O**), and zero (**Z**).

- **Carry Flag (C)**

  The **C** flag is useful for unsigned arithmetic and indicates an unsigned overflow. It is the carry out during addition and the borrow flag during subtraction or comparison. The **C** flag is the ALU carry from bit 7 to 8, 15 to 16, or 23 to 24 on 8-, 16- and 24-bit operation sizes respectively. This flag is set only under the following conditions; if none of these conditions is true, the flag is cleared:

  a. When adding two operands results in a value that exceeds the operation size;

  b. When subtracting two operands and the first operand is smaller than the second operand;

  c. When shifting a register left, register right, or rotate right which results in a carry out of 1.

- **Negative Flag (N)**

  The **N** flag simply reflects the most significant bit of the destination operand. It is used in signed arithmetic along with the **V** bit to determine if a result is positive or negative. The **N** flag may also be useful in routines that use unsigned numbers. For example, the most significant bit of a parameter can be treated as a binary flag by loading the parameter, latching the condition codes, and testing the **N** flag. The **N** flag is set only under the following condition; if this condition is false, the flag is cleared:

  a. After an arithmetic operation, the most significant bit of the result is set.

- **Overflow Flag (V)**

  The **V** flag is useful for signed arithmetic. It is the overflow flag, similar to the **C** flag for unsigned arithmetic. The **V** flag is set only under the following conditions; if none of these conditions is true, the flag is cleared:

  a. When adding two positive operands results in a negative value in the destination operand (i.e., the most significant bit of the result equals 1);

b. When adding two negative operands results in a positive value in the destination operand (i.e., the most significant bit of the result equals 0).

- **Zero Flag (Z)**
  The **Z** flag is set only under the following conditions; if none of these conditions is true, the flag is cleared:

    a. If two equal operands are subtracted;

    b. If there is only one operand, and it is zero;

    c. If two operands are added and the result in the destination is zero;

    d. If two equal operands are compared.

The arithmetic unit shifter influences the condition code results in subtle ways. **C**, **Z**, and **N** always reflect the output of the arithmetic unit shifter, but **V** always reflects the result before the arithmetic unit shifter.

The eTPU does not automatically update condition codes after each arithmetic command, so if you would like to check the result of an ALU operation, use the condition code set (**CCS**) or condition code set valid (**CCSV**) fields. The **CCS** field, when specified, will update all 4 flags based on the operand size used in the ALU operation. The **CCSV** field allows the eTPU code to specify the size of the flag sampling operation: the options are 8 bits, 16 bits, or as defined by the operation size.

Full information for all ALU instruction fields is provided in *Appendix G. Microinstruction Formats*.

The MAC and Divide Unit

The MDU is a powerful hardware tool that executes more advanced arithmetical operations. These operations, also specified by the **ALUOP** microinstruction field, are signed/unsigned multiply, signed/unsigned multiply-accumulate, signed/unsigned fractional multiplication, and unsigned divide. The MDU supports operand sizes of any combination of 8, 16, or 24 bits on all multiply operations. For divides, the operand sizes are always 24 bits. Depending on the size of operands and the type of operation, the MDU can take more than one microcycle to execute the operation. But because the MDU has its own instruction pipe, the microengine will continue to execute other types of microinstructions in parallel. In other words, the microengine does not stall due to MDU execution of multimicrocycle operations. The time needed to perform a multiply or multiply-accumulate depends on a variety of factors:

- A 24-bit x 8 bit multiply lasts 2 microcycles (1 start-MDU plus 1 execution microcycle);

- A 24-bit x 16 bit multiply lasts 3 microcycles (1 start-MDU plus 2 execution microcycles);

- A 24 bit x 24 bit multiply lasts 4 microcycles (1 start-MDU plus 3 execution microcycles);

- A multiply-accumulate also lasts 4 microcycles (1 start-MDU plus 3 execution microcycles);

- A divide operation is always unsigned and takes 13 microcycles to complete, which means that after the start divide microinstruction, one has to wait for 12 microcycles to read the result.

> **Note:** Multiply-accumulate operations differ from multiply operations in that the contents of **MACH** and **MACL** registers are added to the result. When multiply or multiply-accumulate operations complete, **MACH** and **MACL** hold the most and the least significant 24-bit words, respectively.

The result of an MDU operation is always placed in **MACH** and **MACL** registers. During calculations, **MACH** and **MACL** hold temporary values and should not be written; if they are, the result is unpredictable. One must check the MDU busy flag (**BF**) when attempting to issue multiple MDU operations. The **BF** indicates if it safe to issue the next MDU operation when this flag is cleared. An attempt to issue an MDU operation while the MDU is busy will result in unpredictable behavior for both the ongoing operation and the started one.

If eTPU code issues an **END** command, any MDU operation currently executing terminates immediately and is left incomplete.

MDU Flags

As with the ALU, the MDU has its own condition code flags that allow the microengine to make decisions based on the result of all multiply and divide operations by using conditional branch subcommands. There are five flags associated with the MDU:

> **Note:** None of the MDU operations effect the ALU flags, and, conversely, none of the ALU operations effect the MDU flags.

- **MDU Negative Flag (MN)**
  This flag always holds a copy of **MACH** bit 23 at the end of the operation (signed or unsigned). Note that **MACL** holds the quotient and **MACH** holds the remainder of a division operation, which is always unsigned.

- **MDU Carry Flag (MC)**

  The **MC** flag indicates if the result cannot be represented by a 48-bit number, in signed and unsigned multiply-accumulate operations. This flag may be checked at the end of a series of multiply-accumulate operations.

- **MDU Overflow Flag (MV)**

  In multiply operations, the **MV** flag is negated and stays negated, because the result of a multiplication can always fit in a 48-bit result (**MACH** and **MACL** concatenated). In a multiply-accumulate operation, **MV** is asserted if the result size is greater than 48 bits. The **MV** flag works in both signed and unsigned operations. In divide operations, **MV** is asserted only if a divide-by-zero operation is executed.

- **MDU Zero Flag (MZ)**

  In multiply and multiply-accumulate operations, the **MZ** flag is asserted if **MACH** and **MACL** are equal to 0 at the end of an operation. In divide operations, this flag is asserted if **MACL** (the result) is equal to 0.

- **MDU Busy Flag (MB)**

  This flag indicates if the MDU is currently busy with a multiply or divide operation. When there is a need to execute multiple back-to-back MDU operations this flag should be checked to determine if the MDU is busy or free. This flag may also need to be checked prior to exiting the executing thread, for if the thread ends execution before the MDU completes its operation, the result will be unpredictable.

Full information for all MDU instruction fields is provided in *Appendix G. Microinstruction Formats*.

Channel Configuration and Control Operations

The instruction fields described in this section configure and control the channel logic of a specified channel (indicated by **CHAN**). You'll find that in many cases the field name is identical to a register that the field controls.

- **Flag Control (FLC)**

  FLC is a 3-bit field that sets **Flag0** and **Flag1** for the channel in question, as shown in Table 8.2.

FLC	Meaning
000	Clear **Flag0**.
001	Set **Flag0**.
010	Clear **Flag1**
011	Set **Flag1**.
100	Copy **Flag1:Flag0** from **P[25:24]**.
101	Copy **Flag1:Flag0** from **P[27:26]**.
110	Copy **Flag1:Flag0** from **P[29:28]**.
111	No operation.

Table 8.2 Field FLC Settings

- **Time Base A and Time Base B Fields (TBS_A and TBS_B)**
  TBS_A and **TBS_B** are each four-bit fields that configure the type of comparator and time base(s) to use for match and capture for, respectively, action unit A and action Unit B. See Table 8.3 for details.

TBS	Meaning
0000	Greater or equal; capture on **TCR1**; match on **TCR1**.
0001	Greater or equal; capture on **TCR1**; match on **TCR2**.
0010	Greater or equal; capture on **TCR2**; match on **TCR1**.
0011	Greater or equal; capture on **TCR2**; match on **TCR2**.
0100	Exactly equal; capture on **TCR1**; match on **TCR1**.
0101	Exactly equal; capture on **TCR1**; match on **TCR2**.
0110	Exactly equal; capture on **TCR2**; match on **TCR1**.
0111	Exactly equal; capture on **TCR2**; match on **TCR2**.
1000 - 1110	Reserved.
1111	Do nothing.

Table 8.3 TBS Field Settings

- **Input Pin Action Control Fields (IPAC_A and IPAC_B)**
  As you might expect, the **IPAC_A** and **IPAC_B** fields control, respectively the

IPAC_A and **IPAC_B** registers. See Table 8.4 for details on this 3-bit field. In the case where a match affects the transition detection, MatchA is used for **IPAC_A** and MatchB for **IPAC_B**.

IPAC	Meaning
000	Do not detect transitions.
001	Detect rising edge only.
010	Detect falling edge only.
011	Detect both edges.
100	"Detect" a transition when the input signal = 0 on match.
101	"Detect" a transition when the input signal = 1 on match.
110	Reserved.
111	Do not change **IPAC**.

Table 8.4 IPAC Field Settings

- **Output Pin Action Control Fields (OPAC_A and OPAC_B)**
  The **OPAC_A** and **OPAC_B** fields control, respectively, the output pin action for action units A and B. See Table 8.5 for details on this 3-bit field. In the case where a match affects the output pin, MatchA is used for **OPAC_A** and MatchB for **OPAC_B**.

OPAC	Meaning
000	Do not change output signal.
001	Match sets output signal high.
010	Match sets output signal low.
011	Match toggles output signal.
100	Input action sets output signal low.
101	Input action sets output signal high.
110	Input action toggles output signal.
111	Do not change **OPAC**.

Table 8.5 OPAC Field Settings

- **Immediate Pin State Control Fields (PSC and PSCS)**
  The PSC and PSCS fields work together to change the output signal state immediately or set the output signal as defined by **OPAC_A** or **OPAC_B**. See Table 8.6.

PSC	PSCS	Meaning
00	0	Set signal as specified by **OPAC_A**.
00	1	Set signal as specified by **OPAC_B**.
01	x	Set signal high.
10	x	Set signal low.
11	x	Don't change signal state.

Table 8.6 PSC and PSCS Field Meanings

- **Write Match Register (ERW_A and ERW_B) Fields**
These 1-bit fields indicate whether a match value is to be written to the respective match register (**MatchA** or **MatchB**) thereby enabling matches for that action unit. For instance, a value of 0 for **ERW_A** writes **ERT_A** to **MatchA** and enables matches against **MatchA** by setting **MRLE_A** to 1.

- **Clear Transition/Match Event Registers Fields (MRL_A, MRL_B, and TDL)**
Each of these 1-bit fields clears the event register by the same name. For instance, **MRL_A** = 0 clears the **MRL_A** event register.

- **Match Recognition Latch Enable (MRLE) Field**
This 1-bit field disables match recognition on both action units. That is, when **MRLE**=0, both **MRLE_A** and **MRLE_B** event registers are set to 0.

- **Disable Match and Transition Service Request Field (MTD)**
This 2-bit field disables match and transition service requests for the selected field by setting or re-setting the service request inhibit (**SRI**) latch. See Table 8.7.

MTD	Meaning
00	Enable match and transition service requests (**SRI** = 0).
01	Disable match and transition service requests (set **SRI**=1).
10	Reserved.
11	Don't change **SRI**.

Table 8.7 MTD Field Meanings

- **Predefined Channel Modes (PDCM) Field**
The **PDCM** instruction field sets the **PDCM** channel register, thereby establishing the channel mode for the channel. See Table 8.8 for details on this field, and

Chapter 9. Channel Hardware and Modes for details on the channel modes themselves.

PDCM	Meaning
0000	Either match, blocking, single transition
0001	Either match, blocking, double transition
0010	Either match, non-blocking single transition
0011	Either match, non-blocking, double transition
0100	MatchB, single transition
0101	MatchB, double transition
0110	Both matches, single transition
0111	Both matches, double transition
1000	MatchB, ordered, single transition
1001	MatchB, ordered, double transition
1010	Reserved
1011	Reserved
1100	Single match, single transition
1101	Single match, double transition
1110	Single match, single transition, enhanced
1111	Keep current channel mode.

Table 8.8 PDCM Field Settings

- **Channel Interrupt and Data Transfer Requests (CIRC) Field**
  eTPU code can issue interrupt requests, data transfer requests, and a global exception through the 2-bit **CIRC** field. See Table 8.3 for details.

CIRC	Meaning
00	Channel interrupt request.
01	Data transfer request.
10	Global exception.
11	Do nothing.

Table 8.9 CIRC Field Settings

- **Clear Link Service Request (LSR) Field**

  This 1-bit instruction field is used to clear the **LSR** flag of the serviced channel. (Note that the serviced channel might not be the one selected by **CHAN**!) If the **LSR** field is set to 0, the **LSR** flag is cleared. If a channel receives a new link request during a thread that is handling a prior link request, the **LSR** flag will be set again. However, if the **LSR** flag is tested in the first thread it will appear clear. When that thread ends, the channel will find that another link is pending, causing the channel to issue another service request. Since only one channel can execute its thread at any given time for a given engine, this situation occurs only one channel links to itself or, in a dual-engine implementation, where one engine thread issues a link service request to a channel in the other engine.

Flow-Control Operations

Just as the program counter points and sequences through a CPU program, the eTPU program counter (PC) behaves the same way. Its sequence can be altered when evaluating a condition to determine whether the program should branch or not. There are numerous conditions that can be evaluated by the microengine to determine thread execution flow. Conditional and unconditional branches as well as subroutine calls and nestings are supported. As the thread executes a subroutine call, the hardware automatically stores the return address into the return address register (**RAR**). The **RAR** is accessible by eTPU code and may be saved on the stack when subroutine nesting is needed. Stacking and unstacking operations are achieved by using **DIOB** register and indirect addressing with pre-decrement and post-increment modes. The following table shows all flags that can be tested for conditional branches:

Flag	*Meaning*	*Flag*	*Meaning*
V	ALU overflow flag	**FM[0]**	Channel function mode flag 2
N	ALU negative flag	**PSS**	Channel pin status
C	ALU carry flag	Less than	ALU **V** Xored **N** (signed)
Z	ALU zero flag	Lower equal	**Z** ored **C** (unsigned)
MV	MDU overflow flag	**P[24]**	P register bit 24 flag
MN	MDU negative flag	**P[25]**	P register bit 25 flag
MZ	MDU zero flag	**P[26]**	P register bit 26 flag
MC	MDU carry flag	**P[27]**	P register bit 27 flag
MB	MDU busy flag	**P[28]**	P register 28 bit flag

Flag	Meaning	Flag	Meaning
TDL_A	Channel transition detect flag 1	**P[29]**	P resister 29 bit flag
TDL_B	Channel transition detect flag 2	**P[30]**	P register 30 bit flag
MRL_A	Channel match recognition flag 1	**P[31]**	P register 31 bit flag
MRL_B	Channel match recognition flag 2	**PSTO**	Channel pin state output flag
LSR	Channel link service request flag	**PSTI**	Channel pin input flag
FM[0]	Channel function mode flag 1	**SMLCK**	Semaphore lock flag

Table 8.10 Branch Conditions

When a branch condition uses a channel flag (**TDL_A**, **TDL_B**, **MRL_A**, **MRL_B**, **LSR**, **FM[0]**, **FM[1]**, **PSS**, **PSTO**, or **PSTI**), the channel context is related to the channel number written in the **CHAN** register. Recall that when a time slot-transition occurs, the channel number of the channel to be dispatched for execution is written into the **CHAN** register. If the executing thread writes a different channel number into the **CHAN** register, then channel conditions evaluated will reflect the new channel.

Full information for all flow controls instruction fields is provided in *Appendix G. Microinstruction Formats*.

Lab 8

The purpose of this lab is not to have you solve problems per se but to familiarize you with the relationship between the eTPU's "C" code, the assembly code, microinstructions, instruction formats, SCM, and SPRAM. You will use the information provided in this chapter to debug your code. When things go right quickly, you might not use many or any of the tricks provided in this lab, but when things go wrong and seem intractable, you will be desperate to delve into the bowels of the eTPU—the SCM, the SPRAM, the execution unit's registers, the channels' configuration settings, etc.—and this lab describes how to do just these things.

1. Open Lab8.ETpuSimProject to see source code, logic analyzer, and execution unit windows, as well as a channel 0 window, for the PulseTrigger and DelayedPulse functions described earlier in *Chapter 6. Moving to Multiple Channels*.
2. Select the source code window and right-click to show mixed assembly, as shown in Figure 8.2.

Figure 8.2 Viewing Mixed Assembly

The source code is shown with the mixed assembly, a portion of which is shown in Figure 8.3.

```
          pin = pin_low;
0128: 0x49500DE8   chan   FutureOutputPin high on ma
    : 0x49500DE8          CurrentOutputPin = low, mo
          act_unitA = Mtcr1_Ctcr1_ge;
0128: 0x49500DE8   chan   FutureOutputPin high on ma
    : 0x49500DE8          CurrentOutputPin = low, mo
```

Figure 8.3 Mixed Assembly View of the Source Code

Maximize this source code window. You'll notice that the lines underneath each of the `if` statements contains triplets of information: an offset from the entry table base address, a 4-bit hexadecimal number, and some assembly code. Underneath each of the remaining instructions you'll find quadruplets of information: an offset from the entry table base address, an 8-bit hexadecimal number, some assembly code, and a specification of the instruction format. Let's check out the actual memory.

3. Click on the Mem workshop.

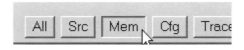

Figure 8.4 Opening the Mem Workshop

You'll see that no windows are open in this Workshop, so let's fix that. Click on the View/Memory submenu option.

Figure 8.5 Opening a Memory Window

The default memory window, SPRAM, opens. But since we want to see SCM, right-click on the memory window and choose the Address Space/Program option.

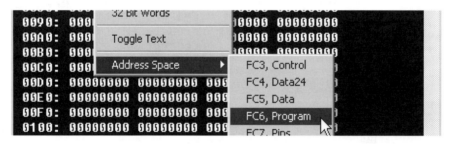

Figure 8.6 Opening an SCM Window

The SCM window opens. You can see starting at address space 0000 the entry table, and starting at address space 0100 the start of the program code.

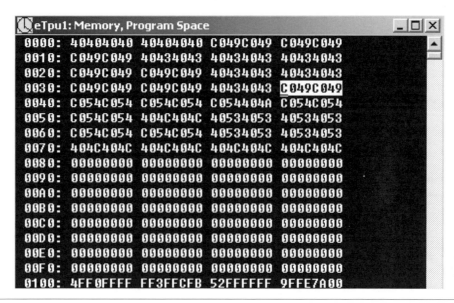

Figure 8.7 Viewing an SCM Window

Since the entry table is in 16-bit words while the program code is in 32-bit words, you may wish to change this window to 16-bit wide words (by left-clicking on the window and choosing the 16-bit words option). Alternatively, you may wish to open multiple SCM windows and set one to 16-bit words and the other to 32-bit words.

Note: Once you open a memory window in any workshop, by default it will appear also in the Src workshop; if you want to change that you can right-click on the memory window, select the Occupy Workshop option, and uncheck the Src checkbox.

You'll notice in the SCM window that the instruction at address 0108 is hexadecimal 0x52FFFFFF. Let's see exactly what this means. Refer to the list of microinstruction formats as shown in *Appendix G. Microinstruction Formats*. First we need to determine which format is in use with this instruction. 0x52FFFFFF hexadecimal is 0101 0010 1111 1111 1111 1111 1111 1111 binary. Since the first three digits in this instruction are 010, we're looking at instruction format C1 or C2, and since the fourth digit is 1, we know we're looking at instruction format C2. See Figure 8.8 for the C2 microinstruction format.

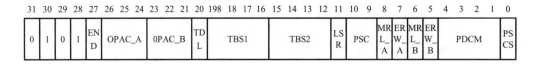

Figure 8.8 Microinstruction Format C2

Now we can map the binary instruction itself to this format.

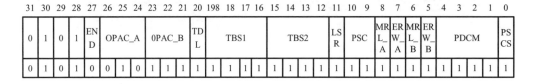

Figure 8.9 Microinstruction Format C2 with Microinstruction

So this instruction has fields **END** = 0, **OPAC_A** = 010, **OPAC_B** = 111, and so on. If you compare these values for these fields to the respective sets of options as displayed in the tables above, you will see that all fields in this instruction except for **END** and **OPAC_A** are set to do, or change, nothing. What this instruction does do is cause an **END** to occur in the current thread and the **OPAC_A** register to be set to detect a falling edge.

4.   Go back to the Src workshop and scroll to this same instruction on the source code window.

You'll see that it all maps out.

```
    DetectAFallingEdge();
    0x52FFFFFF    chan    detectA = falling input pin edge; FormatC2
    0x52FFFFFF    seq     end;;            FormatC2 [4]
```

Figure 8.10 Detect Falling Edge on Action Unit A Code

5.   Step through the code until this instruction (either by pressing F8 repeatedly as necessary or by setting a breakpoint and running) is highlighted (not executed). Before this instruction (the last instruction in the HSR thread) occurs, you'll notice that the **CHAN** specified in the execution unit window is 0 and that the **IPAC_A** setting of channel 0, shown in the channel 0 window, is "do not detect

transitions." Immediately after this instruction is executed, you'll notice that the **CHAN** is now 1 (to respond to the HSR for that channel) and that the **IPAC_A** setting for channel 0 has been changed to "detect falling edge only."

6. Set a breakpoint in the first microinstruction at address 010C, which is in the second thread of the first function. You'll notice that this microinstruction performs two things: sets the **P** register to **ERT_A** and then writes **P** to an absolute address in memory.

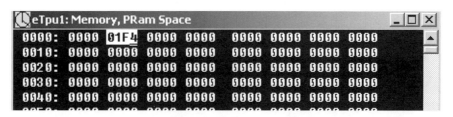

```
          TriggerCount = erta;
010C: 0x9FFE7A00   au    p = erta+nil, SampleFlags
    : 0x9FFE7A00   ram   *((absolute U24 *) 0x0) =
          LinkToChannel( PulseChan0 );
0110: 0xBFEFFB80   ram   p_23_0 = *((relative U24
          LinkToChannel( PulseChan1 );
0114: 0xBFA81A81   au    link = p+nil, SampleFlags
    : 0xBFA81A81   ram   p_23_0 = *((relative U24
```

Figure 8.11 Detect Falling Edge on Action Unit A Code

7. Run (F9) to this breakpoint. Note the current value of **ERT_A**.

8. Step (F8) once through the code and notice, in the execution unit window, that **ERT_A** has been copied into **P**.

Let's see if this value has been copied into memory.

9. Move back to the Mem workshop and open an SPRAM window. You'll notice that the appropriate place in memory has been updated to contain this same value.

```
eTpu1: Memory, PRam Space                    _ □ ×
0000:  0000 01F4 0000 0000   0000 0000 0000 0000
0010:  0000 0000 0000 0000   0000 0000 0000 0000
0020:  0000 0000 0000 0000   0000 0000 0000 0000
0030:  0000 0000 0000 0000   0000 0000 0000 0000
0040:  0000 0000 0000 0000   0000 0000 0000 0000
```

Figure 8.12 Setting RAM

10. Move back to the Src workshop. You'll notice that the `link =` instructions, which are coming up next, correspond to two different microinstructions, the first one of which performs a RAM operation and the second of which performs (perhaps among other things) a **LINK** operation.

11. Continue to step (F8) through the code. Notice as you do that the **LINK** value in the execution unit window changes to 01, then 02, 03, and 04. On the *next* step, notice that **CHAN** changes from 00 to 01. You have moved from the last instruction in the second thread of the first function (running on channel 0) to the first instruction in the second thread of the second function (running on channel 1)! Link requests to channels 2, 3, and 4 await servicing.

You'll notice that with few exceptions the SPRAM addressing registers, the channel configuration and control instruction fields, the ALU and MDU condition codes, and indeed all branch condition codes discussed in this chapter appear either in the execution unit window, a channel window (there is some overlap as the execution unit window will always display the value for the current channel while the channel window displays values for the channel specified), or in the global conditions window of the Simulator.

CHAPTER 9

Channel Hardware and Modes

This chapter[1] describes how each channel mode affects the interaction between the two action units on a channel as well as the service requests that match and transition events produce. An explanation of the benefits and usage of the dual-action modes is also given. It is assumed that the reader is already familiar with the concepts of scheduling a timeout match and output transition, responding to an input transition, the interaction between a match event and a capture event, and service requests, all of which are discussed in earlier chapters.

Introduction to Channel Modes

Previous chapters described the fundamental operations of the match and capture hardware and how they could be used to generate simple output waveforms and measure the duration of input waveforms.

Recall that each channel contains an input signal path, an output signal path, and two action units. These two action units, action unit A and action unit B, each contain one of each of the following registers: match enable, match recognition, transition detection, capture, input pin action control, and output pin action control. In addition, there are hardware connections from the match and transition detection circuits of one action unit to the match and transition enable circuits of the other match unit.

---

1. This chapter was written by Richard Soja from Freescale Semiconductors, Inc.

Which paths are connected between the various hardware blocks is selected by the channel mode. There are a total of 13 channel modes available on the eTPU. A channel mode is enabled by writing to a special register, the predefined channel mode (**PDCM**) register, in the eTPU hardware. Details of all the channel modes, and the application uses of selected modes are described later in this chapter.

The following section describes the general operation of channel hardware interactions and provides an explanation of the naming convention used.

Channel Hardware and Naming Conventions

The **PDCM** determines the channel mode assigned to a channel. Each channel has its own **PDCM** register which is initialized to 1100 (*single match, single transition*, described below) on reset. The channel mode defines much of the channel logic behavior, especially how matches block and enable transitions and vice-versa, as well as the occurrence of time base captures and service requests caused by matches and transitions.

The output signal control logic uses **OPAC_A/B**, the pre-defined channel mode (**PDCM**), and the pin state control (**PSC** and **PSCS**) fields. The **PDCM** control register is write only, which means that software either must be written in a way that assumes the initial value or should maintain a copy or representation of the **PDCM** value in parameter ram. In most cases, software would be designed so that the initialization state writes the **PDCM** value and subsequent states in the eTPU function use other state information to determine what the **PDCM** value is and whether it should be dynamically changed. Any change in **PDCM** takes immediate effect.

Changing **PDCM** may set or reset any of the channel flags, so care must be taken when switching channel modes. On the other hand, an event flag asserted in one mode may stay asserted when **PDCM** is changed, even if the flag is impossible to be set at the new mode. The same applies to the channel service requests, as a consequence. Captures may also occur on mode changing if transitions and/or match flags are asserted. It is advisable to clear **MRLE_A/B**, **TDL_A/B**, **MRL_A/B** flags before changing modes.

Channel modes are used differently for input and output signals. Modes also allow combining input processing and output generation in a single channel. Channel modes are divided into two categories, based on the way they treat transitions:

- **Single Transition Modes** (mnemonic suffix _st): All single transition modes except sm_st_e behave as follows. The first transition asserts flag **TDL_A**, captures two time bases selected by **TBS_A** and **TBS_B** and issues a service request. The second transition asserts flag **TDL_B**, captures the time base selected by **TBS_B**, but doesn't issue a service request.

- **Double Transition Modes** (mnemonic suffix _dt): In these modes the second transition asserts flag **TDL_B** and issues a service request, and each transition captures its own selected time base (The first transition and second transition capture time bases selected by **TBS_A** and **TBS_B**, respectively).

> **Note: sm_st_e** is a special mode that allows eTPU software to determine the input signal delay caused by the input digital filter. A qualified transition captures the filtered signal in **CaptureA** and the unfiltered signal in **CaptureB**. In a quiet environment, the two captures provide the delay of the digital filter in a granularity of two system clocks. In a noisy environment, false transitions may be detected at the input of the digital filter due to the noise and the delay measurement may be reduced, especially if **IPAC_B** selects both edge detections.

In single transition modes, **TDL_A** assertion may capture both time bases at once, while in double transition modes each transition captures its related time base in its related capture register. Double transition mode is always ordered, i.e **TDL_A** enables **TDL_B** and the occurrence of **TDL_B** generates the service request. Detection of the second transition may also be enabled by certain match events. Match detection may be ordered (modes **m2_o_st** and **m2_o_dt**) or unordered. A match event never overwrites the time base captured by a transition event, while a transition event will always overwrite the time base captured by a previous (or simultaneous) match event.

Input signal channel modes can be classified into the following categories:

- Single Transition, Single Match: **em_b_st, sm_st, sm_st_e**
- Single Transition, Double Match: **em_nb_st, bm_st, m2_st, m2_o_st**
- Double Transition, Single Match: **em_b_dt, sm_dt**
- Double Transition, Double Match: **em_nb_dt, bm_dt, m2_dt, m2_o_dt**

Output signal channel modes can be classified into the following categories:

- Single Match: **em_b_st, sm_st, sm_st_e, em_b_dt, sm_dt**
- Double Match: **em_nb_st, bm_st, m2_st, m2_o_st, em_nb_dt, bm_dt, m2_dt, m2_o_dt**

Table 9.1 provides the channel mode names used in the software examples, their equivalent names used in the hardware definition, and their typical application usage.

Channel Mode (Software)	Channel Mode (Hardware)	Input Applications	Output Applications
Single Match Single Transition();	sm_st	Equivalent to TPU3 configuration	TPU3 compatibility
SingleMatchDoubleTransition();	sm_dt	One time-out conditioned by two transitions	
EitherMatchBlockingSingleTransition();	em_b_st	Transition blocks both matches	First to occur match blocks the other
EitherMatchBlockingDoubleTransition();	em_b_dt	Each transition blocks a match	
EitherMatchNonBlockingSingleTransition();	em_nb_st	Matches and captures independent	Unrelated transition and time-out
EitherMatchNonBlockingDoubleTransition();	em_nb_dt	Independent time-outs for captures	Used for fast pulses
BothMatchSingleTransition();	bm_st	Transition detected after time and angle	Pulse now, service later
BothMatchDoubleTransition();	bm_dt	Two transitions after time and angle	Narrow pulses
MatchBSingleTransition();	m2_st	Transition detection in window	Transition conditioned on a match
MatchBDoubleTransition();	m2_dt	Second transition blocks second match	
MatchBOrderedSingleTransition();	m2_o_st	Tests for a transition in a window	Conditional pulse extension
MatchBOrderedDoubleTransition();	m2_o_dt	Tests for two transitions in a window	
SingleMatchSingleTransitionEnhanced();	sm_st_e	Measures digital filter delay	

Table 9.1 Channel Mode Names and Typical Uses

The timing diagrams in the next section show graphically how the dual action hardware operates for input and output modes.

Additionally each channel hardware contains logic that allows an input signal to interact directly with the generation of an output signal. A detected input transition can trigger an output signal edge, without software servicing using **OPAC** options 1xx. Details are provided in the next section.

Application Uses for Dual-Action Modes

There are a number of benefits of having two action units. One is that more than one event can be processed in hardware before a service request is issued to the scheduler. This reduces the loading on the eTPU and helps to minimize the latency of service for all channels. Two good examples of using dual action modes are described in chapter 5, where the dual match mode, **m2_st**, was used to generate a PWM output and the dual transition mode, **em_nb_dt**, was used to measure short input pulses.

Note: The m2 vernacular is a holdover from when the two action units were called action unit 1 and action unit 2, with corresponding register names (i.e., Match2, Capture 1, etc.)

Another benefit of most dual action modes is that they can eliminate software conditional tests that might otherwise be needed before scheduling an output edge. An example of this is when an output transition must normally occur at a point defined by an offset from a reference position but also its maximum offset must be limited to another pre-determined value. Figure 9.1 shows the timing diagram that represents this type of scenario. The limit value of the offset may be defined in terms of the same time base as the normal offset or alternatively, the limit value and normal offsets may use separate time bases.

The hardware modes that provide this functionality are **m2_st** or **m2_dt**. Because we're using the mode as an output, the type of transition (_st or _dt) doesn't matter. The key attribute of the **m2_** modes is that MatchB always blocks MatchA, but the converse is not the case. So, provided that MatchA occurs before MatchB, the action defined by MatchA will occur and then be followed by a service request at MatchB. This situation is shown in the top timing diagram of Figure 9.1. If MatchB occurs first, the action specified by MatchB will occur and MatchA will be prevented from occurring, as shown in the lower timing diagram of Figure 9.1. The way this could be used in an application is to make MatchB a constant value defining the limit case with MatchA representing the requested duration of the pulse, bounded by MatchB. The service request occurs only on MatchB.

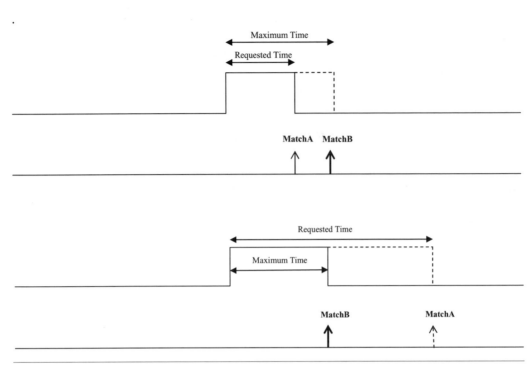

Figure 9.1 m2_st Dual-Match Mode

This type of pulse control could be used to limit the maximum energy supplied to a spark plug coil in a vehicle engine or limit the drive to an electric motor.

The above example places a condition on whether MatchA occurs or not, but MatchB occurs unconditionally. Some applications require both matches to be conditioned equally, where, for example, MatchA blocks MatchB and MatchB blocks MatchA. The **em_b_st** and **em_b_dt**) modes provide this capability. These modes can be used to schedule two independent events that cause a change in pin state, for example (though the event does not necessarily have to change the pin, of course). Whichever event occurs first will affect the pin, and the other event will be effectively cancelled. Obviously, there is the possibility that both events occur simultaneously. Under this circumstance, if a pin change was requested for both events the pin action that prevails is described by the rules given in "Resolving Conflicts in Action-Control Definitions" on page 139. The advantage of using an **em_b_** output mode is that eTPU software does not have to perform conditional tests and branches prior to scheduling the output pulses or events. This improves the efficiency of code especially when each match is referenced to a different counter. Figure 9.2 shows an example of using **em_b_st** to force a pulse to terminate at the first occurrence of a match on either a time base clocked by **TCR1** or an angular position defined by **TCR2**. The MatchA event is scheduled for a time that is offset from the rising edge of the pulse, and defines the pulse width, while the MatchB event is scheduled for an absolute angular position at which to unconditionally terminate the pulse.

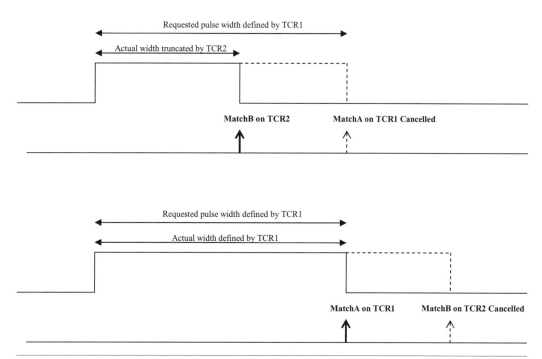

Figure 9.2 em_b_st Output Mode to force pin state on first event

Note that since either match blocks the other, only one service request is generated, by the match event that wins (or prevails).

The **em_nb_st** (or **em_nb_dt**) mode, when used as an output can provide two independent time and/or angle based events to be scheduled on a single channel. For example, a channel can schedule both a task wake-up event and an output pin transition at the same time. This mode is particularly useful in applications in which the output pin transition position must be recalculated by a task that is allowed to run at regular intervals in order to adapt to changing application conditions. The task makes the output rescheduling algorithm run at a desired rate, marked by the dotted vertical lines in Figure 9.3. The **em_nb_dt** mode can be used to schedule a task to run when the MatchB event occurs and at the same time also schedule a rising edge to occur on the MatchA event. Because this is a non-blocking mode, both match events generate service requests. When a service request for MatchB occurs, the task runs to recompute both the position of the rising edge of the pin and the next task wake-up point. The dual action hardware allows the task and pin control to be independent of each other, which minimizes the latency that software rescheduling might cause when the task runs close to the position in which the pin changes state.

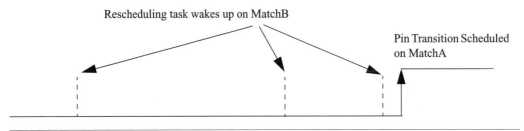

Figure 9.3 em_nb_dt Dual Match Mode

Ordered match modes (**m2_o_st** or **m2_o_dt**) can be used to enforce the minimum width of an output pulse. This feature is useful in applications that could operate incorrectly if the pulse width becomes less than some set value, such as the drive to a spark plug coil or solenoid actuator for example. Figure 9.4 shows the timing of a pulse whose minimum width is limited by the value defined in **MatchA**, while the desired pulse width is defined in **MatchB**. The dotted line represents the demanded pulse width, and the solid line of the pulse shows the actual pulse delivered. The falling edge pin action is assigned only to the MatchB event.

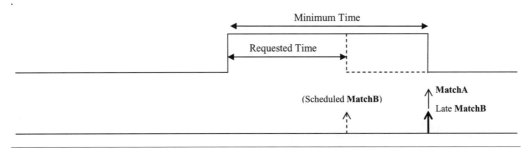

Figure 9.4 m2_o_dt Dual Match Mode

Contrary to what seems to happen in Figure 9.4, a MatchA event does not change the pin state. Because the matches are ordered, MatchB cannot occur until MatchA occurs. Under normal conditions, the **MatchB** register will have a greater value than the **MatchA** register and so MatchB will lie to the right of MatchA in Figure 9.4. In that case, which is not shown, the falling edge of the pulse would be defined by **MatchB**. The abnormal case, shown in the figure, represents the situation where **MatchB** is less than **MatchA**. MatchB is blocked because MatchA has not yet occurred. Once MatchA does occur, MatchB occurs immediately, provided it uses the greater-than-or-equal-to comparator option. The pin changes state on MatchB event. The MatchA event simply provides the boundary condition but has no effect on the pin state.

Input modes can be more complex than output modes because input transition detection may be enabled or disabled by match events. Apart from the trivial case of simply measuring the time of one or two edges using the single or double transition hardware in a channel, all input modes may be combined with match scheduling to qualify the detection of one or two input transitions. The term often used to describe this process is *windowing*. The dual match capability of channels operating in input mode can also be used to provide a time base for a task or output that is completely unrelated to the input signal. Bear in mind that input transitions block matches, so for the match function to operate successfully, it must use a greater-than-or-equal-to comparison and have relatively low resolution and accuracy requirements. The match will be undetected if it occurs between the time the pin transition occurred and the time its **TDL** is cleared, after which point a late match will occur.

Windowing functions have two main uses: to exclude (block) or permit (enable) edge detection. A blocking window filters noise from an input signal by preventing recognition of one or both input edges during a specific period of time. The other windowing use is just the opposite, which is to permit detection of one or both input transition only during specific periods of time.

Figure 9.5 shows the timing of a blocking window to filter noise that might occur immediately following a valid edge. When the valid edge is serviced, the thread schedules a timeout match using the **m2_st** channel mode because this mode blocks the detection of transitions until the timeout occurs.

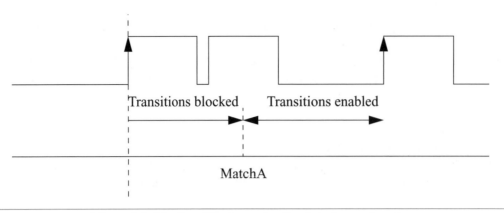

Figure 9.5 Blocking Window using Dual Action mode m2_st

Figure 9.6 shows the timing of an enabling window to permit detection of a signal within a window of time defined by **MatchA** and **MatchB**. This window is set up using channel mode **m2_st** as well. Prior to MatchA occurring, transition detection is blocked. The occurrence of MatchA causes transitions to be enabled in hardware, with no software intervention because no service request is issued. After this point, if a transition occurs before the time defined by **MatchB**, the transition time is captured and a service request is issued. If, however, MatchB occurs before the transition, it will generate the service request first. Note that the occurrence of MatchB does not disable transition detection in the **m2_st** mode, so a transition service request could also exist when eTPU software responds. Software may determine whether MatchB or the transition occurred first by reading the match event register and comparing it to the equivalent captured time base value.

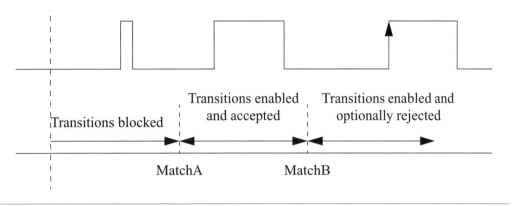

Figure 9.6 Enabling Window Using Dual Action Mode m2_st

The only real difference between the blocking and enabling examples is that in the latter case a MatchB is used to indicate the lack of a signal within the acceptance window. Signals outside the acceptance window are detected, and software must decide whether to accept or reject them.

If a true software-free enabling window is required, then one of the ordered match modes, **m2_o_st** or **m2_o_dt** may be used. In these cases, MatchB disables further transition detection. Of course, some method of re-enabling transition detection may be needed. An auxiliary timeout mechanism running on another channel could be used, or the windowing function on the same channel could be rescheduled when processing the MatchB event.

Hardware-Activated I/O Combinations

As stated previously, each eTPU channel contains hardware that allows input signals to directly interact with output signal generation, with no need for software servicing. This feature is useful in applications that require instant response to certain hardware conditions and cannot wait for software to service them. An example is the generation of an output disable signal in the event of an input signal that indicates excess current in a power switch.

The example in Figure 9.7 implements a fast short-circuit protection feedback mechanism for driving high-current output devices. The input is a feedback signal from the high-current output driver. This input signal is normally delayed from the output signal by the device turn-on delay. After the channel output turns on, the channel logic checks if the driver output (connected to the channel input) follows the driven value after the maximum device turn-on delay. If it doesn't, the channel output is turned off immediately to avoid damaging the device. MatchB occurs after the expected driver delay and causes a service request.

```
IPAC_A = 001; OPAC_A = 001; MatchA = OutputEdgeTime;
IPAC_B = 100; OPAC_B = 100; MatchB = MatchA + MaxTurnOnDelay;
PDCM = m2_o_dt;
```

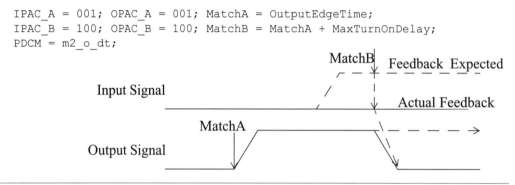

Figure 9.7 Short Circuit Protected Output

In the example shown in Figure 9.8, a low-going output pulse is generated depending on the value sampled on the input signal at a predetermined time. The input signal is sampled upon the occurrence of MatchA, and if the input is low then the output pulse is immediately asserted; otherwise the output stays negated. The output is negated upon the occurrence of the MatchB event. In both cases, a service request is optionally issued at the beginning (MatchA) and at the end (MatchB) of the pulse.

```
IPAC_A = 100; OPAC_A = 100; MatchA = Input Sampling time (Pulse start);
IPAC_B = 000; OPAC_B = 001; MatchB = MatchA + PulseWidth;
PDCM =em_nb_dt;
```

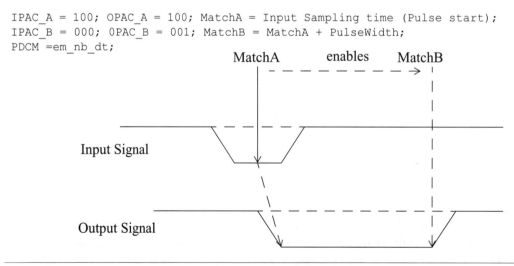

Figure 9.8 Output Pulse Enable/Disable

Resolving Conflicts in Action-Control Definitions

Matches and transitions automatically cause pin actions defined by the **OPAC_A/B** and **IPAC_A/B** channel control registers. Because each channel has two action units, it is possible that simultaneous matches and transitions may occur on the two action units. To ensure determinicity of the pin action, a priority order is assigned between the action unit **OPAC**s. The priority order depends on the channel mode selected, as follows:

- For all channel modes except **m2_** modes, **OPAC_A** has priority over **OPAC_B**.
- For **m2_st** and **m2_dt** modes, **OPAC_B** has priority over **OPAC_A**.
- **m2_o_st** and **m2_o_dt** cannot generate simultaneous matches, so in these modes **OPAC_A** always takes effect before **OPAC_B**.

Note that, if a prevailing **OPAC** is set to 0, indicating no pin action, then the simultaneous occurrence of match events on both action units results in no output pin action. Note also that when an input event causes an output action (i.e., when **OPAC**=1xx), the **OPAC** priority order still applies.

Detailed State Operation of All Channel Modes

Figure 9.9 and Figure 9.10 show all combinations of transition and match events that apply to each of the 13 channel modes that may be selected by the **PDCM** control register.

Mode	initially blocked	1st event: event type	1st event: [blocks] (enables)	1st event: Cap	2nd event: event type	2nd event: [blocks] (enables)	2nd event: Cap	3rd event: event type	3rd event: [blocks] (enables)	3rd event: Cap	4th event: event type	4th event: [blocks] (enables)	4th event: Cap
em_nb_st	none	MatchA/B	none	A/B	MatchB/A	none	B/A	Trans.A	[matches]	both	Trans.B	none	B
					Trans.A	[matches]	both	Trans.B	none	B			
		Trans.A	[matches]	both	TransB	none	B						
em_nb_dt	none	MatchA/B	none	A/B	MatchB/A	none	B/A	Trans.A	none	A	Trans.B	none	B
		MatchA	none	A	Trans.A	none	A	MatchB	none	B	Trans.B	none	B
								Trans.B	[MatchB]	B			
		MatchB	none	B	Trans.A	[MatchA]	A	Trans.B	[MatchB]	B			
		Trans.A	[MatchA]	A	MatchB	none	B	Trans.B	none	B			
					Trans.B	[MatchB]	B						
em_b_st	none	MatchA	[MatchB]	both	Trans.A	[matches]	both	Trans.B	none	B			
		MatchB	[MatchA]	both									
		Trans.A	[matches]	both	Trans.B	none	B						
em_b_dt	none	MatchA	[MatchB]	both	Trans.A	none	A	Trans.B	none	B			
		MatchB	[MatchA]	both									
		Trans.A	[MatchA]	A	MatchB	none	B	Trans.B	none	B			
					Trans.B	[MatchB]	B						
bm_st	none	MatchA/B	none	A/B	MatchB/A	none	B/A	Trans.A	[matches]	both	Trans.B	none	B
					Trans.A	[matches]	both	Trans.B	none	B			
		Trans.A	[matches]	both	Trans.B	none	B						
bm_dt	none	MatchA/B	none	A/B	MatchB/A	none	B/A	Trans.A	none	A	Trans.B	[matches]	B
					Trans.A	none	A	MatchB/A	none	B/none	Trans.B	[matches]	B
								Trans.B	[matches]	B			
		Trans.A	none	A	MatchA/B	none	None/B	MatchB/A	none	B/none	Trans.B	[matches]	B
								Trans.B	[matches]	B			
					Trans.B	[matches]	B						

Service Request on this event

Figure 9.9 Channel Mode Event Handling With No Events Initially Blocked

Figure 9.9 contains the category of channel modes that do not initially block any events, while the modes in Figure 9.10 initially block either one or two events. The grayed cells in the tables indicate when a service request occurs. The event name in square brackets, for example [MatchA], means the event that occurred, indicated by the column heading, blocks the named event. The event name in parenthesis, for example (TransitionA), means the event that occurred enables the named event. These two figures provide a good reference for determining what mode you should select for your particular application. The tables are used by first selecting a specific mode and then following the appropriate rows for that mode from left to right, switching between rows when necessary to match the expected behavior of the application. For example, if the channel is selected to operate in **em_b_dt** mode, the behavior of the channel might be as follows:

1. The first event that occurs is a MatchA event, which blocks MatchB, captures the time base specified by **IPAC_A** in **CaptureA**, captures the time base specified by **IPAC_B** in **CaptureB**, and generates a service request.

2. The second event that occurs is a TransitionA event which doesn't block anything and captures the time base specified by **IPAC_A** in **CaptureA**.

3. The third event that occurs is a TransitionB event which again doesn't block anything, captures the time base specified by **IPAC_B** in **CaptureB** and generates a service request.

By inspecting all the other rows, it can be seen that the **em_b_dt** mode rules are:

1. The second transition always generates a service request.
2. Matches will never block a transition.
3. If the second transition occurs before any match, no matches will occur, and otherwise there will be a match.
4. Only one of the match events will generate a service request.
5. If the first transition occurs before MatchA, then MatchA will never occur.
6. The first transition never generates a service request.

There are three important points to note about the channel mode event handling tables that may not be obvious:

1. Transitions are always ordered—that is, the first transition will use action unit A hardware, and the second will use action unit B hardware. In essence, TransitionB detection is blocked until TransitionA occurs.

2. All single transition modes (except **sm_st_e**) also capture the selected time base if a second transition occurs, but no service request is generated. This feature can be

used to advantage when the latency of servicing an input edge is greater than the time between consecutive edges.

3. eTPU code can override the automatic blocking and enabling that is performed by the hardware. So, in our example above, if eTPU code services the first match event, it could re-enable further match events after hardware had disabled them. This of course would defeat the intent of the hardware designers, but that's the power of software!

Figure 9.10 Channel Mode Event Handling With Some Events Initially Blocked

Mode	initially blocked	1st event type	[blocks] (enables)	Cap	2nd event type	[blocks] (enables)	Cap	3rd event type	[blocks] (enables)	Cap	4th event type	[blocks] (enables)	Cap
m2_st	Trans.A	MatchA	(Trans.A)	A	MatchB	none	B	Trans.A	[matches]	both	transB	none	B
		MatchA and MatchB	(Trans.A)	both	Trans.A	[matches]	both	Trans.B	none	B			
		MatchB	[MatchA]	B	Trans.A	[matches]	both	Trans.B	none	B			
m2_dt	Trans.A	MatchA	(Trans.A)	A	Trans.A	none	A	Trans.B	[MatchB]	B	Trans.B	none	B
		MatchA and MatchB	(Trans.A)	both	MatchB	none	B	MatchB	none	A	Trans.B	none	B
		MatchB	[MatchA]	B	Trans.A	none	A	Trans.B	none	B			
m2_o_st	Trans.A, MatchB	MatchA	[MatchB] (Trans.A)	A	Trans.A	[matches]	both	transB	none	B			
					MatchB	[Trans.A]	B	Trans.B	[MatchB]	B			
m2_o_dt	Trans.A, MatchB	MatchA	(MatchB) (Trans.A)	A	Trans.A	none	A	MatchB	[Trans.B]	B			
					MatchB	[Trans.A]	B	Trans.B	none	B			
sm_st	MatchB	MatchA	none	both	Trans.A	none	A	Trans.B	none	B			
		Trans.A	[MatchA]	both	Trans.B	none	B						
sm_dt	MatchB	MatchA	none	both	Trans.A	none	A	Trans.B	none	B			
		Trans.A	none	A	Trans.B	none	B						
sm_st_e	MatchB, Trans.B	MatchA	none	A	MatchA	[MatchA]	B						
		Trans.A	[MatchA]	A	Trans.A	none	A						

Service Request on this event

Programming Example—Detecting a Pulse in a Window

Suppose we wish to detect a pulse only if it occurs within a given window of time. Here, we want to open the window, capture any detected rising input edge time, capture any detected falling input edge time, and close the window. The falling edge and the window closing should gate one another and should each request servicing so that we can see which one occurred first. If the thread is called due to window closure, we know that the pulse didn't occur within the window (because window closure gates the second transition); on the other hand if the thread is called due to the second transition, we know that the pulse did occur within the window (because the second pulse gates window closure).

The channel mode we want to use, then, should have the following characteristics:

- Input transitions should be ignored until the first match (MatchA).
- Two input transitions should then be detected, the first (TransitionA) asserting flag **TDL_A** and the second (TransitionB) asserting **TDL_B.**
- Servicing must occur on the second match (MatchB) and/or TransitionB.
- TransitionB must block MatchB so that if **TDL_B** is asserted the pulse occurred entirely within window.
- MatchB must block TransitionB so that if **MRL_B** is asserted the pulse did not occur entirely within the window.

This functionality may be obtained from a double-transition channel mode that issues a service on **MRL_B**. A suitable mode is **m2_dt**. The following pages show the code that implements the example function and provides a detailed explanation of how the code works.

```
#include <ETPUC.H>

#pragma ETPU_function DetectPulseInWindow;

int24 RisingEdge, FallingEdge;
int IsValidPulse;

void DetectPulseInWindow() {
int24 CurrentTime;
    if (hsr == 1) {
        pdcm = m2_dt;                 // Select match 2, double transition mode
        act_unitA = Mtcr1_Ctcr1_eq;   // For action unit A use TCR1 for match and
                                      // capture; match on equality
        act_unitB = Mtcr1_Ctcr1_eq;   // For action unit B use TCR1 for match and
                                      // capture; match on equality
        ipacA = low_high;             // Detect a rising edge on action unit A
        ipacB = high_low;             // Detect a falling edge on action unit B
        CurrentTime = tcr1;
        erta = CurrentTime + 0x10;    // Set up MatchA - defines start of window
        ertb = CurrentTime + 0x20;    // Set up MatchB - defines end of window
        erwA = 0;                     // Enable MatchA
        erwB = 0;                     // Enable MatchB
        mtd = 0;                      // Enable match, transition event transition
        IsValidPulse = 0;
    }
    else if ((m1 == 1) && (m2 == 1)) { // If both matches or both transitions
                                      // occurred
        if (mrlB == 1)                // If MatchB occurred then input pulse
                                      // did not occur in widnow
        IsValidPulse = 0;             // Clear flag

        else if (tdlB == 1) {         // If both transitions occurred
            IsValidPulse = 1;         // Set flag
            RisingEdge = erta;        // Store time of rising edge
            FallingEdge = ertb;       // Store time of falling edge
        }
        CurrentTime = tcr1;           // Re-arm window based on current time
        erta = CurrentTime + 0x10;    // Set up MatchA - defines start of window
        ertb = CurrentTime + 0x20;    // Set up MatchB - defines end of window
        erwA = 0;                     // Enable MatchA
        erwB = 0;                     // Enable MatchB
        tdl = 0;                      // Clear transition flag
        mrlA = 0;                     // Clear MatchA flag
        mrlB = 0;                     // Clear MatchB flag
    }
    else ()
}
```

Example 9.1 Code That Detects a Pulse Occurring in a Window of Time

This function, DetectPulseInWindow, sets global flag IsValidPulse, and updates global variables RisingEdgeTime and FallingEdgeTime only if a pulse occurs within a specified window. The function consists of two threads (ignoring the error recovery thread): one initialization thread, executed when the host issues an HSR of 1 on the channel to which the function is assigned; and one thread that is executed when both **m1** and **m2** conditions are satisfied.

- An **m1** condition occurs when **MRL_A** and/or **TDL_B** is asserted.
- An **m2** condition occurs when **MRL_B** and/or **TDL_A** are asserted.

Note that **m2_dt** prevents **MRL_A** and **TDL_A** from generating service requests but does not prevent **MRL_A** and **TDL_A** from being asserted. The **m1**, **m2** compound conditional statement makes use of this fact. Because the code in Example 9.1 always schedules MatchA to occur before MatchB, when **MRL_B** generates a service request **MRL_A** must also be asserted. Moreover, this mode ensures that if **TDL_B** is asserted, **TDL_A** is also asserted but **MRL_B** cannot be asserted. So the **m1/m2** thread always executes when either the window times out on MatchB (which asserts **MRL_B**) or the pulse is detected on TransitionB (which asserts **TDL_B**). The thread then discriminates between the two types of event by checking their respective flags. Finally, the thread schedules the next transition detection window and clears all flags. In Figure 9.11, the two time-slot transitions that occur immediately after the input pin falls indicate the point at which the pulse is detected. The threads are executed as a result of the falling transition. The first wholly visible time slot transition on the logic analyzer is executed as a result of a timeout match when the window closes: it does not occur after an input edge, thus indicating no pulse was detected.

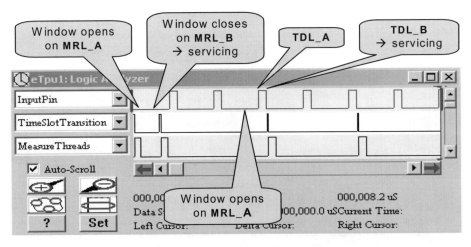

Figure 9.11 Measuring Windowed Pulses

CHAPTER 10

Clocking and Angle Clock

eTPU Time-Base Clocking

Because the eTPU has multiple time-base clocking options to meet automotive and industrial application requirements, the system designer may choose a clocking configuration that is the best fit for the target application needs. As previously stated, the eTPU engine has two timer count registers, **TCR1** and **TCR2**. These 24-bit counters are shared by all 32 channels for matches and captures. eTPU software may read these counters to get the current time, an activity that is usually performed during the initialization thread of a channel. The capture values reflect the relative time of match or input transition events and may be used to calculate future output events. **TCR1** and **TCR2** clocking is controlled by the eTPU time base configuration register (**ETPUTBCR**), which provides distinct clocking options for each counter.

TCR1 Clocking

TCR1 operation and clock selection is shown in Figure 10.1. **TCR1** clocking is controlled by the **TCR1CTL** field, which offers three options:

- Externally clocked by the **TCRCLK** input, after the digital filter;
- Driven from the system clock divided by 2;
- Driven by the STAC bus.

Note: The maximum rate of a time base driven to or imported from the MPC5554 STAC bus is the system clock divided by 4.

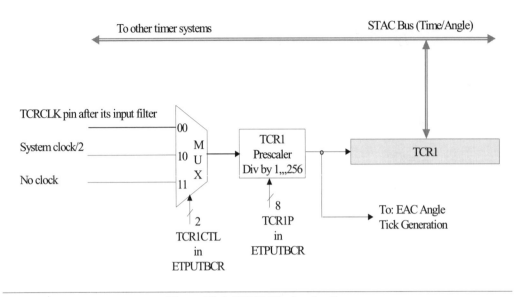

Figure 10.1 TCR1 Clock selection

When the **TCR1** clock source is either the system clock/2 or the **TCRCLK** input pin, a prescaler from 1 to 256 can be chosen, as set in the **TCR1P** bit field. When **TCR1** is a shared time and counter (STAC) bus client, the **ETPUTBCR** clock selection and the presaging logic is void and becomes ineffective. **TCR1** is referred to as *a client* when it receives time or angle information from the STAC bus, which in turn may be driven by another timer system. For example, in the MPC5554 implementation there are two integrated eTPU engines. In such an implementation, one eTPU may drive the STAC bus (called *server*) and the other eTPU may use it as its time base (called *client*). The STAC bus implementation in the eTPU allows multiple timer systems to share a common time base or angle information, which allows for synchronization between channels. The STAC bus selection is determined by the eTPU stack bus configuration register (**ETPUSTACR**). A detailed explanation of this appears later in this chapter.

For additional information on **TCR1** clocking, refer to *Chapter 7. Host Interface*.

TCR2 Clocking

TCR2 clocking, as shown in Figure 10.2, is controlled by the **TCR2CTL** field and has numerous choices of clock selection to meet certain requirements.

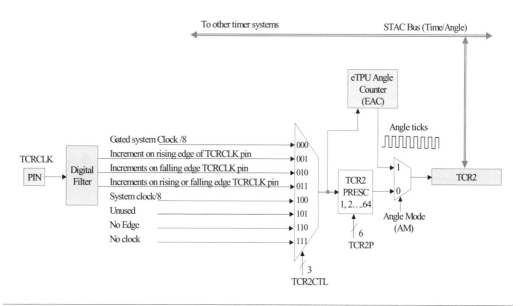

Figure 10.2 TCR2 Clock Selection

The **TCRCLK** digital filter can be programmed to use the system clock divided by two or to use the same filter clock of the channels, controlled by the **TCRCF** field in **ETPUTBCR**. It contains an up-down counter which operates as a digital integrator to optimize signal latency in the selected mode and clock rate. See Table 10.1 for **TCRCLK** pin filter modes.

TCRCF	Filter Clock	Filter Mode
00	System clock/2	Two samples
01	Filter clock of the channels	Two samples
10	System clock/2	Integration
11	Filter clock of the channels	Integration

Table 10.1 TCRCLK Pin Filter Mode

When **TCR2** is driven from the system clock divided by 2, the synchronizer and the digital filter are guaranteed to pass pulses that are wider than four system clocks (two filter clocks). Otherwise the **TCRCLK** is filtered with the same filter clock as the channel input signals as controlled by the channel digital filter (**CDFC**) of the eTPU engine configuration register (**ETPUECR**). Note that the channel digital filter is a common filter for all channels that are configured as inputs.

In angle-based engine-control applications, the tooth signal generated from the flywheel is applied to the **TCRCLK** input pin as the clock source to increment **TCR2**. The input signal edge is software programmable, which allows incrementing **TCR2** on rising edge, falling edge, or either edge. The input signal is also fed to channel 0 input logic although the channel 0 pin is unused. This means that on some MCUs, such the MPC5554, the pin itself may be assigned to an alternate function such as GPI/O. Note that the channel 0 input detection logic must match the input detection mode for **TCR2**. For example, if the host software sets the input detection mode for **TCR2** to rising edge only, eTPU software should set the input detection mode for channel 0 to rising edge only also.

When in angle mode, the **TCR2CTL** = 110 setting selects "no edge" for **TCRCLK** detection by the eTPU angle counter (EAC). In this setting, **TCR2** will still be incremented by the tick generator and can be kept running by the code asserting insert physical tooth (IPH). This is useful when the TCRCLK signal becomes unreliable. In such a situation, the eTPU code can use the CAM signal instead of the crank signal to calculate engine angular position.

Refer to *Chapter 7. Host Interface* for more details on **TCR2** clocking.

Angle Mode Operation

Angle mode is targeted for angle-based engine control in automotive applications in particular but may be used in any application that requires high-resolution angular placement of pulses or events such as interrupts to the host processor or DMA requests to the DMA controller. In angle mode, a pulse signal derived from a toothed wheel attached to an automobile crankshaft, for example, is applied to the **TCRCLK** input pin, as shown above in Figure 10.2. The signal passes through a programmable input filter to remove noise. After the input filter validates the signal, it is applied to the eTPU angle tick (EAC) generator.

The angle tick generator operates like a rate multiplier: the output of the generator is a clock that runs at a frequency that is a multiple of the input frequency of pulses from the toothed wheel. The angle tick generator output increments **TCR2** at a rate defined by eTPU software. The result is that **TCR2** represents a higher resolution angular position of the crankshaft than can be represented by the physical teeth alone. **TCR2** effectively interpolates between teeth.

The resolution of the interpolation is user programmable and is defined by the combination of:

- the number of angle ticks (increments of TCR2) required per physical tooth period.
- the rate at which angle ticks should be generated.

eTPU software should write the required number of angle ticks per tooth to the 10-bit **TICKS** field of the tooth program register (**TPR**). The frequency at which the angle ticks occur is a function of the value that eTPU software writes to the **TRR** register and would typically be based on the last measured period between physical teeth. However, because the next physical tooth could arrive earlier or later than anticipated, the EAC contains hardware that halts or accelerates the angle ticks to ensure that exactly **TICKS** counts are generated between physical teeth.

If the anticipated tooth arrives sooner than expected and before all programmed ticks are counted, the angle ticks automatically accelerate to count all ticks, ensuring that all values of **TCR2** are generated. The acceleration of angle ticks is referred to as *high-rate mode*. In this mode, angle ticks are generated at a rate of system clock/8. If the anticipated tooth arrives later than expected and all programmed ticks have been counted, **TCR2** is stopped until the next tooth arrives. This is called *halt mode*. The next actual physical tooth generates an angle tick that increments **TCR2** and then normal operation commences where **TCR2** is again incremented by EAC angle ticks. Figure 10.3 depicts angle clock ticks during engine acceleration and deceleration.

The rate at which angle ticks should be generated is very much a function of the expected behavior of the engine. Predictive models or filtering algorithms may be used to more accurately represent the expected time until the next physical tooth. For the sake of simplicity, the algorithm described here assumes the tooth period is constant and that the most recently obtained period may be used without modification to calculate the value written to **TRR**, representing the desired angle tick rate.

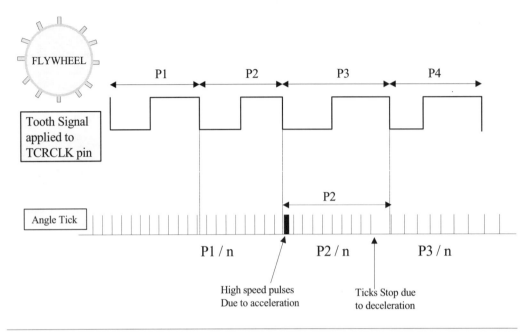

Figure 10.3 Angle Clock Acceleration and Deceleration

The value stored in the 24-bit **TRR**, as shown in Figure 9.4, is composed of two portions: a 15-bit integer and a 9-bit fraction. The integer portion defines the period, in **TCR1** counts, of angle ticks from the tick rate generator. The fractional portion is used to increase the average tick rate accuracy by compensating for the fact that the tick rate generator can be clocked only by an integral value of **TCR1** counts, derived from the division of two integers. The fractional portion is added to itself after each angle tick is generated. When the accumulated fraction overflows (which means it exceeds the value of 1.0), the angle tick generator is halted for one **TCR1** count to extend the duration of one angle tick by one **TCR1** count only.

The final accuracy of the angle ticks depends on the used resolution of the fraction. The best accuracy is obtained using two divides, two shifts and a logical OR, as follows:

- divide the tooth period by the number of angle ticks per tooth and left-shift the result (contained in the **MACL** register) by 9 bits to give the integer portion for the **TRR**;
- take the remainder from the previous divide (contained in the eTPU **MACH** register) shift it left 9 bits and divide that by the number of angle ticks per tooth. The

result, in **MACL**, represents the 9-bit fraction for the **TRR**. The remainder in **MACH**) may be discarded;

- logically OR the result values of the two previous steps.

eTPU software should then write the OR-ed value to the **TRR** to generate a new tick rate. The new rate is effective immediately after the next angle tick generated by the angle tick generator.

Note that for high engine speeds, the algorithm for determining **TRR** may be simplified: first shift the tooth period 9 bits to the left then divide the shifted value by the number of angle ticks per tooth. The 24-bit result (in eTPU **MACL**) contains the integer and fraction portion in the correct bit positions.

For example, on a 60 teeth flywheel running at 1000 RPM, the tooth period is 1 msec. If **TCR1** counts at 25 MHz, it counts 25,000 times in a tooth, which can be represented by 15 bits. Therefore the tooth period can be shifted 9 bits to the left prior to the divide operation and still be represented in 24 bits.

Other algorithms may be used. The key is to ensure that the integer part of the algorithm's result is justified in the most significant 15 bits of the **TRR**. For applications that do not require the accuracy provided by all 9 bits of the fraction portion, the resolution of the fractional calculation may be reduced or the fractional portion may contain the value 0.

For example the algorithm **((ToothPeriod << 3)/ TicksPerTooth) << 6)** yields a correctly justified result with only one divide, one three-bit left shift and one six-bit left shift (giving a total of 9 bits of left shift). The final six-bit left shift produces a **TRR** value with only three bits of fractional resolution. This may be acceptable in many applications.

23..9	8................0
INTEGER[0:14]	FRACTION[0:8]

Figure 10.4 Tick Rate Register (TRR)

- **INTEGER[0:14]**
  This is the integer part of the angle tick period;

- **FRACTION[0:8]**
  This the fractional part that determines the angle tick period.

In angle mode, channel 0 must be used to measure periods between crankshaft teeth. When the tooth signal is detected by channel 0, eTPU software recalculates the next expected tooth time by adjusting the duration of the programmed ticks using the previous algorithm.

The tooth program register (**TPR**), which contains the 10-bit **TICKS** field, also includes a number of bit fields which may be used to control the operation of the angle clock hardware. The following is a detailed explanation of how each field is used for angle-based engine control.

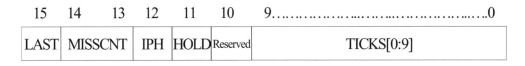

Figure 10.5 Tooth Program Register (TPR)

- **TICKS[0:9]**
  This 10-bit field holds the number of programmed ticks (less 1) to interpolate between crank shaft teeth. For example, to generate 100 ticks, write 99 to the **TICKS** field. The angle clock hardware can be programmed by the eTPU code to generate up to 1024 ticks. If the number of ticks is set to 128, say, in a 60-tooth flywheel, angle ticks per tooth provides a resolution of approximately 0.05 degrees per tick. Most automotive applications require an accuracy of 0.1 degree. The interpolation resolution between adjacent teeth can be increased by simply increasing the number of programmed ticks.

- **MISSCNT[0:1]**
  Most flywheels implement one or more missing teeth to accurately detect the engine angular position. For this reason, the eTPU angle clock (EAC) supports up to three missing teeth and is able to insert the required number of dummy teeth to replace the missing teeth of the flywheel. **MISSCNT** field options are shown in Table 10.2.

MISSCNT[0:1]	*Meaning*
00	No missing tooth
01	One missing tooth
10	Two missing teeth
11	Three missing teeth

Table 10.2 MISSCNT Field Encoding

- **LAST**

  The **LAST** bit is used in combination with the value of **MISSCNT** to indicate when hardware should reset **TCR2**. This bit is set by eTPU software to indicate that the last physical tooth edge has occurred prior to the occurrence of the missing tooth position. The last physical tooth edge may be followed by one, two, or three missing teeth, according to the crankshaft implemented in the application. There are two methods of handling missing teeth:

    a. On the last physical tooth arrival, eTPU software writes the **TICKS** field in the program tooth register to double, triple, or quadruple the number of ticks according to the crack shaft type (one, two, or three missing teeth). For example, if the **TICKS** field is set to 99 ticks for the physical tooth interpolation, on the last physical tooth detected eTPU software writes the **TICKS** field with 199, 299, or 399 depending on the number of missing teeth (1, 2, or 3) in the crank shaft. With this method, missing teeth are not counted and the eTPU angle clock hardware works in its regular interpolation manner. When the next tooth edge is detected, eTPU software should restore the **TICKS** field to the original value of 99.

    b. On the last physical tooth arrival, eTPU code sets the **LAST** bit and the indicates the number of missing teeth in the **MISSCNT** field. With this method, the missing teeth are counted as normal teeth by automatic insertion of the required number of dummy teeth as programmed in **MISSCNT** field. For example, for a crankshaft of 58 physical teeth with two missing, the physical teeth will be numbered from 0 to 57 and the missing teeth will be numbered 58 and 59. eTPU software will set the **LAST** bit when tooth number 57 is counted and at the same time sets **MISSCNT** field to 2 to indicate two missing teeth will follow. **MISSCNT** is then decremented with the arrival of each missing tooth. When the first physical tooth after the missing teeth period is detected, the hardware decrements **MISSCNT** to 0, and, because LAST is set, the hardware will also reset **TCR2** to 0.

- **Insert Physical Tooth (IPH)**

  This bit may be set by eTPU software to provide the angle clock hardware a mechanism to insert a physical dummy tooth when there is a need to catch up with the current angular position. For example, if the eTPU code algorithm detects that the angle ticks are lagging or halted, setting **IPH** causes the angle clock to enter the high-rate mode (if in normal mode) or the normal mode (if in halt mode).

- **Force eTPU Angle Clock Halt (HOLD)**

  Setting this bit forces the angle clock to enter halt mode. Halting the angle clock ticks may be required when eTPU code detects that the tick count is ahead of the current angular position. **HOLD** may be set, for example, when the eTPU angle clock hardware detects a tooth that happens to be a spurious tooth (false tooth) due to noise. As the next real physical or the emulated tooth arrives, this bit is automatically negated and normal operation resumes.

Angle mode is enabled by setting the angle mode (**AM**) bit in **ETPUTBCR**. In this mode, **TCR2** may be used to track engine angular position. The **TCR2** angular position can be exported to other eTPU channels in dual-engine implementations as well as the enhanced modular I/O timer system (eMIOS), if integrated on chip. Since **TCR2** reports all angular positions during constant speed, acceleration, and deceleration and since its angle information is made visible to all channels, any channel that needs to reference **TCR2** can read it. Once an eTPU function has scheduled an event to occur on a certain angular position, the channel does not need to be reprogrammed to adjust for engine acceleration and deceleration. This is also applicable to the eMIOS timer system channels. Once channels are set up for angle matches, they will then drive their output pins to fire their respective sparks or fuel injectors at precise angular position. In other words, output channels using **TCR2** as their time base for matches will trigger when there is a match between **TCR2** and their respective channel match registers. As shown in Figure 10.6, channel 0 is used to capture the input signal and to calculate the tooth period. To prevent detection of noise and to guarantee passage of the tooth signal only, channel 0 uses match2 (*m2_st*) channel mode to generate an acceptance window for the anticipated tooth signal arrival. For additional information on channel modes, refer to *Chapter 9. Channel Hardware and Modes*

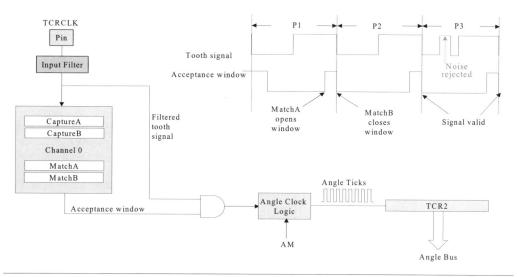

Figure 10.6 Channel 0 Tooth Signal Acceptance Window

Since the previous tooth period is measured by channel 0, the next tooth is anticipated to occur in the future relative to the previous tooth period. Based on this information, eTPU software writes two future match values into channel 0's **MatchA** and **MatchB** registers, producing an acceptance window within which the next tooth signal is predicted to occur. The acceptance window opens when a match occurs between the selected time base and the MatchA event and closes when the selected time base equals the **MatchB** register value, guaranteeing that only the expected signal will pass through to the angle clock hardware logic. Any pulses applied to the **TCRCLK** pin outside the programmed window will be rejected as noise. As stated previously, in angle mode, channel 0 uses **TCRCLK** pin as its input signal and its pin can be used for a secondary function such as GPI/O.

> **Note: TCR1** typically, but not necessarily, is clocked from the prescaled system clock and is used as the time base for channel 0's matches and captures.

STAC Bus Operation

The shared timer and counter (STAC) interface is used to synchronize all timers implemented on the MCU. Since some of the MPC5500 family derivatives integrate two eTPUs and a modular I/O timer system (eMIOS), one eTPU may be used to drive the

STAC bus and the other timers may listen to it as their time base. In such implementations, **TCR1** or **TCR2** in either eTPU_A or eTPU_B can be programmed to drive the STAC bus. The selection of which **TCR** and which engine to drive STAC is made by bit fields in the eTPU STAC configuration register (**ETPUSTACR**), which is shown in Figure 10.7. Bits 0 through 15 configure **TCR1**, and bits 16 through 31 configure **TCR2**.

0	1	2	3	4	5	6	7	8	9	10	11	12	13	14	15
REN1	RSC1	0	0		SERVER_ID1			0	0	0	0			SRV1	

16	17	18	19	20	21	22	23	24	25	26	27	28	29	30	31
REN2	RSC2	0	0		SERVER_ID2			0	0	0	0			SRV2	

Figure 10.7 eTPU STAC Bus Configuration Register (ETPUSTACR)

The **TCR** that drives the STAC bus is referred to as the *server* and those that listen are referred to as *clients*. Each client can receive information from only one server, but a server can provide time base information to a number of clients. The server information is time multiplexed onto the bus. Each server is assigned a fixed (hardcoded) ID, which is driven along with the timing/angle information. These IDs are available in the read-only 4-bit fields **SERVER_ID1** and **SERVER_ID2**. In the MPC5554 implementation, there can be only four servers: **TCR1** and **TCR2** of eTPU_A and eTPU_B.

A client must be given the server ID to which it listens. Once this ID appears on the bus, the client captures the related timing/angle information. The ID is programmed in the **ETPUSTACR** fields **SRV1** and **SRV2** (for **TCR1** and **TCR2** respectively). In MPC5554, the **SRV** options are as follows (hardwired):

- eTPU_A **TCR1** server ID = 0
- eTPU_A **TCR2** server ID = 2
- eTPU_B **TCR1** server ID = 1
- eTPU_B **TCR2** server ID = 3

The **SERVER** and **SRV** fields are meaningful only after enabling the STAC interface for **TCR** operation by setting the resource client/server operation enable bit (**RENx**) in the **ETPUSTACR** and then specifying whether the **TCR** in question is to serve as a client or as a server, which is controlled by the resource server/client assignment bit (**RSCx**) also in the **EPTUSTACR**. The following table explains the server/client selection of **TCR1** and **TCR2**.

REN2	RSC2	*Resource Selection*	REN1	RSC1	*Resource Selection*
0	0	Disabled	0	0	Disabled
0	1	Don't care	0	1	Don't care
1	0	**TCR2** is client	1	0	**TCR1** is client
1	1	**TCR2** is server	1	1	**TCR1** is server

Table 10.3 TCRx Client/Server selection

Note that there are restrictions on which servers can be assigned to a given eTPU client: a client must not be assigned to listen to a server in the same engine. Also, time bases must not be configured as clients when the engine is in angle mode.

If, for example, we want eTPU_B's **TCR2** to receive eTPU_A's **TCR1**, and eTPU_A's **TCR2** to receive eTPU_B's **TCR1**. The settings would be as shown in Table 10.4.

Field	*eTPU_A*	*eTPU_B*
REN1	1	1
REN2	1	1
RSC1	1 (**TCR1** is server)	1 (**TCR1** is server)
RSC2	0 (**TCR2** is client)	0 (**TCR2** is client)
SRV1	Don't care	Don't care
SRV2	1 (so, the server for eTPU_A's **TCR2** is eTPU_B's **TCR1**)	0 (so, the server for eTPU_B's **TCR2** is eTPU_A's **TCR1**)

Table 10.4 Sample ETPUSTACR Settings

Angle Clock Application Example

The following is an application example that uses the eTPU angle clock to provide angle information for a four-cylinder engine. In this section we will examine the basic engine operation first and then provide simple code segments to demonstrate how the eTPU angle clock is used to control the timing of sparks and fuel injectors.

Overview

For a typical automotive engine control, the controller needs to decode the engine angular position according to the crank and CAM sensor inputs. Based on the engine position, the controller delivers the spark and fuel pulse for each cylinder.

The popular four-stroke engine used on most automobiles today completes two revolutions when all cylinders complete all four strokes. This is also referred as an *engine cycle*. The four-stroke engine system is illustrated in Figure 10.8. For the four-stroke internal combustion engine, the fuel can be delivered only when the cylinder is in the intake and/or compression stroke.

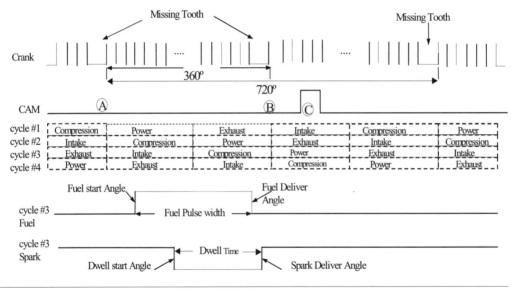

Figure 10.8 Engine System

The spark normally fires at the end of the compression stroke. Since the crank signal can only identify the angular position within 360°, the CAM signal is needed to determine if the engine rotation is on the first or second revolution of the engine cycle. With the help of the CAM sensor, the phases of each cylinder can be described as a range of angular position.

The engine control application requires significant bandwidth for the controller. At 6000 RPM, for 60x-2 tooth engine configuration, the time interval between two adjacent crank teeth is about 167 μs. At each crank tooth, the engine position needs to be decoded and the spark or fuel pulse needs to be scheduled or adjusted for each cylinder. The event-intensive nature of the engine application requires the engine controller to handle frequent interrupts effectively.

The eTPU is designed to off load the main CPU to handle the intensive timing events. One typical application usage for the eTPU is automotive engine control. As illustrated in the simple engine-control examples in the following sections, the eTPU can be used to decode the engine position, deliver the spark and fuel, etc.

Engine Control Application Functional Partition

The typical automotive engine control system consists of engine position decoding, ignition control, and fuel injection control. In this example, the eTPU will be used to decode the engine position based on the crank and CAM sensor inputs. The host CPU will calculate the spark delivery angle (spark advance), and Dwell time based on the engine operation condition. The eTPU is used to control the timing of the ignition and fuel injector events. Similarly, the host CPU will calculate the fuel pulse width and delivery angle based on the engine operation conditions.

The following sections describe the functional requirements of the engine position decoding, the eTPU channel configuration requirements, and spark and fuel control.

Engine Position Decoding Functional Requirement

It is assumed that the target engine is a four-cylinder engine with a 36x-1 crank tooth pattern. The relationship between crank and CAM sensor output is shown in Figure 10.8. The CAM sensor always generates a single pulse at a fixed angular position on the second rotation. One eTPU channel will be used to decode the crank sensor input to generate the angle clock. A second eTPU channel will be used to decode the CAM sensor input. The host CPU will determine the engine synchronization status based on both angle clock and CAM sensor input.

The first step of the engine position decoding is to identify the missing tooth to establish the reference point. The eTPU crank channel monitors the crank sensor input to capture the time stamp of the current input pulse. When the transition is detected, the time interval between the two adjacent teeth (i.e., the *tooth period*) is calculated. The latest tooth period is compared to the previous tooth period to identify the missing tooth. Once the first missing tooth is detected, the eTPU crank channel starts to generate the angle clock.

As shown in Figure 10.8, when the first missing tooth is detected, the engine position is either at Point A or Point B. Since reading the crank signal alone won't indicate if the engine is at its first or second rotation of an engine cycle—that is, at Point A or Point B—the engine system is half synchronized. Cylinder 1 may be in the start of power stroke (at Point A) or intake stroke (at Point B).

The eTPU CAM channel monitors the CAM signal. When the CAM tooth is detected, it will generate a link request to the crank channel. If the missing tooth on the crank channel has been detected at this point (Point C), the engine is fully synchronized. Depending on the position of the CAM pulse, the angle clock may need to be adjusted to reflect the actual engine angular position.

The host CPU will determine the spark and fuel deliver strategy based on the engine synchronization status.

eTPU Angle Clock/CAM Channel Configuration and Software Design

The eTPU CAM input channel can be set to *either match, blocking, double transition* (**em_b_dt**) channel mode. The TransitionA event is programmed to capture a rising edge while the TransitionB event is programmed to capture a falling edge. Matches are not used. In this channel mode, the TransitionA event (i.e., a rising edge) has to take place before the TransitionB event (i.e., a falling edge)—otherwise, transitions will be ignored. When both rising and falling edges of the CAM signal are captured, the angle clock is also

Note: The code examples throughout this chapter utilize complex macros from the etpuc_common.h header file, which comes standard with the eTPU_C Compiler. This header file, including the complex macros, is described in *Appendix A. Byte Craft Limited's eTPU_C Compiler*.

recorded. The CAM signal angular pulse width is used to qualify the CAM signal pulse. The eTPU code example for setting up the CAM decoding is provided below.

```
. . . . .
    if (hsrInitCAM) { // Init Cam HSR -- required to initialize the signal
    InitCam:
        CamStatus = SearchingCam;
        SetChannelMode(em_b_dt);

        SetupCaptureTrans_A(Capture_tcr2, low_high);
        SetupCaptureTrans_B(Capture_tcr2, high_low);
    }

    else if (matchA_transB) {
        ClearTransLatch();

        if ((GetCapRegB() - GetCapRegA()) > VALID_CAM_PULSE)
        {
            CamStatus = CamDetected;
            LinkToChannel(CrankChannel);
        }
    }
. . . . .
```

Example 10.1 Code That Sets Up the CAM Decoding

The crank sensor decoding function has to run on eTPU channel 0, which is connected to the angle clock hardware. The crank sensor input is connected to both the **TCRCLK** pin and channel 0 input. The **TCRCLK** pin is used to drive the angle clock hardware. In addition to the configuration for the angle clock, the eTPU angle clock channel (channel 0) is set up as *both match, single transition* channel mode in order to capture the falling edge of the crank sensor input signal. One match is used to block out the noise when it's too close to the valid transition. When the falling edge is detected, the timestamp is captured. The timestamps between two adjacent edges are used to determine the missing tooth. The eTPU code example for detecting missing tooth is provided below.

```
. . . . .

  if (hsrInitAngleClock) {                // Init_Angle_Clock_HSR

. . . . .
      // Initialize the angle clock to zero degrees
      EngineAngle = 0;

      // Use match2, single transition channel mode
      SetChannelMode(m2_st);
      ClearAllLatches();

      // Set up action unit A to capture high-to-low transition
      SetupCaptureTrans_A(Capture_tcr1, high_low);

      // Set up match to block out transition too close to current time
      SetupMatch_A((tcr1+20), Mtcr1_Ctcr1_ge, match_no_change);
  }

  else if (matchB_transA) {

. . . . .
      // If the last tooth period including a missing tooth
      if (ToothPeriod >= (NUM_MISSING_TEETH + 1) * ToothPeriodLast) {
          AngleClockMode = ANGLE_CLOCK;
```

Example 10.2 Code That Detects a Missing Tooth

Once the first missing tooth is detected (Point A on Figure 10.8), the angle clock channel starts to generate the angle clock. On every crank tooth, the tooth period is calculated. Then, the tick rate register (**TRR**) is updated with the value calculated to control the tick rate between two adjacent teeth. Since the **TRR** is updated on every tooth, the angle clock can be adjusted to reflect the engine speed variation. With slow or fast counting, based on engine acceleration/deceleration, the angle clock will count every tick between teeth to ensure that angular position is reached.

On every tooth, the tooth number is counted. Once the last tooth before the missing tooth is expected, the missing count (**MISSCNT**) field in the tooth program register (**TPR**) is written to inform the eTPU that the next tooth interval includes a missing tooth (or teeth) so that the angle clock can be generated correctly (Point B). When the next missing tooth is detected (Point D), the angle clock will count up to 720° before resetting to 0°.

```
    . . . . .
    case ANGLE_CLOCK:
        ToothPeriodLast = ToothPeriod;
        ToothPeriod = TempToothPeriod;
        ToothCount ++;

        // Calculate the tick rate based on the last period
        TickRate = ((TempToothPeriod*8)/TICKS_PER_TOOTH)*64;
        // Program tooth program register
        tpr = TICKS_PER_TOOTH - 1;

        if (ToothCount == LAST_TOOTH_1) {
            // If the next tooth is expected to be missing,
            // set number of missing tooth to tooth program register
            tpr_reg.MISSCNT = NUM_MISSING_TEETH;

            if (CamDetected) {
                // If the CAM tooth is detected, the engine is fully sync'd
                // to 720 degrees
                CrankStatus = Full_Sync;
                CamDetected = FALSE;
            }
        }
    . . . . .
```

Example 10.3 Code That Makes Angle Clock Count to 720°

Spark Control Functional Requirement

The spark control channel triggers the ignition event at specified engine angular position (spark delivery angle). Before the ignition event, the ignition coil is energized by a voltage that increases current flow through the coil for a period defined by the Dwell time. The spark delivery angle and Dwell time are calculated by the host CPU, based on the engine operating condition, and then passed to eTPU.

The spark delivery angle is normally specified in terms of engine angular position. With the angle clock, the ignition event can be directly scheduled. The Dwell time is normally specified in terms of time. To take advantage of the engine angle clock's ability to compensate for engine speed variation, matching events will be scheduled on the angular position as much as possible. Based on the specified spark delivery angle, the Dwell start angle offset can be calculated by converting the Dwell time to the engine angular position, based on the current engine speed and the spark delivery angle.

Once it is converted to the engine angular position, the Dwell starting angle will change with the engine speed. The Dwell time is bounded by minimum and maximum Dwell time parameters that are also specified by the host CPU in terms of time. The Dwell time is always smaller than the maximum Dwell time. After the Dwell is started, if the engine decelerates rapidly the ignition coil may stay in the Dwell too long before the spark delivery angle is reached. In this case, the spark will fire when the maximum Dwell time is reached.

eTPU Spark Control Channel Configuration and Software Design
The control logic for the spark control is illustrated in Figure 10.9. The control logic is designed as a state machine, and the eTPU channel set up for each state is described in the following sections.

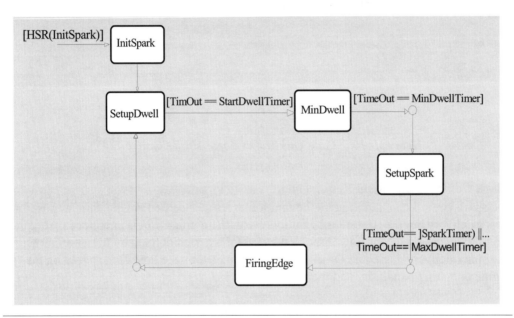

Figure 10.9 Spark Control

InitSpark State
The InitSpark state is executed when the host service request is issued. In the InitSpark state, the spark control function will initialize the state machine, set the output pin to high, and then transition to the SetupDwell state.

SetupDwell State
The Dwell starting angle is calculated based on the specified Dwell time and engine speed. In the SetupDwell state, spark channel is set as *single match, single transition* (**sm_st**)

channel mode. The **MatchA** register is programmed to match the Dwell start angle. Transitions are ignored. Once the Dwell starting angle is reached, the output pin will transition to low.

```
. . . . .
Setup_Dwell:
/* In Setup Dwell state, the match A is setup to start the Dwell at the
 * right ANGLE. Once the Dwell angle is reached, The output pin will be
 * asserted according to the predefined active state,the TCR1 is captured as
 * Dwell Start Time. The match B is setup to peroidically update the angle
 * to start Dwell. Once the match occurs, the Dwell start angle is
 * re-programmed.
      */
   channelState = SetupDwell;

    // Use either match, non-blocking, double trasnition channel mode
   SetChannelMode(sm_st);

    // Calculate the Dwell start angle
   scratchReg1 = DEGREE_PER_TOOTH * DwellTime/ToothPeriod;
   scratchReg2 = Subtract_Angle(SparkAngle, scratchReg1);

    //Setup Match A to start Dwell angle
   SetupMatch_A(scratchReg2, Mtcr2_Ctcr1_eq, start_Dwell);
. . . . .
```

Example 10.4 The SetupDwell State

MinDwell State

The MinDwell state forces the coil to charge for the minimum Dwell time. The channel is set to *single match, single transition* (**sm_st**) channel mode. The minimum Dwell offset is added to the captured Dwell start time then programmed to **MatchA**. Once **TCR1** matches the minimum Dwell time, the status of the output pin does not change. The operation then transitions to the SetupSpark state.

```
. . . . .
Min_Dwell:
   ChannelState = MinDwell;

   // Use single match, single transition channel modemode
   SetChannelMode(sm_st);

   //Enforce the minimum Dwell
   SetupMatch_A((GetCapRegA() + MinDwellTime), Mtcr1_Ctcr2_eq, /
   match_no_change);
. . . . .
```

Example 10.5 The MinDwell State

SetupSpark State

In the SetupSpark state, the channel is set to *either match, block and double transition* (**em_b_dt**) channel mode. The **MatchA** register is set up to match the spark firing angle. The **MatchB** register is set up to match the time of the maximum Dwell time period. Depending on the spark angle adjusted by the host services, the Maximum Dwell time may be reached before the spark angle. When either match occurs, the pin state will be change to fire the spark and the other programmed match is canceled.

```
.....
Setup_Spark:
    channelState = SetupSpark;

    // Use either match, blocking, double transition channel mode
    SetChannelMode(em_b_dt);

    // Set up MatchA to fire on the spark angle
    SetupMatch_A(SparkAngle, Mtcr2_Ctcr1_eq, fire_spark);

    // Calculate and set up Maximum Dwell time
    SetupMatch_B((GetCapRegA() + MaxDwellTime), Mtcr1_Ctcr2_eq, fire_spark);
.....
```

Example 10.6 The SetupSpark State

FiringEdge State

For the FiringEdge state, there are no timer events or output pin actions. In this state, the state variables are updated. The system then transitions to the SetupDwell state.

eTPU Spark Control Channel Setup Summary

The timer and angle match events and output pin state for each state is summarized in Table 10.5.

State	Match/Clock/ Events	Channel Mode	Pin State when match occurs	Next State
InitSpark	No match event	N/A		SetupDwell
SetupDwell	MatchA: match TCR2, Dwell start angle	*sm_st*	Start_Dwell	MinDwell
MinDwell	MatchA: match TCR1, minimum Dwell time	*sm_st*	No change	SetupSpark
SetupSpark	MatchA: match TCR2, spark firing angle	*em_b_dt*	Fire_spark	FiringEdge
	MatchB: match TCR1, maximum Dwell time		Fire_spark	FiringEdge
FiringEdge	No match events	N/A		SetupDwell

Table 10.5 Spark Control Channel Match Event and state Transition Summary

Fuel Control Functional Requirements

The fuel control channel delivers a single-fuel pulse with a specified pulse width to the fuel delivery angle. The fuel pulse width and fuel delivery angle are calculated by the host CPU. The fuel delivery angle is normally specified in terms of engine angular position. However, the fuel pulse width is normally specified in terms of time. To take advantage of the engine angle clock's ability to compensate for the engine speed variation, the fuel pulse width can be converted to the engine angular offset based on the fuel pulse width and engine speed. Thus the fuel pulse can be started at an engine angular position.

For each cylinder, there is a fuel limited angle at which the fuel injector has to be turned off. When the engine operated at constant speed, the fuel limit angle always occurs after the fuel delivery angle. After the fuel pulse is started, if the engine accelerates or decelerates, the fuel pulse ending angle will be changed to ensure that the specified pulse width will be delivered. The fuel pulse ending angle will be retarded or advanced. In the case of rapid acceleration, the fuel pulse end angle may be greater than the limit angle. In this case, the fuel pulse width will be terminated at the limit angle.

eTPU Fuel Control Channel Configuration and Software Design

The control logic for the fuel control is illustrated in Figure 10.10. The control logic is designed as a state machine, and the eTPU channel set up for each state is described in the following sections.

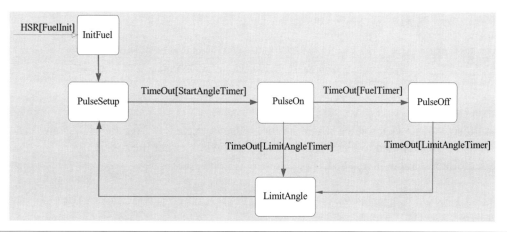

Figure 10.10 Fuel Channel High Level Functional Logic

InitFuel State

The InitFuel state is executed when the host service request (HSR(InitFuel)) is issued. In the InitFuel state, the pin state is set to inactive and the state variables are initialized. There is no match event in this state. Once it is initialized, the operation transitions to the PulseSetup state.

PulseSetup State

In the PulseSetup state, the channel is set as *single match, single transition* (**sm_st**) channel mode. The **MatchA** register is set up to match the angle to start fuel pulse. Transition detection is not used. The fuel pulse starting angle is calculated based on the fuel delivery angle and the current engine speed. Once the engine angle (**TCR2**) to start fuel pulse is reached, the output pin is asserted to start the fuel pulse.

```
.....
Pulse_Setup:
    channelState = PulseSetup;

     // Use single match, single trasnition channel mode
    SetChannelMode(sm_st);

    // Calculate the fuel pulse start angle
    scratchPadReg1 = FuelPulseWidth / ToothPeriod;
    scratchPadReg2 = DEGREE_PER_TOOTH * scratchPadReg1;
    scratchPadReg1 = Subtract_Angle(InjectionAngle, scratchPadReg2);

    // Set up MatchA to start fuel pulse on the starting angle, capture pulse
    // start time
    SetupMatch_A(scratchPadReg1, Mtcr2_Ctcr1_eq, fuel_on);
.....
```

Example 10.7 The PulseSetup State

PulseOn State

The PulseOn state is activated when the fuel pulse is started. At the PulseOn state, the channel is programmed to terminate the fuel pulse when either the fuel delivery angle or the fuel limited angle is reached.

```
.....
Pulse_On:
    channelState = PulseOn;

    //Capture time to start fuel pulse
    pulseStartTime = GetCapRegA();

     // Use either match, blocking, double transition channel mode
    SetChannelMode(em_b_dt);

    // Set channel to turn fuel pulse off when the pulse width is delivered
    SetupMatch_B((pulseStartTime + FuelPulseWidth), Mtcr1_Ctcr1_eq, fuel_off);

    // Set channel to turn fuel pulse off at limit angle
    SetupMatch_A(LimitAngle, Mtcr2_Ctcr1_eq, fuel_off);
.....
```

Example 10.8 The PulseOn State

The channel mode is set to *either match, blocking, double transition* mode (em_b_dt). The **MatchA** register is set up to match the limit angle. The **MatchB** register is set up to match the fuel delivery angle. When either match occurs, the status of the output pin is changed to end the fuel pulse. The match that occurs first will cancel the second match so that no additional eTPU service request will be generated.

PulseOff State

In the PulseOff state, the channel is set as *single match, single transition* (sm_st) channel mode. The **MatchA** register is set up to match the limit angle. Once the limit angle is reached, the output pin state will not change. The channel state is then transitioned to the LimitAngle state.

```
.....
Pulse_Off:
    channelState = PulseOff;

     // Use single match, single transition channel mode
    SetChannelMode(sm_st);

    // Set up MatchA to the fuel limit angle, no pin state change
    SetupMatch_A(LimitAngle, Mtcr2_Ctcr1_eq, fuel_off);
.....
```

Example 10.9 The PulseOff State

LimitAngle State

The LimitAngle state is activated when the fuel limit angle is reached. The LimitAngle state is a transit state. Neither timer events nor channel pin state changes are scheduled for the LimitAngle state. The state variables are updated then the system transitions to the PulseSetUp state.

eTPU Fuel Control Channel Setup Summary

The timer and angle match events, output pin state for each state is summarized in Table 10.6.

State	Match/Clock/ Events	Pin State when match occurs	Next State
InitFuel	No match event		PulseSetup
PulseSetup	MatchA: match TCR2, Fuel pulse start angle	Fuel_On	PulseOn
PulseOn	MatchA: match TCR1, Limit angle	Fuel_Off	LimitAngle
	MatchB: match TCR2, Fuel injection angle	Fuel_Off	PulseOff
PulseOff	MatchA: match TCR2, Limit angle	Fuel_Off	LimitAngle
LimitAngle	No match events	No change	No change

Table 10.6 Fuel Driver Match Events and State Transition Summary

We have provided this application example on this books CD-ROM. The read-me file should be read especially when there is a need to modify and rebuild the project. You can test, run, single step, and view the result on the production version of the ASH WARE Simulator (not provided with this book) to verify the figure below.

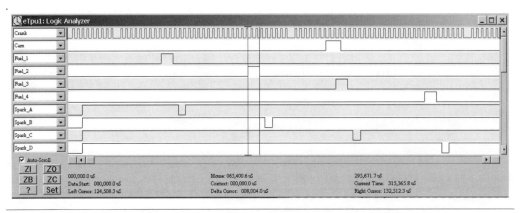

Figure 10.11 Angle Clock Application Example Shown in Logic Analyzer

CHAPTER 11

Threads and the Entry Table

This chapter, which is a follow-on to *Chapter 4. Handling Events*, provides more information on threads, the entry table, entry points, and entry table encoding schemes.

Threads

Recall that a thread is a service routine that executes in response to a specific event or combination of events on a given channel. Each thread corresponds to the set of

> **Note:** In the TPU, a thread was known as a *state*.

code that follows each `if` statement in the eTPU function's top-level `if-else` statements and consists of one or more instructions that handles the event(s) that prompted the thread's execution. Typically a thread is code that calculates the next phase of waveform to be input to, or output from, a given channel. A thread finishes when an **END** microinstruction executed (see *Appendix G. Microinstruction Formats* for details on this flow control instruction.)

Once started, a thread will normally execute to completion; there is no mechanism for another channel request to preempt or halt it. One advantage of this design decision is that the eTPU has extremely fast context switch since there is no thread-state information that needs to be saved off. On the other hand, a pending thread needs to wait until the current thread finishes in order to start up. A "runaway" thread can literally lock up the eTPU.

Each thread has its entry point. An entry point is a field in the entry table that contains the SCM address of the thread's first instruction. See the next section for details.

The Entry Table and Entry Points

The entry table is a vector table, created by the compiler and residing in shared code memory (SCM), that contains thread start addresses (i.e., entry points). It is a mapping of an event (or set of events) to the first line of code, elsewhere in the SCM, that services the event(s). See Figure 11.1.

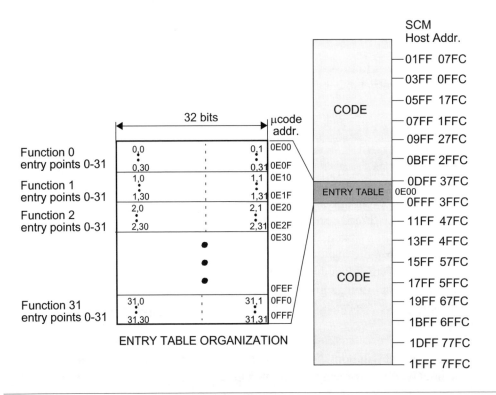

Figure 11.1   Entry Table Organization

As you can see from the above figure, the entry table is organized by functions. Each function can have up to 32 entry points of 16 bits each, corresponding to 32 possible threads per function. A single thread can be associated with more than one event/condition combination, in which case multiple entry points will be assigned to the single thread. Each 32-bit word in the entry table holds two entry points.

The location of the entry table in code memory is specified both in eTPU and in host code, and the two specifications must match one another. eTPU code requires a `#pragma` statement such as `#pragma entryaddr 0x00`. For the host, the entry table base (**ETB[4:0]**) in the eTPU engine configuration register (**ETPUECR**) specifies the location of the entry table. The entry table can be placed in any SCM address multiple of the entry table size. However, it is recommended to place the entry table at the start of the SCM in order to get continuous code memory and to ease the eventual migration of the code from larger parts down to smaller ones without rearranging the binary image. Unused entry points may be used for eTPU code, so function numbers should be selected from 0 up to 31. If, for example, only eight functions are implemented, only the entry table locations for function 0 to 7 are used, and the entry table locations for function 8 to 31 can be used as microinstruction memory (thereby providing an extra contiguous 1536 bytes for microprogram usage). For instance, an entry table for the standard eTPU automotive mask might be constructed as in Table 11.1

Function $00 AngleClock	32 AngleClock entry points
Function $01 CamDecode	32 CamDecode entry points
Function $02 FuelControl	32 FuelControl entry points
Function $03 SparkControl	32 SparkControl entry points
Function $04 AnglePulse	32 AnglePulse entry points
Function $05 PWM	32 PWM entry points
Function $06 SM	32 SM entry points
Function $07 unassigned	
...	
Function $1F unassigned	

Table 11.1 A Sample Entry Table

One way of implementing different sets of functions is to have more than one entry table and to configure the eTPU with the appropriate one for the application by changing the **ETB** field of the **ETPUECR** register. Note that multiple engines can use different entry tables, with or without the same set of functions.

Each entry point in the entry table has the following format:

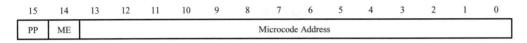

15	14	13	12	11	10	9	8	7	6	5	4	3	2	1	0
PP	ME	Microcode Address													

Figure 11.2 Entry Point Format

The fields in this format are described below:

- **Preload Parameter (PP)**
  If **PP** = 0, then channel parameters 0 and 1 are to be preloaded into **P** and **DIOB**, respectively, during the time slot transition. If PP = 1, then channel parameters 2 and 3 are to be preloaded into **P** and **DIOB**, respectively. The numbers specified are the offsets in SPRAM from the channel parameter base address (**CPBA**) in the eTPU channel configuration register (**ETPUCxCR**).

- **Match Enable (ME)**
  The contents of the ME field are copied into the match enable flag (**MEF**) during the time-slot transition. The **MEF**, which is an engine flag and not part of channel hardware, enables assertion of **MRL_A** and **MRL_B**, depending, respectively, on the **IPAC_A** and **IPAC_B** fields for the channel currently in execution. This field, in other words, allows matches to be recognized during thread execution; there are important consequences to this, as described in *Chapter 9. Channel Hardware and Modes*. See this chapter for more information about the relationships among these fields.

- **Microcode Address**
  This field is of course just the address in SCM that begins the thread in question. That is, it is the start address of the thread that will execute when the conditions that define this entry point are recognized by the microengine, as described in the next section.

Entry Table Encoding Schemes

Recall that there are four types of events (HSRs, LSRs, matches, and transitions) and that eTPU code executes *only* in response to one or more of these events. In addition to events, the states of two programmatically driven channel flags (**Flag0** and **Flag1**) as well as the state of that channel's input pin are used to determine which thread to execute. These latter pieces of information (i.e., flag and pin states) are *channel conditions*. When a channel is to be serviced, hardware obtains that channel's function number from the channel function select (**CFS**) field of the channel's configuration register, **ETPUCxCR**. With the function number, the choice of

> **Note:** eTPU hardware decodes the function number for a channel in a single clock cycle. Hardware then uses the decoded function number as part of the address to select one of 32 entry points. The use of hardware rather than software to perform these decoding operations significantly reduces the context switch latency of the eTPU system.

entry points is narrowed to 32. The microengine then looks at the channel conditions to choose a single entry point from the possible 32.

As mentioned earlier, an encoding scheme is the set of rules that: a) specify which event/ condition combinations are recognized and b) govern which event/condition combinations map to which rows in the physical entry table in code memory. There are two entry table encoding schemes for the eTPU: the standard encoding scheme, which is HSR/LSR-centric and does not support the **Flag1** condition at all, and the alternate encoding scheme, which is **Flag**-state-centric. The latter encoding scheme is therefore better suited for functions that need more states and/or faster state decoding, without needing many HSRs. See Figure 11.3 and Figure 11.4 for the two encoding schemes.

In both encoding schemes, HSRs take precedence over other types of events. So, for instance, if an HSR and an LSR are both awaiting service, the HSR will get serviced first. Also in both encoding schemes, the MatchA and TransitionB events are combined to form a single recognized event, sometimes called *matchA_transB*; analogously, the MatchB and TransitionA events are combined to form a single event, sometimes called *matchB_transA*. What this means is that the matchA_transB entry is taken when either or both MatchA or TransitionB event(s) occur. Likewise, the matchB_transA entry is taken when either or both MatchB or TransitionA event(s) occur.

No.	Encoded Channel Conditions [C4-C0]	Host Service Request Bits	Link Request	Match A / Trans.B	Match.B / Trans.A	In/Output Pin State	Channel Flag1	Channel Flag0
0	00000	001	x	x	x	0	x	0
1	00001	001	x	x	x	0	x	1
2	00010	001	x	x	x	1	x	0
3	00011	001	x	x	x	1	x	1
4	00100	010	x	x	x	x	x	x
5	00101	011	x	x	x	x	x	x
6	00110	100	x	x	x	x	x	x
7	00111	101	x	x	x	x	x	x
8	01000	110	x	x	x	x	x	x
9	01001	111	x	x	x	x	x	x
10	01010	000	1	1	1	x	x	0
11	01011	000	1	1	1	x	x	1
12	01100	000	0	0	1	0	x	0
13	01101	000	0	0	1	0	x	1
14	01110	000	0	0	1	1	x	0
15	01111	000	0	0	1	1	x	1
16	10000	000	0	1	0	0	x	0
17	10001	000	0	1	0	0	x	1
18	10010	000	0	1	0	1	x	0
19	10011	000	0	1	0	1	x	1
20	10100	000	0	1	1	0	x	0
21	10101	000	0	1	1	0	x	1
22	10110	000	0	1	1	1	x	0
23	10111	000	0	1	1	1	x	1
24	11000	000	1	0	0	0	x	0
25	11001	000	1	0	0	0	x	1
26	11010	000	1	0	0	1	x	0
27	11011	000	1	0	0	1	x	1
28	11100	000	1	0	1	x	x	0
29	11101	000	1	0	1	x	x	1
30	11110	000	1	1	0	x	x	0
31	11111	000	1	1	0	x	x	1

Host Service Request

Figure 11.3 Standard Entry Table Encoding Scheme

No.	Encoded Channel Conditions [C4-C0]	Host Service Request Bits	Link Request	Match A / Trans.B	Match.B / Trans.A	In/Output Pin State[1]	Channel Flag1	Channel Flag0
0	00000	01x	x	x	x	0	x	0
1	00001	01x	x	x	x	0	x	1
2	00010	01x	x	x	x	1	x	0
3	00011	01x	x	x	x	1	x	1
4	00100	10x/001	x	x	x	x	x	x
5	00101	11x	x	x	x	x	x	x
6	00110	000	1	0	0	0	x	x
7	00111	000	1	0	0	1	x	x
8	01000	000	x	1	0	0	0	0
9	01001	000	x	1	0	0	0	1
10	01010	000	x	1	0	0	1	0
11	01011	000	x	1	0	0	1	1
12	01100	000	x	1	0	1	0	0
13	01101	000	x	1	0	1	0	1
14	01110	000	x	1	0	1	1	0
15	01111	000	x	1	0	1	1	1
16	10000	000	x	0	1	0	0	0
17	10001	000	x	0	1	0	0	1
18	10010	000	x	0	1	0	1	0
19	10011	000	x	0	1	0	1	1
20	10100	000	x	0	1	1	0	0
21	10101	000	x	0	1	1	0	1
22	10110	000	x	0	1	1	1	0
23	10111	000	x	0	1	1	1	1
24	11000	000	x	1	1	0	0	0
25	11001	000	x	1	1	0	0	1
26	11010	000	x	1	1	0	1	0
27	11011	000	x	1	1	0	1	1
28	11100	000	x	1	1	1	0	0
29	11101	000	x	1	1	1	0	1
30	11110	000	x	1	1	1	1	0
31	11111	000	x	1	1	1	1	1

Host Service Request

Figure 11.4 Alternate Entry Table Encoding Scheme

You'll notice that both encoding schemes utilize the state of either the input or output pin. Which signal is to be used for a given channel depends on the value of that channel's entry table pin direction (**ETPD**) bit in the **ETPUCxCR** register.

Which entry table encoding scheme is to be used for a given eTPU function needs to be specified in eTPU code, and this must match the encoding scheme assigned by the host to the channel(s) that are going to run that eTPU function. (When none is specified, the standard encoding scheme is assumed.) The compiler is told using either the following `#pragma` statements:

```
#pragma ETPU_function SomeStandardFunc, standard;

#pragma ETPU_function SomeAlternateFunc, alternate;
```

When an eTPU function declaration does not specify either encoding scheme, the standard encoding scheme will be used.

For the host, the entry table condition select (**ETCS**) field within the eTPU channel x configuration register (**ETPUCxCR**) specifies either the standard or alternate encoding scheme for each channel. A common error is a mismatch between the **ETCS** bit for a given channel and the encoding scheme specified in the eTPU code of that channel's function.

Coding and the Entry Table

Some important challenges related to the entry table face the programmer when designing eTPU functions. All of the following mistakes will result in compiler errors or warnings.

> **Note:** This is not to say that you must write only eTPU functions. On the contrary, normal "C" functions can be written and then called from an eTPU function. The problems described in this section apply only to eTPU functions.

First, it is easy to make logical errors by writing an invalid event/condition combination. There can be no ambiguity, in terms of which thread to execute, that applies to any given (recognized) event/condition combination. For instance, the following will produce a compiler warning because it would be unclear whether the second or third thread should be executed as a result of a match on action unit A.

```
#include <etpuc.h>

#pragma entryaddr 0x00;

#pragma ETPU_function AmbiguousFunction;

void AmbiguousFunction () {
   if (hsr == 3){
   ;
   }

   else if (m1 == 1){
   ;
   }
   else if (m1 == 1){
   ;
   }
   else {}  // Error recovery code ...
}
```

Example 11.1 Ambiguous Code

Second, there can be no event/condition combination for which code is not written (hence the catch-all `else` statement at the end). The following code example will also produce a compiler warning:

```
#include <etpuc.h>

#pragma entryaddr 0x00;

#pragma ETPU_function IncompleteFunction;

void IncompleteFunction (){
   if (hsr == 3){
   ;
   }
   else if (m1 == 1){
   ;
   }
}
```

Example 11.2 Incomplete Code

Third, conditional logic not included in any event/condition combination is not allowed in the series of top-level `if-else` statements of an eTPU function; such logic needs to placed inside the thread itself. The following code will not compile:

```
#include <etpuc.h>

#pragma entryaddr 0x00;

#pragma ETPU_function SuperfluousConditionalFunction;

void SuperfluousConditionalFunction ( int24 HighTime ) {
   if (hsr == 3){
   ;
   }
   else if ( HighTime = 0x100 ){
   ;
   }
   else {}
}
```

Example 11.3 Uncompilable eTPU Function Containing a Superfluous Conditional

Finally, any code found inside an eTPU function (a function is an eTPU function if (and only if) it is declared with a `#pragma ETPU_function <function name>` statement), but outside the function's series of top-level `if-else` statements cannot be executed. For instance, the following will produce a compiler error:

```
#include <etpuc.h>

#pragma entryaddr 0x00;

#pragma ETPU_function SuperfluousCodeFunction;

void SuperfluousCodeFunction ( int24 HighTime ) {
   HighTime = 0x100;
   if (hsr == 3){
   ;
   }
   else {}
}
```

Example 11.4 Uncompilable eTPU Function Containing Superfluous Code

The input pin state condition is also potentially the source of errors because the condition is based on the input pin state *at the beginning of the thread* and *not when the event occurred*. Since, the input pin could toggle between these two times, unexpected results can occur. Be very careful when coding a thread that utilizes this condition!

Remember also, as noted above, that the type of entry table encoding scheme (standard or alternate) specified for a channel by the eTPU must match the encoding scheme specified by the programmer for that channel's function.

CHAPTER 12

The Scheduler

Scheduling Service Requests

Recall from the previous chapter that an eTPU function is composed of one or more routines, each of which may consist of one or more instructions and each of which executes in response to a particular event or set of events that occurs in the channel to which the function has been assigned. A *thread* is the execution of a single service routine. When a channel needs to execute a routine in response to an event or events, it issues what is called a service request to the scheduler. A channel will generate a service request to the scheduler for any of the following reasons: the channel logic detects an input or an output event, eTPU code issues a link service request, or host application software issues a host service request. That is, a channel requests service as a result one or more of the following events:

1. The host CPU issues a service request to the channel (**HSR** is set);
2. A match event on that channel results in match recognition (**MRL** is set);
3. A transition event on that channel results in transition detection (**TDL** is set):
4. Another channel issues a link service request to that channel (**LSR** is set).

At any time, an arbitrary number of channels can request service. The task of the scheduler is to recognize and prioritize the channels' service requests and to grant execution time to each request. The time given to an individual thread for execution or service is called a *time slot*. The duration of a time slot is determined a host of factors, as described in the worst-case-latency sections below, and may vary in length. Since one microengine handles several channels operating concurrently, the function threads are executed one at a time. That is, only one request is serviced per time slot. The scheduler must ensure frequent servicing of high-demand functions and as well as a minimum time allocation to all channels requesting service. To do this, the scheduler employs primary and secondary priority schemes. The primary scheme prioritizes requesting channels that have different priority levels; the secondary scheme prioritizes requesting channels that have the same priority level.

Each time slot is assigned a priority—high, middle, or low. Time slots are divided into sets of seven with a repeating pattern of high, middle, and low priorities, as shown in Figure 12.1.

1	2	3	4	5	6	7	1	2	3	4	5	6	7
H	M	H	L	H	M	H	H	M	H	L	H	M	H

Figure 12.1 Time Slot Priority Levels

You'll notice that in each set of seven time slots, four are assigned a high priority, two are assigned a middle priority, and one is assigned a low priority. These three priority levels match the priority levels available to the host to assign to each active channel. That is, each active channel is assigned a priority of either high, middle or low by the host application software. Once a channel is assigned a priority, it can request service upon the detection of some event or events. The channel service request is intercepted by the hardware scheduler, which then allocates a service time slot to the requesting channel according to its priority. During a high-priority time slot, a high-priority channel that is requesting service will be handled. If service is pending for multiple high-priority channels during a high-priority time slot, the channel with the lowest number will be handled (i.e., channel 0 will be handled before channel 1). The others must wait until the next high-priority time slot. During a middle-priority time slot, a middle-priority channel that is requesting service will be handled, and mutatis mutandis for a low-priority time slot and channel. Figure 12.2 illustrates the numbered time slots in sets of seven (windows 1 and 2), identifies their assigned default priority level, and shows the servicing of channels according to their assigned priority.

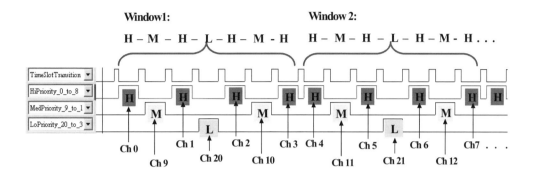

Figure 12.2 Time Slot Assignments

In the example shown in the figure above, it is assumed that channels 0 through 8 are assigned high priority, channels 9 through 19 are assigned middle priority, and channel 20 through 31 are assigned low priority. It is also assumed that all channels are requesting service simultaneously. After the first window completes, the scheduler starts a new window and the process is repeated allowing a service time for each channel and thus ensuring that all are serviced.

If no high-priority channel is awaiting service during a high-priority time slot, a waiting middle-priority channel will be serviced. If no middle-priority channel is awaiting service, a low priority channel will be serviced. And if no low-priority channel awaits service, the scheduler returns to time slot 1 to await the next service request. A similar algorithm applies to middle- and

Note: The only difference between the eTPU and TPU schedulers is that the TPU does not return to time slot 1 when encountering an empty time slot.

low-priority time slots, as shown in Table 12.1, whereby the order of service passing always gives priority to the higher of the remaining two priorities. Passing service to a different-level channel is called *priority passing*. Priority passing ensures that the eTPU will not sit idle in a particular time-slot when there is no requests pending at that priority level but there are requests pending at a different priority level.

Assigned Priority Level	*Next Priority Level*	*Next Priority Level*
High	Middle	Low
Middle	High	Low
Low	High	Middle

Table 12.1 Priority Passing

Time slot priority assignment is fixed, but the servicing priority is not. When priority is passed to another level, that level is serviced and the fixed-priority-level sequence is resumed with the next time slot.

What happens if, for instance, a high-level channel requests service constantly while another high-level channel requests service relatively infrequently? If the demanding channel has a lower channel number than the more passive one, the first channel would effectively screen out the servicing of the second. To prevent this from happening, the scheduler must ensure that if a channel that has been just serviced and generates a second request, that channel will not be serviced again until all other channels at the same priority level have been serviced first. To do this, the scheduler employs internal flags located in the service request register (**SRR**) and the service grant register (**SGR**) to keep track of the service requested and granted for all channels at the same level. Each of these two registers consists of 32 bits, one for each of the engine channels. When a channel requests service, its corresponding bit in the **SRR** is set. When that channel is serviced, its **SRR** bit is cleared and its **SGR** bit is set. The scheduler will continue to clear **SRR** bits and set **SGR** bits until no remaining **SRR** bits for channels at a given priority level are set, at which point all **SGR** bits are cleared. In other words, **SGR**s are not cleared individually by the scheduler, but rather as priority level groups. A **SGR** group is cleared on the condition that all channels at the same priority level have been serviced, and no other channel of that priority level is requesting service (has a set **SRR**) but has not been granted service (has a clear **SGR**). The clearing of a group of **SGR**s begins a new cycle for that priority level. A channel whose **SGR** bit is set may request service (thereby setting its **SRR** bit) but it will not be serviced until its **SGR** bit is cleared. This mechanism ensures that all channels at the same level are serviced before any one of those channels is serviced a second time. Figure 12.3 depicts the equivalent logic of a given channel's request and acknowledgment.

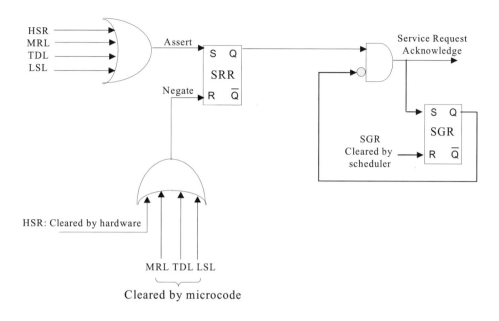

Figure 12.3 Channel Service Requests and Aknowledgments

In short, we have two priority schemes—the primary one ranking inter-priority-level requests and the secondary one handling intra-priority-level requests—working simultaneously to ensure both fairness and efficiency. The following example shows how these two schemes interact during execution.[1]

1. During time slot 1 (high priority), service is requested by one high-priority channel and one low-priority channel and no other channels. Having its **SRR** bit asserted, the high-level channel is granted the time slot, its **SRR** bit is cleared, and its **SGR** bit is set. At the end of the thread, that channel's **SGR** is cleared, as no other requests of high-priority channels are outstanding (i.e., no high-level **SRR** bits are set).

2. The scheduler proceeds to time slot 2, which has middle-level priority. However, no middle-level channel is requesting service. Priority is passed to the high level, but no high-level channel is requesting service. Therefore, priority is passed again, and service is granted to the single requesting low-level channel. Having its **SRR** bit asserted, the low-level channel is granted the time slot, its **SRR** bit is

---

1. This example is a modified version of that found in the Freescale Semiconductor block guides.

cleared, and its **SGR** bit is set. At the end of the thread, that channel's **SGR** is cleared, as no other requests of low-priority channels are outstanding (i.e., no low-level **SRR** bits are set).

3. The scheduler proceeds to time slot 3, which has a low-level priority. However, no low-level channels are requesting service. Priority is passed to the high and then the middle level, on both of which occasions no channels at that priority level are requesting service. So the scheduler returns to time slot 1 (which is high priority) and waits for the next request.

4. Two high-level and two middle-level channels simultaneously request service. Since it is time slot 1, a high-priority time slot, the scheduler services the lower-numbered high-level channel. This channel's **SRR** bit is cleared, and its **SGR** bit is set. At the end of the thread the scheduler finds that at least one remaining high-priority channel is awaiting service (i.e., its **SRR** bit is set), so no **SGR** bits are cleared.

5. The scheduler proceeds to time slot 2, which has middle priority and allocates that slot to the lower numbered of the two middle-level channels requesting service. Again, this channel's **SRR** bit is cleared, and its **SGR** bit is set. At the end of the thread the scheduler finds that at least one remaining middle-priority channel is awaiting service (i.e., its **SRR** bit is set), so no **SGR** bits are cleared.

6. The scheduler proceeds to time slot 3, which has high priority. This slot is allocated to the remaining unserviceable high-priority channel. This channel's **SRR** bit is cleared, and its **SGR** bit is set. At the end of the thread the scheduler finds that no remaining high-priority channels await service (i.e., no high-level **SRR** bits are set), so all **SGR** bits for high-priority channels are cleared.

7. The scheduler proceeds to time slot 4, which has low priority. However, no low-level channel is requesting service, so priority is passed to the high level. Since no high-level channels are requesting service, priority is passed again, to the middle level. At this level there is one remaining channel requesting service. This channel's **SRR** bit is cleared, and its **SGR** bit is set. At the end of the thread the scheduler finds that at least no remaining middle-priority channels await service (i.e., no middle-level **SRR** bits are set), so all **SGR** bits for high-priority channels are cleared. Before the scheduler transitions to the next time slot, a new request for service is received from a low-priority channel.

8. The scheduler proceeds to time slot 5, which has high priority. Since there are no more requests from high- or middle-priority channels, the single low-level channel that required service is granted this slot. Once serviced, the channel's **SRR** bit is cleared and its **SGR** bit is set and then negated again.

9. The scheduler proceeds to time slot 6, which has middle priority. Since no channels are requesting service, the scheduler returns to time slot 1 and waits for incoming requests.

Introduction to Worst-Case Latency

Worst-case latency (WCL) for a channel is defined as the longest period of time that can elapse between the execution of any two function threads on that channel. For example, if in a particular system, channel 3 is running a PWM function, the worst-case latency for channel 3 is the longest possible time between the execution of two PWM threads. The worst-case time includes the time that the execution unit takes to execute threads for other active, intervening channels. It also includes other delays, described later in this chapter. Figure 12.4 depicts non-detailed worst case latency for channel 3 running a PWM function.

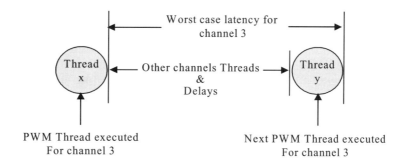

Figure 12.4 Worth-Case Latency

To calculate the WCL with accuracy, one must examine all the factors that affect latency. These factors are:

1. The number of active channels (typically but not necessarily all 32 channels are active);
2. The number of channels on a priority level;
3. The number of available time slots on a priority level;
4. The number of microcycles required to execute a function thread;
5. The number of parameter RAM accesses during the function thread;

6. System clock frequency;

7. The number of engine-to-engine semaphore RAM accesses. This factor is relevant only in dual-eTPU implementations.

Priority passing is implemented in hardware and does not contribute to worst-case latency.

Worst-case latency for a channel depends both on the function running on that channel and on the activity on other channels. For instance, changing the priority scheme and channel number assignments can change performance for a function even if the same set of functions are still active. Further, since the 32 eTPU channels share a single execution unit, execution speed of a particular function varies with each implementation. The PWM, for instance, runs faster if it is the only active channel than if other channels are also active. WCL calculation always considers full load—where all channels requesting service simultaneously—but realistically only a few channels requests will be pending at any given time.

Figure 12.5 shows several functions as divided into threads. The eTPU execution unit executes one thread of a function at a time. For example, the execution unit might execute thread one of PWM, then thread three of DIO, then thread two of PWM, then thread two of SM, and so on. The amount of time the eTPU spends in a thread varies with the number of microcycles in the thread. This in turn depends on the number of instructions in the thread; an instruction is capable of performing multiple operations and always executes in two system clock cycles with exception of multiply and divide. Since there is only one execution unit, the eTPU cannot execute the software for multiple functions simultaneously. However, the hardware for each of the 32 channels is independent. This means that, for example, all 32 channel pins can change state at the same moment, provided that the function software sets up the channel hardware to do so beforehand.

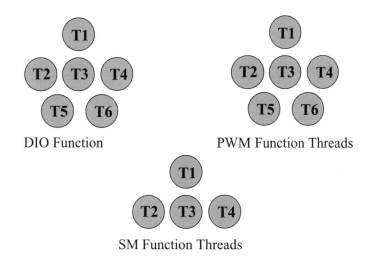

DIO Function

PWM Function Threads

SM Function Threads

Figure 12.5 Threads of Three eTPU Functions

Time-Slot Transition
After each time slot, the eTPU engine prepares for the next time slot. This preparation time between each pair of adjacent time slots is called a *time-slot transition*. A time-slot transition (TST) is a context switch and takes six system clock cycles to complete. During each TST, the eTPU engine performs the following steps:

1. The appropriate entry point is selected, based on the condition or conditions currently present at the channel;
2. Up to two parameters are read from the shared parameter RAM (SPRAM);
3. The state of the channel input signal is latched;
4. The channel register (**CHAN**) is written with the channel number being dispatch for execution;
5. The capture registers (**CaptureA** and **CaptureB**) are transferred into the event register temporary (**ERT_A** and **ERT_B**, respectively).

Shared Parameter RAM Accesses And Collisions
Most function threads read or write to the eTPU shared parameter RAM (SPRAM) at least once. Because both the host and the eTPU microengine can access the SPRAM but not at the same time, the microengine may suspend its thread execution for two system clock

cycles if the host is currently accessing the SPRAM. Likewise, the host receives two wait states if tries to access the SPRAM while the microengine performing its accesses. The attempt by the host and the microengine to access the SPRAM simultaneously is called *collision*. Since SPRAM collision may impose a two system-clock cycle delay on the microengine, this delay must be included in WCL calculations. The system designer should estimate the percentage of SPRAM accesses in the system that will result in microengine wait-states. This percentage is called the RAM collision rate (RCR).

A second SPRAM access consideration must be taking into account when calculating WCL. Often, the host CPU needs to transfer two parameters coherently to the SPRAM. To ensure coherent accesses the eTPU implements a coherent dual-parameter controller (CDC) to allow for atomic transfer. Atomic transfers by the CDC always consists of four consecutive accesses (read, write, read, and write), each of which takes one clock cycle. If the microengine attempts to access the SPRAM during CDC transfers, a four system-clock cycle delay is imposed. The designer should estimate of the percentage of SPRAM accesses in the system that will result in a microengine wait due to coherent transfer, and multiply it with the average number of system clocks the microengine waits for each transfer. This percentage is called coherent parameter collision rate (CPCR). More information on CDC operation is provided later in this chapter.

A dual-engine implementation results in yet another factor that affects WCL. In such a system, the shared parameter RAM (SPRAM) is accessed by both engines. There are no collision or delays imposed when one engine attempts to access the SPRAM while other engine is in the process of executing a data transfer. This implies that a single parameter of microengine-to-microengine communication does not affect performance. But often one engine may need to transfer multiple parameters to the other engine coherently. For this purpose, the eTPU implements a hardware semaphore mechanism. If one engine has a semaphore locked and the other engine is waiting for it to unlock, thread execution will be delayed. Note that the delay in this case is due to a software loop and not hardware wait-states. In other words, the microengine that waits for the semaphore to unlock will loop until it is freed by the other microengine. The system designer must estimate the percentage of microengine-to-microengine coherent parameter transfer that will result in thread execution delay, and multiply it with the average number of system clocks the microengine loops for each transfer. This percentage is called communication collision rate (CCR). More information on semaphore operation is provided later in this chapter.

After the collision rate for a system is found, it can be applied to the WCL calculations for each channel by using an approximate collision percentage rate and the number of

SPRAM accesses (with and without semaphores). We will utilize variables to represent the factors that effects latency and use them in a formula to calculate WCL.

- N1 = Number of simple RAM accesses in the longest thread
- RCRWait = Maximum clock wait time for simple RAM collision = 2
- CPCRWait = Average system clocks for coherent parameter transfer (using CDC).
- N2 = Number of eTPU-eTPU semaphore RAM accesses in the longest thread.
- CCRWait = Average system clocks for microengine-microengine communication transfer.

Given, the above, we obtain:

Estimated wait time = N1 * (RCR * RCRWait + CPCR * CPCRWait) + N2* CCR * CCRWait.

Once the WCL is found for a channel, the user must determine how to use this number to analyze performance. To analyze the performance of a channel running the PWM function, for example, some information about what happens in each thread is necessary.

In a PWM, thread one is the initialization thread, and threads two and three are used during normal function execution. (PWM threads four, five, and six are for special modes and will be assumed to be unused on channel 3.) Thread two writes a time into the channel's **Match** register and performs other operations that will cause the channel 3 pin to go from low to high at the time indicated in the **Match** register (match time). At match time, the pin goes high and channel 3 requests service from the eTPU execution unit to execute thread three. Thread three writes a time into the channel 3 **Match** register and performs other operations that will cause the channel 3 pin to go from high to low at match time. At match time, the pin goes low and channel 3 requests service from the eTPU execution unit to execute thread two. A PWM waveform is kept running on the system by the eTPU executing thread two, then thread three, then thread two, then thread three, and so on. Since the definition of WCL assumes a fully loaded running system, initialization threads are not part of worst-case calculations. For the channel 3 example, the two PWM threads in Figure 12.4 are thus the two normal running threads, threads two and three. This figure does not define which thread is thread two and which is thread three. Since the WCL derived from the first-pass analysis is the worst-case between *any* two threads (not counting initialization threads), it is safe to say that the WCL shown in this figure represents both the worst-case high time and the worst-case low time. Notice in Figure 12.4 that WCL is drawn from the end of the execution of the first PWM thread to the end of the execution of the next PWM thread. It is drawn from end to end because the eTPU code instructions that make up the threads control the channel hardware. To ensure that all the eTPU code instructions needed to change the pin state have been executed, it is necessary to include the execution time of the second thread.

First-Pass Worst-Case Latency Analysis

The first-pass WCL analysis is based on a deterministic, generalized formula that is easy to apply. Because of the generalizations in the formula, the first-pass result is almost always much worse than the real worst case. If the desired system performance is within the limits of this first analysis, then no further analysis is required; the system is well within the performance limits of the eTPU. If the desired system performance exceeds that indicated by the first analysis, the second-pass WCL analysis should be applied. The second-pass analysis is not a generalized formula but rather uses specific system details for a realistic worst-case estimation.

To estimate first-pass WCL for a channel, assume this worst-case condition: the channel has just been serviced in a time slot of its priority level, and all other channels in the system are continuously requesting service and have cleared SGRs. The WCL is the time from the end of the channel's service until the end of the channel's next service, including the time taken to service intervening channels. Refer to Figure 12.6.

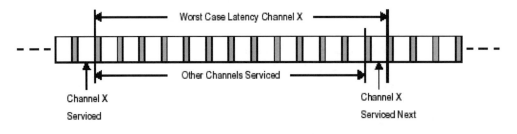

Figure 12.6 First-Pass Worst-Case Latency

To estimate worst-case latency:

- Find the worst-case service time for each active channel.
- Using the **H-M-H-L-H-M-H** time-slot sequence, map the channels that are granted for each time slot. To know when a channel just serviced will be serviced

again, it is necessary to determine which other channels will be serviced first. We can do this by assuming all channels are continuously requesting service and mapping the channels into the time-slot sequence.

- Add 6 clocks for each time-slot transition.

To find the worst-case service time for each active channel, a table for eTPU functions should list the longest threads (not counting initialization threads) for the functions, and the number of eTPU SPRAM accesses in the longest thread (semaphored and non semaphored). These figures will be used for estimating microengine wait time.

The worst-case service time for each channel = Longest thread + ((number of RAM accesses in longest thread + 1) * RCR * 2 clocks)

Note that this formula adds 1 RAM access for the parameter preload that occurs during TST. Also it is assumed that CPCR=CCR=0.

The following table provides worst-case services times for old TPU functions in which there are only simple parameter RAM accesses. It does not take into consideration the CDC operation and microengine-to-microengine communication.

Function	Longest Thread	RAM Accesses
DIO	10	4
ITC	40 (no linking)	7
	42 (linking)	
OC	40	7
PWM	24	4
PMA	94	8
PMM	94	8
PSP		
Angle-Angle Mode	76	6
Angle-Time Mode	50	3
SM	160	21

Function	Longest Thread	RAM Accesses
PPWA		
Mode 0	44	9
Mode 1	50	10
Mode 2	44	9
Mode 3	50	10
SPWM		
Mode 0	14	4
Mode 1	18	4
Mode 2	20 (no linking)	4
	22 (linking)	4

Table 12.2 Old TPU Longest Thread and RAM Accesses

At this juncture we are ready to look at some examples that will give the reader a relatively close estimate of worst-case latency to servicing channels. Since the TPU and eTPU scheduler almost identical in functionality and the TPU functions longest threads execution times are known, we will be using in our examples the eTPU functions shown in Table 12.2.

We will assume that only three channels are configured to execute the eTPU functions, as shown in Table 12.3, with system clock frequency of 100Mhz and RAM collision rate of 9%

.

Channel	Priority	Function
0	High	PWM (driving a DC motor)
1	Middle	PPWA (mode 0, measuring DC motor speed
2	Low	DIO (input)

Table 12.3 Channel Configuration Example

Example 1: First-Pass WCL for Channel 0

The following example is used to find the worst case latency for channel 0, which is executing a PWM function.

1.   Find the worst-case service time for each active channel.

Longest thread of PWM is 24 CPU clocks with four RAM accesses.

24 + ((4 RAM accesses+1) * 0.09 * 2 CPU clock waits) = 24.9 CPU clocks, rounded up to 25 CPU clocks.

Channel 0 worst-case service time = 25 CPU clocks.

Longest thread of PPWA in mode 0 is 44 CPU clocks with nine RAM accesses.

44 + ((9 RAM accesses+1) * 0.09 * 2 CPU clock waits) = 45.8 CPU clocks, rounded up to 46 CPU clocks

Channel 1 worst-case service time = 46 CPU clocks.

Longest thread of DIO is ten CPU clocks with four RAM accesses.

10 + ((4 RAM accesses+1) * 0.09 * 2 CPU clock waits) = 10.9 CPU clocks, rounded up to 11 CPU clocks.

Channel 2 worst-case service time = 11 CPU clocks.

2. Assume channel 0 has just been serviced and that channels 1 and 2 are continuously requesting service. Using the H-M-H-L-H-M-H time-slot sequence, map the channels that are granted for each time slot.

Channel 1 will be serviced in the middle-priority time slot before channel 0 is serviced again.

3. Add six system clock cycles for each TST.

Conclusion: In this example channel 0 worst case latency is 83 clock cycles.

Channel 0 worst-case service time	25 clocks
Channel 1 worst-case service time	46 clocks
2 time-slot transitions	12 clocks
Total clocks	83 Clocks

Table 12.4 First-Pass WCL, Example 1

Channel 0 worst-case latency = 83 clocks * 10ns = 830 nanoseconds

Since the eTPU is a double action capable system, the PWM needs servicing from the microengine only once each period and thus offer no latency for minimum high time.

Example 2: First-Pass WCL for Channel 1

Channel 1 is configured to execute a PPWA function.

1. Find the worst-case service time for each active channel. See step 1 of previous example.

2. Assume channel 1 has just been serviced and that channels 0 and 2 are continuously requesting service. Using the H-M-H-L-H-M-H time-slot sequence, map the channels that are granted for each time slot. Channel 0 will be serviced twice and channel 2 once before channel 1 is serviced again.

3. Add six system clock cycles for each TST.

2 channel 0 worst-case service times	50 clocks
1 channel 1 worst-case service time	46 clocks
1 channel 2 worst-case service time	11 clocks
4 time-slot transitions	24 clocks
Total clocks	131 clocks

Figure 12.7 First-Pass WCL, Example 2

Channel 1 worst-case latency = 131 clocks * 10 ns = 1310 nanoseconds

Conclusion: In this system configuration PPWA can measure a period or pulse of minimum 1310 ns.

Note that PPWA function is optimized for eTPU hardware and can use double transition mode to measure very narrow pulses with one service after the second transition. Latency affects only the minimum gap between two input pulses.

Example 2: First-Pass WCL for Channel 2

Channel 2 is configured to execute a DIO function.

1. Find the worst-case service time for each active channel. See step 1 of previous examples.

2. Assume channel 2 has just been serviced and that channels 0 and 1 are continuously requesting service. Using the H-M-H-L-H-M-H time-slot sequence, map the channels that are granted for each time slot.

Channel 0 will be serviced four times and channel 1 twice before channel 2 is serviced again.

3. Add six system clock cycles for each TST.

4 channel 0 worst-case service times	100
2 channel 1 worst-case service times	92
1 channel 2 worst-case service time	11
Seven 6-clock time-slot transitions	42
Total clocks	245

Figure 12.8 First-Pass WCL, Example 3

Channel 2 worst-case latency = 245 clocks * 10ns = 2,450 nano-seconds

Conclusion: In this example, DIO channel 2 can track minimum pulse time of 2,450 nano-seconds.

Note that DIO function is optimized for eTPU hardware and can use double transition mode to measure two pin transitions at a time and reduce the service time which improves overall system performance and latency.

Second-Pass Worst-Case Latency Analysis

The second-pass analysis is useful for higher-performance systems, since it gives a more realistic WCL result than first-pass analysis. Second pass analyses stipulate the following:

- Determine a realistic service request rate for each channel;
- If a function is active during system initialization but not during the high-speed running mode of the system, then that function does not need to be included in the calculation;
- Use a realistic SPRAM collision rate;

- Try different assignments of priority levels to channels to see how it affects the system;
- When mapping out channels to the sequence, choose a worst-case slot to start the mapping;
- Instead of using the longest thread in a function as the worst-case state, evaluate the threads in the function that will be used in the system and use the appropriate worst case threads.

The examples in this section assume 24 active channels. Channels 0 through 7 are configured to execute PWM function and are assigned high priority, channels 8 through 15 are configured to execute PPWA and are assigned middle priority and channels 16 through 23 are configured to execute DIO function and are assigned a low priority. See Figure 12.9

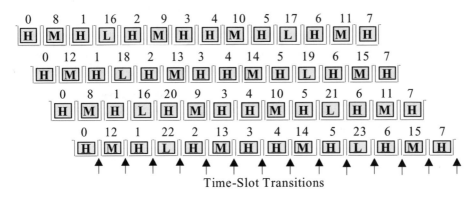

Channels: 0-7 = high priority
Channels 8-15 = Middle priority
Channels 16-23 = Low priority

Figure 12.9 Time-Slot Sequencing for 24 Channels

We will calculate WCL for channels 0, 8, and 16.

Example 1: Second-Pass WCL for Channel 0

1. Find the longest thread in a PWM function.
2. Assume channel 0 has just been serviced and all other channels are continuously requesting service.
3. Map all 24 channels to time-slot sequence shown in Figure 12.9.

4. Add 6 system clock cycle for each time-slot transition.

Because the scheduler uses round-robin priority scheme, channel 0 will not be serviced again until all channels at the same priority level (in this example, channels 1 through 7) are serviced first.

8 high-priority worst-case service times for PWM channels	8*25 = 200
4 middle-priority worst-case service times for PPWA channels	4*46=184
2 low-priority worst-case service times for DIO channels	2*11= 22
14 time-slot transitions	14*6 = 84
Total clocks	490

Figure 12.10 Second-Pass WCL, Example 1

Example 2: Second-Pass WCL for Channel 8

1. Find the longest thread in a PPWA function.
2. Assume channel 8 has just been serviced and all other channels are continuously requesting service.
3. Map all 24 channels to time-slot sequence shown in Figure 12.9.
4. Add 6 system clock cycle for each time-slot transition

8 middle-priority worst-case service time for PPWA channels	8 * 46= 368
16 high-priority worst-case service time for PWM channels	16 * 25 = 400
4 low-priority worst-case service times for DIO channels	4 * 11= 44
28 time-slot transitions	28 * 6 = 168
Total clocks	980

Figure 12.11 Second-Pass WCL, Example 2

Example 3: Second-Pass WCL for Channel 16

1. Find the longest thread in a DIO function.
2. Assume channel 16 has just been serviced and all other channels are continuously requesting service.
3. Map all 24 channels to time-slot sequence shown in Figure 12.9.
4. Add 6 system clock cycle for each time-slot transition

8 low-priority worst-case service times for DIO channels	11*8 =88
32 high-priority worst-case service times for PWM channels	32* 25 =800
16 middle-priority worst-case service times for PPWA channels	16*46 =736
56 time-slot transitions	336
Total clocks	1960

Figure 12.12 Second-Pass WCL, Example 3

Conclusion: Since we assumed that the eTPU clock frequency is 100Mhz, each clock period is equal to 10ns. As shown in the table above the worst-case latency for channel 16 is 1960 clocks or 19,600ns.

As stated earlier in this chapter, SPRAM accesses can be affected by the coherent dual-parameter controller and the use of semaphores. Semaphores are applicable only in dual-eTPU engine implementations. This section will cover the CDC and semaphore operation and the potential latency that must be accounted for when calculating worst case latencies.

Coherent Dual-Parameter Controller (CDC)

The CDC is provided to allow transfer of two parameters from or to eTPU shared parameter ram (SPRAM) coherently. The eTPU is capable of transferring two parameters coherently by executing two back-to-back SPRAM accesses and actually does not require any assistance from the CDC. However, multiple-word host transfers are not coherent in the MPC5500 implementations because the peripheral bus physical implementation does not support coherent transfer of multiple words. In other words, there is no locking of the bus between one 32-bit transfer and the next, so the eTPU can access SPRAM between consecutive CPU accesses to the SPRAM. This condition must be avoided to permit coherent parameter transfer by the host. For this reason the CDC is implemented for the purpose of allowing the host to read and write to the SPRAM for atomic transfer of two parameters when needed. All atomic transfers are requested by the host by signaling a read/write command to the CDC. Upon receipt of the command from the host, the CDC initiates two parameter transfers by executing four consecutive accesses: read followed by write, and a second read followed by write. During this time any attempt to access the SPRAM by the eTPU engine will be blocked for at least 2 microcycles (4 system clocks) until the CDC completes its transfer. Figure 12.13 depicts the basic structure of the CDC and its operation. In the meantime, if the host attempts to access SPRAM while CDC access in progress, the host may suffer from 3 and up to 11 wait states (system clocks).

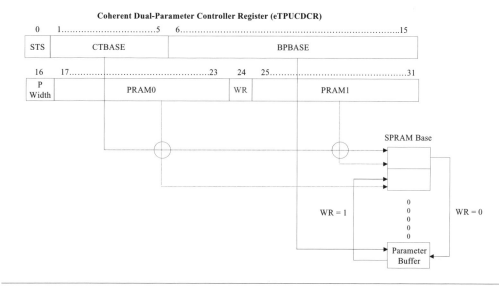

Figure 12.13 Coherent Dual-Parameter Controller Operation

For a CDC transfer to be initiated, the host writes the coherent dual-parameter control register (**ETPUCDCR**) with the following bit fields:

- **Channel Transfer Base (CTBASE)**
  This 5-bit field pointer is concatenated with the seven-bit field of parameter number 0 (**PRAM0**) and the 7-bit field of parameter 1 (**PRAM1**) to form the absolute word offset from the SPRAM base address. The two offsets, **PRAM0** and **PRAM1**, are used by the CDC after concatenating them with **CTBASE** to select which two-word (parameter) locations to be transferred. The transfer direction of the two parameters is controlled by the read/write (**WR**) bit.

- **Buffer Parameter Base (BPBASE) Address**
  This 10-bit field is used by the CDC to point to the source or destination parameter buffer (PB) in SPRAM area. **PBBASE** has a granularity of two parameters (8 bytes). If the **PBBASE** = 0, the CDC will transfer two parameters from location 0 and 1 to or from the parameter buffer when CDC is commanded to execute the transfer. Likewise, if **PBBASE** =1, the CDC will transfer two parameters from or to parameter buffer from parameter locations 2 and 3, etc. Based on the value of the read/write (**WR**) control bit, the two parameters will be transferred from two

consecutive or non-consecutive locations from the memory location pointed by concatenated fields of **CTBASE | PRAM0** and **CTBASE | PRAM1**. If **WR** = 0, the transfer will be a read operation from the selected address of **PRAM0** and **PRAM1** and written into the parameter buffer (PB); otherwise the transfer will be from the **PB** to **PRAM0** and **PRAM1**. The actual transfer operation by the CDC is executed when the start (**STS**) bit is set by the host. Note that the host can write the entire 32-bit word to the **ETPUCDCR** in one write cycle.

- Parameter Width (**PWIDTH**)
  Since parameter transfers between the host and the eTPU engine are either 24 bits or 32 bits wide, the parameter width (**PWIDTH**) control bit is used to select the desired size.

Semaphores

Semaphores provide a means for two separate engines to synchronize code execution by setting and testing the locked state of a common semaphore number. Normally the code that executes will eventually access SPRAM after the engine is able to lock the semaphore. If the engine cannot lock the semaphore, it will cither wait in a software loop until it can lock it, or give up, quit the thread and try again at the next service time. In the eTPU, there are four semaphores to allow code to use different semaphores for different locking.

For example, if both microengines had to access channel 2 and channel 4 parameters, semaphore 0 could be used by both engines to indicate they want to access channel 2 parameters and semaphore 1 could be used by both engines to indicate they want to access channel 4 parameters. So, if eTPU_A wants to access channel 2 parameters it sets semaphore 0. eTPU_B will not be able to lock semaphore 0 until eTPU_A has freed it. However, eTPU_B can immediately lock semaphore 1, because eTPU_A has not locked it. This means, in our example, that eTPU_A has immediate access to channel 2's parameters and does not stall eTPU_B's access to channel 4 parameters. If there were only one semaphore, the unrelated data accesses would stall each other.

When a function is written in "C," one may not know beforehand what other functions are written and which semaphores are being used. Ideally it should be left to the compiler and linker, and there would be special statements and functions to declare and access a protected area, so that semaphores would be hidden to the "C" code to further hide some of the complexity that is not truly needed by the programmer.

Appendices

Byte Craft Limited's eTPU_C Compiler

eTPU engines are implemented as peripheral processors attached to a host CPU.[1] The eTPU serves as an interface between the host CPU and the physical I/O pins. The software running on an eTPU processor is organized as up to 32 independent eTPU functions, supporting up to 32 channels and I/O pin pairs.

An eTPU function formalizes the interface between the host CPU and one or more channels. During eTPU initialization, the host CPU ties an eTPU function to a channel and assigns an area of dual-port RAM, or shared parameter RAM (SPRAM), to serve as control and data registers. The host can use this area to pass information to and retrieve information from the eTPU. eTPU functions are independent of the channels that they support. For example, an eTPU function that emulates a pulse width modulator (PWM) may be attached to several channels by the host, with each supported channel having its own control and data space.

An eTPU function argument list is the interface to the host CPU processor through SPRAM. The meaning of the arguments is defined by the eTPU function. Information about the arguments can be (optionally) exported through *host interface files,* to be formally included in the host CPU application code. Each supported channel, tied to a specific eTPU function, has its own argument list.

---

1. This appendix was written by Kirk Zurell from Byte Craft Limited.

An eTPU function is organized as series of event-driven processes. An event initiates the execution of a code thread (much like an interrupt service routine in many processors). The events supported by the eTPU functions are host service requests (HSRs), match or transition events, and link service requests (LSRs) from other channels; the actual state of the I/O pin and state resolution Boolean flags also contribute to the interpretation of events. The eTPU supports entry tables that identify 32 possible event combinations for each available eTPU function, encoded in one of two ways as described below.

The general form of the eTPU function is a series of `if-else` statements, each part of which tests for one or more events and has a code body to be associated with that event. In practical terms, the eTPU_C compiler matches the `if-else` logic with entry table combinations. The execution threads are tied to the entry points in that function's portion of the entry table, as shown in Figure A.1.

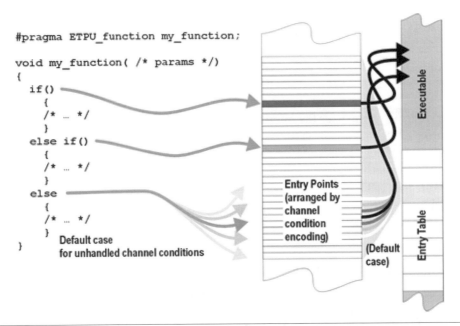

Figure A.1 The Entry Table and eTPU Functions

The eTPU compiler was designed to export its code image, along with calling information for eTPU functions, to be included in the host CPU application code. The host interface files contain eTPU-specific application information that is taken from host interface macros. These interface files create a development environment that will generate a host CPU application including eTPU code in a single build process.

In 2003, the ISO C standards for embedded systems were adopted by the majority of ISO member countries (ISO/IEC TR 18037, "Extensions for the Programming Language C to support Embedded Processors"). Many elements of this standard were included in the eTPU_C compiler to provide direct "C" access to the underlying eTPU architecture. All of the eTPU registers can be declared and accessed as if they were variables. And an implementation-defined structure provides access to all of the channel-specific flags and fields of the eTPU. These rather simple language extensions provide the full flexibility of the lowest-level access to the eTPU hardware.

This appendix introduces the essential steps for using eTPU_C and BCLIDE to compose and build complete eTPU programs.

Introduction to the Compiler

eTPU_C is an optimizing cross-compiler for Freescale Semiconductor's eTPU. It parses the "C" language, analyzes the input program to perform a series of optimizations, and performs resource allocation and code generation. eTPU_C generates executables and reports for debugging. It packages the executables in forms suitable for use by the host processor's compiler as well as by the rest of the toolchain (simulators and emulators). Finally, eTPU_C generates host interface files from host code embedded in the eTPU_C program and compiler-supplied information.

With its moving subinstruction fields and parallelism, eTPU was designed for computer-generated code. The eTPU_C compiler offers many advantages that far surpass hand optimization in assembly language. For instance, the eTPU_C compiler tracks actual demand on resources far more closely than a programmer doing so manually. The compiler uses a rule-based expert system for code generation: "programmers' tricks," once added to the knowledge base in the eTPU_C compiler, are applied to every program. Furthermore, the compiler is capable of applying both these techniques to generate expressions not previously anticipated.

Finally, the constraints of the instruction set and eTPU architecture are embedded in the compiler. This leaves application developers free to think in the problem space—what they intend to accomplish—rather than in the solution space—the obstacles they must overcome.

eTPU_C offers some intrinsic variables and functions and special data types to give access to the eTPU's microengine and channel registers. The intrinsics are designed to present an intuitive interface to the programmer. For instance, channel-specific features are grouped as members of a channel structure. Reading and writing the members of this structure resolve to two completely different approaches in code. Writing channel structure members creates `chan` subinstructions to implement the desired output. Reading channel structure members creates conditional branch subinstructions and code paths that work with the desired result value.

eTPU_C performs two levels of optimization: within eTPU instruction words and within the entire program. eTPU_C combines subinstructions wherever possible to take advantage of the eTPU's parallelism. There are limits to this type of optimization, and eTPU_C is fully aware of situations in which parallelism is inappropriate, arising either from the eTPU hardware or from the "C" language. The compiler will avoid combining subinstructions where side-effects would prevent correct code.

Installing and Using the Compiler

The demonstration version of eTPU_C accompanying this book is limited to creating two eTPU functions, of a maximum 0.5 KB including space for entry tables. This software can generate small executables to run with ASH WARE's eTPU Stand-Alone Simulator, a demonstration version of which also accompanies with this book.

To install the compiler, double click the **SETUP.EXE** in the eTPU_C Compiler (Demo) folder on the CD accompanying this book, and then follow the on-line directions.

There are three ways to work with eTPU_C: using BCLIDE, through a built-in compiler console, or from the command line. All three create the same results.

BCLIDE
BCLIDE organizes your work into projects with several source files and displays them in a multiple document interface (MDI) environment in Windows, as shown in Figure A.2.

Appendix A. Byte Craft Limited's eTPU_C Compiler

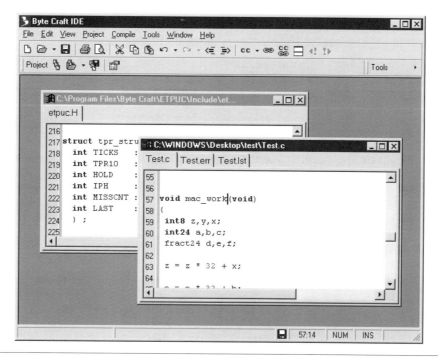

Figure A.2 BCLIDE's GUI

BCLIDE is an integrated development environment specifically matched to eTPU_C:

- It groups a "C" source file with several related secondary files: a similarly-named header file, any listing file or error file generated during compilation, and any resulting hex (executable) file. When BCLIDE opens the C source file, it opens the other files you select in the same tabbed editor window.

- BCLIDE handles the onerous chore of creating a linker command file for BClink, based on information given in the Project Properties window. For more on linking, see below.

- BCLIDE has programmer-oriented code template functionality. It can bind a named boilerplate code fragment to a keystroke. In addition, it can auto-correct a customizable list of common typing errors.

Full documentation ships with BCLIDE; choose **Help|BCLIDE Help** to view it. Here are some hints on using BCLIDE:

- BCLIDE will display the compiler's error output in the progress window at the bottom of the main window. You can navigate to an error in the source code by double-clicking on the error message in the progress panel.
- You can also copy one or more lines to the clipboard by selecting them, right-clicking and choosing **Copy selected lines to clipboard**. This is useful when composing e-mail or documentation.
- If you are used to line numbers in your editor or on printouts, use the following steps to enable them:
    - For line numbers in the editor, choose **Project|Properties**, select the **Editor** tab, and choose one of the **Edit Highlighting Options** buttons. An Editor Options dialog opens.
    - Choose the **Options** tab, and check **Line numbers in gutter**. The line numbers will appear in a gutter in the edit window.
    - For printouts with line numbers, choose **File|Print Setup**. Under **Print Options**, check **Print line numbers**. Choose the **Preview** button to see the appearance.
- If you're working with a specialized preprocessor, BCLIDE can accommodate some types of special notation. Choose **Project|Properties**, and select the **Tools** tab. At the bottom, set start and end character sequences for the notation you want to navigate. Click the **Add** button to add them to the list. When the cursor sits at the beginning of a block of text delimited by the start and end sequences, choose either **Tools|Find start/end of block** or **Tools|Mark block**. BCLIDE will move the cursor or mark the block as appropriate.

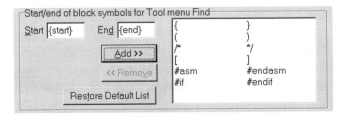

Figure A.3 Accommodating Special Notation

- After you create a new code module, you will likely need to add `#include` statements for some standard header files. Choose **Tools|Include header file.** BCLIDE displays a window with several paths and header files, as shown in Example A.4.

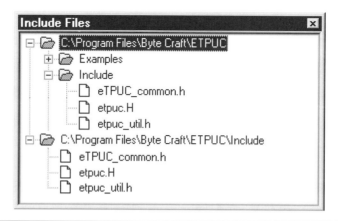

Figure A.4 Including Standard Header Files in Compiler Project

This dialog explores the header files available at each point in the INCLUDE path (specified in the General tab of the Project Properties dialog). In this example, the same files are shown, but with different roots. Each root is a folder listed in the INCLUDE path, and used as the base of a relative path in the `#include<>` statement.

- When you're calling for technical support, consult the **Help|About** dialog box. It presents serial number and version information for BCLIDE, the compiler set in the project, and BClink:

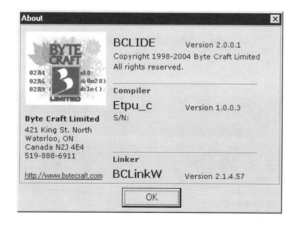

Figure A.5 BCLIDE's About Screen

Creating a Project

Open BCLIDE. The initial information that appears is part of a default project. At startup, BCLIDE re-opens the last open project. Choose **Project|New Project**. BCLIDE opens the Project Properties dialog. Fill in the information as described in the online help. To get the project compiling, all you need is the Working, Include, and Library folders on the General tab as shown in Figure A.6, and the Compiler on the Compiler tab, as shown in Figure A.7.

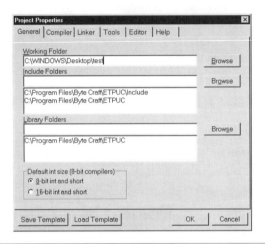

Figure A.6 Setting a Project's General Properties

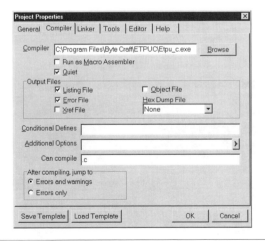

Figure A.7 Setting a Project's Compiler

Choose **Project|Save Project**. Give the new project a name and save it in a central place. (BCLIDE suggests the working folder.)

To create the first program module, choose **File|New**.

Standard Builds
Ensure the BCLIDE project specifies the ELF Hex Dump File format, or has **Object File** selected (compiling to an object file is used to create a library). Press **F9** to compile the file. Pressing **Alt-F9** links, and **Ctrl-F9** compiles and links in one step. If the compile encounters errors, it will report them in the progress window at the bottom of the BCLIDE window.

Information on building and linking multiple files is provided below.

Invoking the Compiler Directly
If you invoke the compiler from a script, a makefile, the DOS prompt, or a cmd.exe shell, it will compile the file specified on the command line. If you invoke the compiler without a file name, it presents the console shown in Figure A.8.

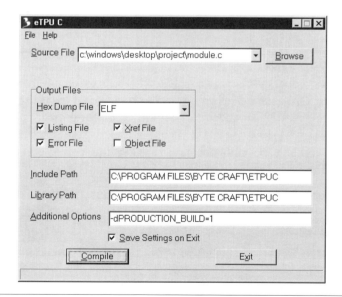

Figure A.8 The Compiler Console

Browse for a source file, and then click **Compile** to compile it. You can't invoke the linker using this console; only sources using Absolute Code Mode (`#include` statements) will compile.

The Include and Library paths are semicolon-separated paths.

You can specify command-line options in the Additional Options field. Valid command line options are described in the online documentation. To prevent this console from appearing (for instance, when compiling from make), use the +q command line switch (Quiet mode).

The Compiler and eTPU_C Programming

You can develop full-fledged eTPU programs completely in "C." eTPU_C offers header files with a convenient API for common eTPU operations. The "C" compiler translates program statements into eTPU subinstructions, reorders them, and assembles them into an executable image. One important note: the eTPU is a word-oriented machine, but "C" is (essentially) byte-oriented. Byte Craft Limited has continued to respect the byte-oriented nature of "C." The compiler addresses memory as an array of bytes.

The Standard Header Files

Byte Craft Limited products use separate header files to provide device-specific information to the compiler. This practice simplifies support, makes retargeting software easier, and allows the developer to customize device information for project-specific reasons.

At time of writing, eTPU_C has only one device header file, named etpuc.h. This file supplies numerous definitions required for all eTPU_C programs:

- Register variable declarations for direct access to the eTPU ALU and channel logic registers. Operations on these variables translate into references to the underlying registers.
- A variable declaration channel of type `chan_struct`. This is described below.
- Some helpful identifiers allowing for faster access to channel structure members, and constants to use in conjunction with them.
- The `tpr_struct` structure, the bit fields present in the tooth program register (**TPR**).

A second header file, etpuc_common.h, offers programmer-friendly macros commonly used in eTPU_C programs. This file is the union of several source files; several equivalent files have been used since the start of eTPU_C development. In order to avoid wholesale rewrites of existing code, these files have been combined. This file contains some redundant declarations, which vary by programming style and length and descriptiveness of the identifiers. Canonical versions appear first, followed by a tag SYNONYMS in a "C" comment, and then alternate versions. (Identifiers in this file will be supported in all subsequent updates of the eTPU_C compiler.) For instance:

- `Clear(flag0)` is the same as `ClrFlag0()`, where `Clear()` can be used to clear other latches as well.

- `ClearLSRLatch()` and `ClearLinkServiceRequestEvent()` are synonymous; use either depending upon your preference for descriptive identifiers.

- Some synonyms are interleaved, owing to capitalization or context. These definitions are used as channel condition tests. For example, the three macros in Example A.1 are synonymous with one another.

```
#define MatchA_TransB                (m1==1)
#define matchA_transB                (m1==1)
#define IsMatchAOrTransitionBEvent()  (m1==1)
```

Example A.1 Synonymous Macros in the Standard Header Files

- Some synonyms such as those shown in Example A.2 require attention to etpuc.h.

```
#define SetChannelMode(mode)   (channel.PDCM = mode)
#define channel_setup           channel.PDCM
```

Example A.2 PDCM Macros

- Some complex macros such as those shown in Example A.3 provide a way to set up matches and transition detection quickly, easily, and accurately. These macros are complex because they are defined in terms of other macros. The second and third macro in this example are useful only in initialization threads and if you know which **TCR** you want to use.

```
#define SetupMatchA(reference) \
        erta = reference;           \
        EnableMatchA();             \
        ClearMatchALatch();

#define SetupMatch_A(reference, timebase_comparator, pin_action) \
        erta = reference; \
        act_unitA = timebase_comparator; \
        opacA = pin_action; \
        EnableMatchA();             \
        ClearMatchALatch();\
        EnableEventHandling();

#define SetupCaptureTrans_A(timebase, pin_trans) \
        act_unitA = timebase;\
        ipacA = pin_trans;\
        ClearTransLatch();\
        EnableEventHandling();
```

Example A.3 Complex Macros

Further, some macros require you to consult the **PDCM** constants, as shown in
Example A.4.

```
#define EitherMatchBlockingSingleTransition()  channel.PDCM = em_b_st
#define EitherMatchBlockingDoubleTransition()  channel.PDCM = em_b_dt
```

Example A.4 Macros Setting the Channel Mode

A third header file, etpuc_util.h, has definitions related to the angle clock hardware, as
shown in Table A.1

Definition	Description
Add_Angle(b,c)	Adds two angles and performs a modulo operation if the sum exceeds T_Modulus.
Subtract_Angle(b,c)	Subtracts angle c from angle b and performs a modulo operation if the operation underflows.

Table A.1 Angle Clock Hardware Definitions in etpuc_util.h

As a result, etpuc_util.h requires two definitions in your source code, prior to including the header, as shown in Table A.2.

Definition	Description
TicksPerTooth	The number of **TCR2** ticks that elapse per tooth.
TeethPerCycle	The number of teeth per revolution.

Table A.2 Two Definitions Required by etpuc_util.h

Just `#include` etpuc.h, and perhaps etpuc_common.h, in your main program module. Include etpuc_util.h if you're using the angle clock functionality.

Guidelines for Modifying Standard Header File Definitions
If you want to modify the definitions in the standard header files, follow these guidelines:

- `#undef` and redefine the offending definitions in your source files. The project will properly pick up subsequent versions of the header files when the compiler is upgraded.
- You can always copy the files and modify them, but please rename your modified copies. This practice will make technical support much more straightforward. Rename the "C" directives inside the file that provide `#include` protection. The `#ifdef` and `#define` are at the top, and a comment with the same symbol is at the bottom. This definition will show up in the listing file (in the symbol table report) and in the .cod file, serving as a reminder.

Program Structure
Byte Craft Limited has chosen to use special "C"-language constructions to represent architectural elements of eTPU programming. The compiler recognizes these structures as special and generates different output data as a result.

There are two main differences between "C" programming for the eTPU and typical embedded "C." The first is that the `main()` function is no longer emphasized. Second, the "C"-language functions that implement eTPU channel functions are specially constructed. They are also specially named, here and in eTPU_C documentation, by the directive used to declare them: `ETPU_Function`. eTPU functions are the core of eTPU programming. You can declare other functions (called "C" functions to distinguish them), and call those from eTPU functions or from one other, as you would expect to do in "C."

The main() Function

In eTPU_C, all code execution is initiated by an event. The processor has no reset event, so the `main()` function has no special role. Program execution starts in eTPU functions, described below. A placeholder `main()` function may, however, be present. While the "C" standard does not require a `main()` in a stand-alone environment, it's still a good idea. However, if the body of the function is empty the compiler will not generate any code. Any code in `main()` will be unreachable.

eTPU Functions

The eTPU programmer must define one or more eTPU functions. These become the entry points for the eTPU's microengine code during thread execution. eTPU functions have a special structure that helps make the translation from "C" to the eTPU threads easier while leaving the function intuitively understandable for the programmer. eTPU_C translates each specially-declared eTPU function into the channel condition encoding and the threads. The uppermost code in the eTPU function is a series of `if-else` tests of the channel conditions; these are translated into the position information of the channel condition encoding within the entry table. The bodies of the `if-else` statements structure become the threads' executable code.

The eTPU function declaration requires a `#pragma` instead of a prototype (calling one eTPU function from another is not allowed). The `#pragma` communicates important parameters to the compiler, including (optionally) the channel condition encoding to be used (standard or alternate). For instance:

```
#pragma ETPU_function function_one, standard;
```

The function itself is defined normally, as a void function with parameters. The parameters of the eTPU function are used for communicating with the host's program. The host sets initial values and can read results back through them at will. You can declare as many parameters of different types as the eTPU will accept (128 words). (Note that array parameters will be allocated their full size out of this limit.) Parameters' names are made available to the host through the host interface macros, described below.

```
void function_one(int param_a, int param_b)
```

The top-level scope of the body of the eTPU function cannot contain any code other than the series of `if-else` statements. These statements test the conditions that caused the eTPU channel to receive the attention of the engine: matches (or transitions), host service requests, or link service requests. Each of these statements can also test the state of the channel's input pin (latched rather than sampled0, and the state resolution flags (**Flag0** and **Flag1**). For instance:

```
void function_one(int param_a, int param_b);
{
   if(IsHostServiceRequestEvent(3))
      {
         int one = 23;
         static int two = 45;

         /* C instructions */
      }
   else if(m1 && flag0)
      {
         /* C instructions*/
      }
   else
      {
         /* C instructions */
      }
}
```

Example A.5 The Structure of an eTPU Function

The tests performed in the series of `if-else` statements are highly constrained: only the identifiers, and appropriate constants, shown in Table A.3are allowed. You can combine multiple tests with logical operators as usual in "C," but illegal or meaningless combinations will be flagged by the compiler. Unused channel conditions—combinations not tested in the eTPU function—are routed to the thread of the final `else` statement, or stubbed in with a NOP thread.

Identifier	*Description*	*Values*	*Notes*
hsr	Host service request	Encoding-specific, always 0-7	If not explicitly tested, a test against 0 is assumed; such threads will not run with hsr != 0.
lsr	Link service request	0 or 1	
pin	State of the input pin	0 or 1	Does not cause service request; combines with one that does
m1	MatchA (or TransitionB)	0 or 1	
m2	Match B (or TransitionA)	0 or 1	

Identifier	Description	Values	Notes
flag0	State resolution **Flag0**	0 or 1	Does not cause service request; combines with one that does
flag1	State resolution **Flag1**	0 or 1	Does not cause service request; combines with one that does

Table A.3 Events and Channel Conditions

eTPU_C describes an entry point using a line in the listing file as shown in Example A.9:

```
00D6 40 81   03 SOB P01 ME 0204  HSR 0  lsr 1  m1 1  m2 1  pin x  flag1 x  flag0 1
```

Figure A.9 Listing File Line Showing Entry Point

This line of the listing file, which is essentially a report, describes the position of the entry in the table and the conditions to execute the code, as follows:

- The entry is at 00D6 in the table.
- The value stored at that location (**ME**, **PP**, and entry point) is 0x4081.
- It's part of eTPU function number 3.
- The entry is encoded in standard format, thread 0x0b.
- **P/DIOB** will be preloaded from parameters 0 and 1.
- Match events are enabled.
- The thread start address is 0x0204.

The entry conditions are interpreted as follows: a *1* means the thread responds to that condition, a *0* means it will not, and an *x* means that that condition isn't considered in this entry point.

The compiler will generate errors if any of the tests in an `if` test cannot be compiled into a channel condition encoding. eTPU_C takes care of generating the entry table and entry points, making it only as large as necessary to accommodate the defined eTPU functions.

Advanced Feature: Function Groups
eTPU functions are easily re-usable: the compiler uses channel-relative addressing to access eTPU function parameters and local variables. Each assignment of a function

shares the same underlying code, so as to conserve shared code memory (SCM) resources, but uses its own parameter variables.

eTPU functions can address "C" global variables. This is an effective way to allow logical groups of eTPU functions to communicate (for example, for a communications bus). It isn't always desirable to use the host's intervention or link service requests to communicate; sometimes global variables are the least invasive solution.

Mixing these two cases together, however, introduces a potential conflict. "C" global variables will be shared across all instances of the related eTPU functions. This will interfere with the logical separation between the instances of groups of eTPU functions. The globals will be too global. The solution is to explicitly declare groups of related eTPU functions (and, therefore, related global variables) to the compiler with a `#pragma` directive. The compiler will ensure globals used within the group are global only within each instance of the group. Internally, the compiler adds these group-globals to a union parameter list shared by each member of the group. The groups are named, sharing the same namespace as "C" identifiers. The notation is shown in Example A.6

```
#pragma ETPU_function_group name;

/* global variable declarations */

#pragma ETPU_function fname;

void fname(function argument list)
{
  if /* ... */ else /* ... */
}

/* other eTPU functions */

#pragma ETPU_function_group_end name;
```

Example A.6 Function Groups

Any global variable declared within this block will be treated as global only to the group. Host-based initialization code can continue to use the regular host information macros to allocate SPRAM for the union parameter list.

There are some tradeoffs when using function groups. For one, all eTPU functions within the group will consume parameter positions whether they're actually assigned to a channel or not. More importantly, no eTPU function or "C" function within the block may call any

"C" function in another block; called "C" functions outside of any block may not use the group-global variables.

For more information on this advanced feature, see the eTPU_C documentation.

Intrinsics and Values

Compiler writers attempt to find ways of addressing exceptional or non-orthogonal processor features within the general spirit of the "C" language. Some functions that translate directly to processor features are intrinsic to the compiler and avoid distracting excursions into assembly language. In eTPU_C, using intrinsics generates several different types of code: channel-specific subinstructions, conditional branches (with code paths), ALU subinstructions, and others. But the point of the intrinsics is to make using exceptional features as intuitive as all other "C" programming.

Intrinsic Instructions

eTPU_C offers a `NOP()` function, which translates directly to a NOP subinstruction.

`enable_match()` and `disable_match()` are two very special commands and appear only in eTPU functions. They do not generate any code: eTPU_C sets or clears the value of the **ME** field to be placed in the entry table for that thread. The eTPU passes this value to the **ME** flag that governs match events during thread execution. `enable_match()` is the default.

For signaling an exception to the host, the **CIRC** member of the channel structure is used. This is described below.

Types and Registers

eTPU_C offers direct access to user-serviceable registers through specialized data types. The compiler enforces the restrictions on the hardware. These initial declarations are made in etpuc.h as shown in Example A.7

```
register_erta      erta;      // 24 bits
register_ertb      ertb;      // 24 bits
register_tcr1      tcr1;      // 24 bits
register_tcr2      tcr2;      // 24 bits
register_tpr       tpr;       // 16 bits
register_trr       trr;       // 24 bits
register_chan      chan;      //  5 bits
register_link      link;      //  8 bits
```

Example A.7 Register Data Types

Assignments to or from these variables (**CHAN** and **LINK**, especially) cause all the expected side effects that are mentioned in Freescale Semiconductor's documentation of the underlying registers.

Other registers (the general-purpose registers, **P, DIOB**, etc.) have equivalent types and can be used to declare variables in the same way. The types are documented, but since the compiler uses the underlying registers for performing "C" calculations, no declarations are included by default. Should you choose to declare variables of these types and use them explicitly, the compiler will not take your operations into account as it generates code. Such usage must be considered on a case-by-case basis.

Condition Codes

The ALU flags (carry (**C**), overflow (**V**), and so on) appear as fields in a variable of special type. Variables of type register_cc all address the ALU flags through a structure. The members of this structure include:

- CC.C, CC.N, CC.C, and CC.Z, the integer ALU flags
- CC.MB (busy), CC.MC, CC.MN, CC.MV, and CC.MZ, the MAC flags

The compiler uses these in its calculations (and watches the **MB** busy bit itself). Other members of register_cc are listed in Table A.4.

Field	*Description*
CC.TDLA	Transition detection latch A
CC.TDLB	Transition detection latch B
CC.MRLA	Match recognition latch A
CC.MRLB	Match recognition latch B
CC.LSR	Link service request (in the serviced channel)
CC.FM1	Function mode bit 1 (set by host)
CC.FM0	Function mode bit 0 (set by host)
CC.PSS	Sampled state of input pin (set from selected channel at writing of **CHAN**)
CC.LT	Less than ALU flag combination (signed)
CC.LS	Lower or same ALU flag combination (unsigned)
CC.P_24	Bit 24 of the **P** register.
CC.P_25	Bit 25 of the **P** register.
CC.P_26	Bit 26 of the **P** register.
CC.P_27	Bit 27 of the **P** register.

Field	Description
CC.P_28	Bit 28 of the **P** register.
CC.P_29	Bit 29 of the **P** register.
CC.P_30	Bit 30 of the **P** register.
CC.P_31	Bit 31 of the **P** register.
CC.PSTO	Current output pin state (of the selected channel)
CC.PSTI	Current input pin state (of the selected channel)
CC.SMLCK	Semaphore lock for the engine
CC.GE	Greater or equal ALU flag combination (opposite of 'less than'; signed)
CC.GT	Greater than ALU flag combination (opposite of 'lower or same'; unsigned)

Table A.4 The register_cc Fields

If you test any of these structure members, eTPU_C generates a conditional branch subinstruction, with code paths determined by the context.

The Channel Structure
The centerpiece of eTPU_C programming is the channel structure. The channel structure collects the eTPU code-controlled registers of the channel into one logical structure. Use this structure (or the helpful macros in etpuc_common.h) to perform the channel I/O for the eTPU function.

The channel structure variable is declared in etpuc.h. The underlying type is named chan_struct, and is intrinsic to the compiler. There is little reason to declare other variables of type chan_struct. Example A.8 shows the equivalent declaration.

```
struct {
  CIRC    int : 2 ;
  ERWA    int : 1 ;
  ERWB    int : 1 ;
  FLC     int : 3 ;
  IPACA   int : 3 ;
  IPACB   int : 3 ;
  LSR     int : 1 ;
  MRLA    int : 1 ;
  MRLB    int : 1 ;
  MRLE    int : 1 ;
  MTD     int : 2 ;
  OPACA   int : 3 ;
  OPACB   int : 3 ;
  PDCM    int : 4 ;
  PIN     int : 3 ;
  TBSA    int : 4 ;
  TBSB    int : 4 ;
  TDL     int : 1 ;
  SMPR    int : 2 ;
  FLAG0   int : 1 ;
  FLAG1   int : 1 ;
  FM0     int : 1 ;
  FM1     int : 1 ;
  PSS     int : 1 ;
  PSTI    int : 1 ;
  PSTO    int : 1 ;
  TDLA    int : 1 ;
  TDLB    int : 1 ;
}
```

Example A.8 The Channel Structure

Assignments to channel structure members translate directly into microinstructions, addressing the fields of the same names. etpuc.h and etpuc_common.h include numerous helpful declarations that make assigning values to channel members easier.

Tests of channel structure members translate directly to branch condition tests. You can test these members in if() statements like any other variables. Not all of the members are testable, and some that are testable are duplicated in the register_cc structure type.

Table A.5 provides detailed information on the channel members.

Member	Size	Description	Mode	Typical Values and Notes
CIRC	2	Interrupt control: interrupt, data transfer, global fault	WO	00 channel interrupt, 01 data transfer, 10 global exception
ERWA	1	Write **ERT_A** to **MatchA**, and enable matches for MatchA	WO	0 to assert
ERWB	1	Write **ERT_B** to **MatchB**, and enable matches for MatchB	WO	0 to assert
FLC	3	Flag copy immediate or from **P** upper bits	WO	See eTPU_C documentation; note some duplicates below
IPACA	3	Input pin action control, **MatchA** and first transition	WO	See eTPU_C documentation
IPACB	3	Input pin action control, **MatchB** and second transition	WO	See eTPU_C documentation
LSR	1	Clear the link service request flag	RW	Tests **LSR**; 0 to assert
MRLA	1	Match recognition latch for action logic A (similar to **TDL**)	RW	Tests match recognition A; 0 to clear latch
MRLB	1	Match recognition latch for action logic B (similar to **TDL**)	RW	Tests match recognition B; 0 to clear latch
MRLE	1	Disable matches (use **ERW_A/B** to enable)	WO	0 to assert
MTD	2	Enable/disable match/transition service requests	WO	00 to assert, 01 to negate
OPACA	3	Output pin action control, **MatchA**/input action	WO	See eTPU_C documentation
OPACB	3	Output pin action control, **MatchB**/input action	WO	See eTPU_C documentation
PDCM	4	Pre-defined channel mode	WO	See eTPU_C documentation
PIN	3	Combination of **PSC** (2 bits):**PSCS** (1 bit)	WO	000 (**OPAC_B**), 001 (**OPAC_A**), 010 (high), 100 (low)

Member	Size	Description	Mode	Typical Values and Notes
TBSA	4	Comparator and time base selection for action logic A	WO	See eTPU_C documentation
TBSB	4	Comparator and time base selection for action logic B	WO	See eTPU_C documentation
TDL	1	Transition detection latch for both action logics (similar to **MRL_A/B**)	WO	0 to clear **TDL_A/TDL_B**
SMPR	2	Semaphore control and test	RW	Assign 0-3. Test against 0: if not 0, wait.
FLAG0	1	**Flag0** (related to **FLC** above)	WO	1 to assert
FLAG1	1	**Flag1** (related to **FLC** above)	WO	1 to assert
FM0	1	Function mode bit 0	RO	Function mode bit 0
FM1	1	Function mode bit 1	RO	Function mode bit 1
PSS	1	Pin sampled state (governed by **CHAN**)	RO	Changes at will
PSTI	1	Pin state input (part of the channel)	RO	Changes when channel.chan is assigned
PSTO	1	Pin state output (part of the channel)	RO	Changes when channel.chan is assigned
TDLA	1	Transition detect latch A (action logic A)	RO	See **TDL**
TDLB	1	Transition detect latch B (action logic B)	RO	See **TDL**

Table A.5 Channel Members

Other Notes

Values to be used in multiply-accumulate and divide (MDU) operations must be of, or will be automatically typecast to, type int24 or fract24. For instance:

```
0001 0005                                          signed int24 a, b;

0200 9FEFFB00    ram p23_0 = 0001.                 a = a * b;
0204 9FE80A01    alu a = p ,ccs;
                     ram p23_0 = 0005.
0208 3B190FE9    mdu a mults p ,ccs.
                        .
0210 3BF80FB4    alu a = macl ,ccs.
0214 9FEFFB00    ram p23_0 = 0001.
```

Example A.9 MDU Operations

The tooth program register (**TPR**) is exposed to "C" as variables of type `register_tpr`. The register has several fields, which are described in a matching structure in etpuc.h as shown in Example A.10.

```
struct tpr_struct {
   int TICKS   : 10;
   int TPR10   : 1;
   int HOLD    : 1;
   int IPH     : 1;
   int MISSCNT : 2;
   int LAST    : 1;
} ;
```

Example A.10 The TPR Structure

This structure is not intrinsic to the compiler, but is included as a helpful standard definition.

Linking and Libraries

As a rule, linking is simple for embedded systems. Dynamic linking is unnecessary because the executables are monolithic. The complete resources of the system—RAM and ROM—are known at compile time, and there's no reason to provide for any sort of fix-up. Also, with today's personal computers there is little extra cost in re-cross-compiling an entire embedded program at once.

There's another reason to avoid late-stage linking: optimization. Only the compiler has the information to determine whether or not code or data will be used during the program run. Every extra step in the build process risks preserving unnecessary information and leaving the executable larger than necessary.

eTPU_C includes the BClink optimizing linker. BClink accepts a linker command file, which specifies the compiler, object files and libraries, and, most importantly, all `#pragma` directives. Note that this latter includes all `#pragma ETPU_function` and `#pragma ETPU_function_group` directives. An example linker command file is shown in Figure A.10.

```
COMPILER = C:\Program Files\Byte Craft\ETPUC\Etpu_c.exe
#include "C:\Program Files\Byte Craft\ETPUC\Include\etpuc.H"
#include "C:\projectdir\etpucproject.h"
COMMAND  = n="C:\Program Files\Byte Craft\ETPUC;C:\Program
Files\Byte Craft\ETPUC\Include"
COMMAND  = t="C:\Program Files\Byte Craft\ETPUC"
COMMAND  = +delf
HEX      = C:\projectdir\etpuc
OBJECT   = C:\projectdir\etpucproject.obj
LIBRARY  = project_definitions.obj
LIBRARY  = supplem.obj
```

Figure A.10 A Linker Command File

It is a special (and necessary) feature of BClink that, using the etpuc.h header file and a project-specific header file, the linker command file replicates all the information available to the compiler during the initial compilation. One of BClink's tasks is to perform a final optimization pass over the eTPU_C program to ensure that all possible optimizations have been performed. Without the header files, this final optimization would be impossible.

BCLIDE can generate linker command files on its own, simplifying the process somewhat. To configure BCLIDE for linking:

1.   Choose **Project|Properties**, and select the **Linker** tab. Ensure all the files in the link are listed under the Source Files, Include Files, and Library Files tabs.

2.   Choose the **Options** tab, and select the output files you need (especially the type of executable).

3.   The contents of the Command entry become part of the command line. BCLIDE will perform some substitutions on the contents: click the arrow button at right to choose from a list of variables.

4.   The contents of the Option line become part of a `#pragma` option directive understood by the linker. This is a quick way to perform link-time configuration. For instance, the *f 0* entry will turn off page breaks in the listing file.

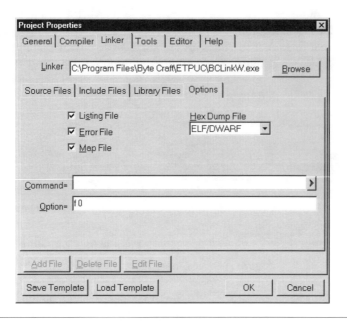

Figure A.11 Configuring BCLIDE for Linking

More usually, however, eTPU_C programs are written to use Absolute Code Mode. The compiler simply generates a final executable in one operation. Use #include statements to include supporting headers (at the top) and supporting C modules (at the bottom) in the eTPU_C program's main module.

```
#include <etpuc.H>
#include <supporting.h>

/* your main module here */

#include <supporting.c>
```

Example A.11 Including Supporting Header Files

Simply compile the main module to an executable (**F9**).

Absolute Code Mode is not just a fancy name for #include: you can #include object files as well as C source files. This may be useful for distributing object files to third parties. In fact, renaming object files with a .lib extension eliminates the need for the second

#include since eTPU_C will try to read in a matching library file (extension .lib) for each .h header file (having the same base name) that is #included at the top of a source file.

Host Interface Files

eTPU_C generates programs for the eTPU. The host CPU is responsible for actually programming and starting the eTPU, so its program must process the eTPU_C-generated executable. Since eTPU_C is the point of origin for the eTPU executable and associated information (for example, the amounts of SPRAM needed and the size of the executable), it makes sense that eTPU_C should direct the generation of host CPU programming that pertains to the eTPU. You can embed the code intended for the host in an eTPU_C program by using #pragma write statements. These statements cause the compiler to emit host interface files and to expand host interface macros with information derived from the generated code. eTPU_C re-generates these files upon every successful compilation, inserting the most current information.

The syntax is as follows:

```
#pragma write letter, ( text to be emitted );
```

letter is a single letter (usually c or h) that becomes the extension of the emitted file's name. The base name itself is the eTPU_C main module base name, with the characters "_CPU" appended, and the single-letter extension. You can use multiple #pragma write invocations, each with a different extension letter; eTPU_C creates each file at the first invocation of a particular extension letter and closes the file automatically at the end of compilation. eTPU_C accepts any code between the parentheses and will expand numerous macros starting with the sequence "::ETPU". A short list appears below; see the eTPU_C documentation for the complete list.

Macro	Description	Sample Use	Sample Output
::ETPU-code, ::ETPUcode 32	The code of the eTPU_C executable, as a list of (byte/word) integer constants	::ETPUcode32	0xFFDFCCF9,0x1C5 F5FF6,0xFFC0101F, 0x6FFFFFFF,0x4FFF FFFF,0x6FFFFFFF, 0xFFC0101F,0x6FFF FFFF, /* ... */
::ETPUco-deimage-size	The size of the eTPU_C executable, in bytes, as an integer constant	::ETPUcodeimag-esize	0x7FFE

Macro	Description	Sample Use	Sample Output
`::ETPU-function-frameram()`	The number of SPRAM bytes needed for an eTPU function (by name or number). Includes parameters and locals.	`::ETPUfunction-fram-eram(function_o ne)`	0x0010
`::ETPU-function-number()`	The number of the eTPU function in the entry table; suitable for use in the host channel configuration register.	`::ETPUfunction-num-ber(function_on e)`	0 /* first one declared */
`::ETPUlit-eral()`	The parameter text, with no host interface macros expanded.	`::ETPUlit-eral(results of ::ETPUcode)`	results of ::ETPUcode
`::ETPU-params()`	The parameters of an eTPU function. Expressed as macro calls with names, unambiguous types, and offsets.	`::ETPU-params(function _one)`	__etpu_param(param_ a, sint24, 0x0001) __etpu_param(param_ b, sint24, 0x0005)
`::ETPUsta-ticinit()`, `::ETPUstat icinit32()`	The initial (byte/word) values for SPRAM for an eTPU function (by name or number). Expressed as a macro call with an offset and a value.	`::ETPUstaticini t32(function_on e)`	__etpu_staticinit32(0x 0008,0x0000002D)

Table A.6 Host Interface Macros

Some host interface macros expand to a sequence of (one or more) macro calls themselves. You can identify them by the double-underscore prefix, as in the examples above. A user-supplied macro is needed: define a macro of the same (expanded) name prior to using the host interface macro in order to implement the operation in a host-specific way.

Make sure that any parentheses that are part of the host code between the outermost pair are balanced. If you need to insert an unbalanced parenthesis, use the `::ETPUliteral` macro. `::ETPUliteral` accepts literal text enclosed in various delimiters: parentheses, square brackets, angle brackets, or braces. Use one of that list that is not part of the literal text to be emitted.

The host interface mechanism is very flexible. You can use it to generate many parts of the host program:

- The loader that writes eTPU code to the SCM.
- The code that assigns eTPU functions to each channel and allocates SPRAM.

- The code that writes initial global and static values to SPRAM.
- A host API for eTPU functions, to set eTPU function parameters, perform host service requests, respond to interrupts and data transfers, and retrieve the results.

Summary

eTPU was designed from the beginning to be suited for compiler-generated programming. The eTPU code-type instruction set, with moving subinstruction fields, makes hand-coding an unnecessary struggle.

The special structure of eTPU functions and the dual nature of the channel structure make eTPU programs easier to understand at first glance. It should be clear, from the expected flow of control in "C," how the program will run under the various events the eTPU will process. The only differences between eTPU programs and other "C" programs are that eTPU programs contain specialized declarations (channel condition identifiers and ETPU_function prototypes) and a placeholder `main()` function.

The host interface files and macros can communicate a tremendous amount of information about the eTPU_C program, all of which is available to the host program at compile time. The `::ETPUcode` macros provide the simplest way to communicate the executable from eTPU_C to the host code; there's no need to deal with an external executable file format. In addition, the programmer can create a host-program API for the eTPU_C program and maintain it alongside the eTPU programming itself. This simplifies code partitioning and dependency management for the programmer.

APPENDIX B

ASH WARE's eTPU Stand-Alone Simulator

Installing the Simulator

1. Insert the installation CD into the computer's CD drive and run the installation file, **mtdt_zip.exe**, from the eTPU Stand-Alone Simulator (Demo) folder.

The dialog box in Figure B.1 should appear. (If it doesn't, run the installation file, "Setup.exe" from the CD drive.)

ASH WARE Inc MtDt Software Installation and Upgrade   ☒

The first step is extraction of the installation files. Later, you will be asked to select both an installation directory and the product that you wish to install or upgrade.

Hit the setup button to procede with this first step.

WinZip® Self-Extractor © Nico Mak Computing, Inc. http://www.winzip.com

[Setup]
[Cancel]
[About]

Figure B.1 Installation Screen

2. Click **Setup**.

The dialog box in Figure B.3 appears.

Figure B.2 Alert Message

3. Click **OK** (there is no need to shutdown all application for this installation).

The dialog box in Figure B.3 appears.

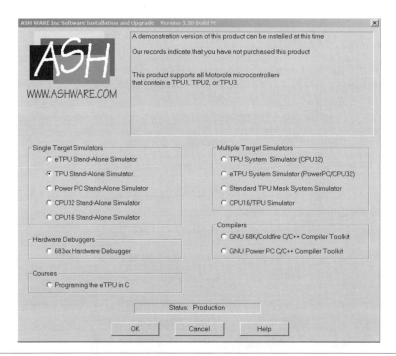

Figure B.3 Selecting the eTPU Stand-Alone Simulator

4. Select **eTPU Stand-Alone Simulator**.
5. Click **OK**.

The dialog box shown in Figure B.4 appears.

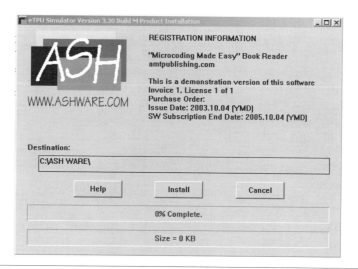

Figure B.4 The Simulator Is Installing

6. Click **Install**.

Installation takes about two minutes. The dialog box in Figure B.5 will then appear.

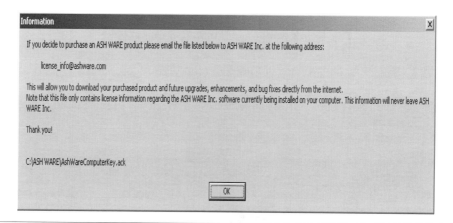

Figure B.5 Informational Screen

7. Click **OK**.

The confirmation dialog box in Figure B.6 appears.

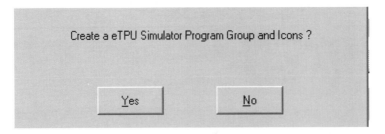

Figure B.6 Confirmation

8. Click **Yes**.

The dialog box in Figure B.7 appears

Figure B.7 Simulator Installation Complete

9. Click **OK**. (Note that you do not need to reboot your computer.)

Congratulations, you have successfully installed ASH WARE's eTPU Stand-Alone Simulator!

Using the Simulator

Launch the Byte Craft compiler demo that is installed with the eTPU Stand-Alone Simulator.

1. From the Windows menu, go to the **Programs** sub-menu, then the **eTPU Simulator** sub-menu, and finally select the **ByteCraft Compiler Demo**.

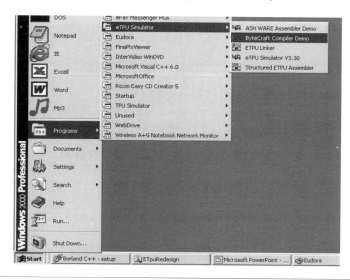

Figure B.8 Launching the Demo

After launching the demo, the application should appear as shown in Figure B.9.

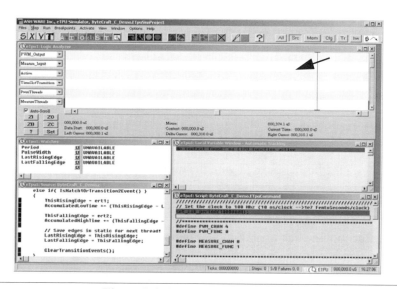

Figure B.9 Running the Simulator

2. Right-click in the Logic Analyzer window, approximately where the arrow is shown.

The following waveform should appear in the Logic Analyzer window.

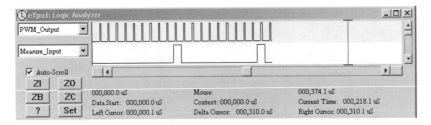

Figure B.10 First Waveform

Single Stepping

3. Hit **F8** a few times until the red line goes to the "LastRisingEdgeCnt" line of code shown in Figure B.11.

```
eTpu1: Source: ByteCraft_C_Demo.c
        else
        {
            ClearMatch1Event();
            ClearMatch2Event();
            LastRisingEdgeCnt = ert1;
            ert1 = LastRisingEdgeCnt + Period;
            ert2 = LastRisingEdgeCnt + Period + Pulse
            WriteErt1ToMatch1AndEnable();
            WriteErt2ToMatch2AndEnable();
        }
    }
```

Figure B.11 Program Counter

The red line shows the line associated with the program counter

Breakpoints

4. Using the mouse click the left mouse button on the "ert1 = LastRisingEdgeCnt + Period" line, which is one below the red line

5. With the "ert1 = LastRisingEdge + Period" line selected, goto the **Breakpoints** menu and select **Toggle**."

A green breakpoint line appears on the line, as shown in Figure B.12.

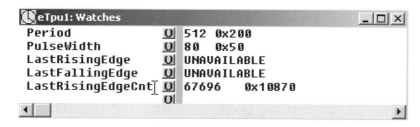

```
eTpu1: Source: ByteCraft_C_Demo.c          _ □ ×
        else
        {
            ClearMatch1Event();
            ClearMatch2Event();
            LastRisingEdgeCnt = ert1;
            ert1 = LastRisingEdgeCnt + Period;
            ert2 = LastRisingEdgeCnt + Period + Pulse
            WriteErt1ToMatch1AndEnable();
            WriteErt2ToMatch2AndEnable();
        }
}
```

Figure B.12 Breakpoint

Watch Window

6.   Free-run the Simulator a few times by hitting the **F9** key.

The waveform in the Logic Analyzer window should grow and the simulation should stop on the breakpoint.

7.   In the Watch window, left-click immediately below the LastFallingEdge row, in order to edt the window. Type the text, "LastRisingEdgeCnt" and hit **Enter**.

The result should look like Figure B.13.

```
eTpu1: Watches                              _ □ ×
Period              □  512  0x200
PulseWidth          □  80   0x50
LastRisingEdge      □  UNAVAILABLE
LastFallingEdge     □  UNAVAILABLE
LastRisingEdgeCnt[  □  67696    0x10870
                    □
```

Figure B.13 Watch Window

8.   Free-run the Simulator a few more times (by hitting **F9**) and verify that the "LastRisingEdgeCnt" value changes.

The watch window can be used for global, function, and local variables. But be careful, because the values displayed in this window will always be in the current context. So a function variable will reflect the channel being serviced, which may not be the one you're interested in!

Local Variable Window

9. Free-run the Simulator a few times by hitting **F9**.

10. View the Local Variable window as shown in Figure B.14.

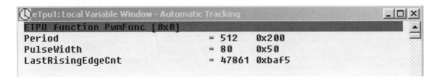

Figure B.14 Local Variable Window

Whereas the Watch window allows the user to type in variable names to watch, the Local Variable window automatically displays all variables that are active in the current context. The local variables window display variables and their values in the current context. That is, if as you step through the code the channel being serviced changes, that will be reflected in the variables displayed in the local variable windows.

Trace Window

11. In the **View** menu, select a **Trace** window.

A window similar to Figure B.15 appears.

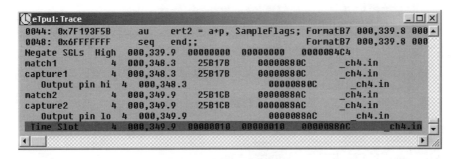

Figure B.15 Trace Window

12. Single step the Simulator using the **F8** key. New data appears in the Trace window.

13. Right-click the mouse on the lowest line in the trace window. Press the up arrow key on your keyboard several times. Observe the Logic Analyzer window and the source code window as you do so.

The yellow lines in these windows are called *context lines*.

Function Frame Window

The function frame window shows function variables on a particular channel.

14. In the **View** menu, select a **Function Frame** window.

A window similar to Figure B.16 appears.

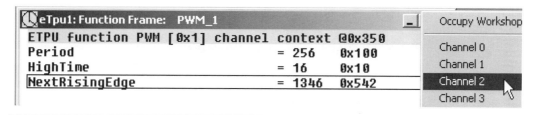

Figure B.16 The Function Frame Window

To change the channel of a function frame, left-click on the window and choose the desired channel. See Figure B.16. (You can open a function frame windows for each channel of interest.)

Code Coverage

Code coverage allows you to see which lines of code have been executed, and which not.

15. Click on the **Options/IDE** menu (see Figure B.17).

Figure B.17 Options/IDE Menu

16. Click the **View Code Coverage** checkbox.

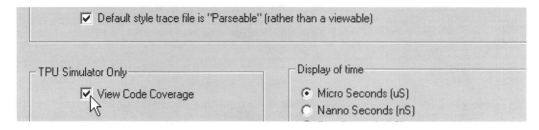

Figure B.18 Setting Up to View Code Coverage

Now as you step through, or simply run, the code, rectangles at the left of the source code file show executed lines (hollow) and unexecuted lines (black). See Figure B.19.

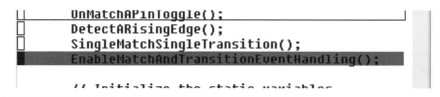

Figure B.19 Viewing Code Coverage

Workshops

As you begin to construct more complicated eTPU functions, the ability to create and configure workshops in the Simulator becomes more important.

17. You can switch to a different set of windows in a project by clicking on the **Src**, **Mem**, **Cfg**, or **Trace** buttons at the upper right. Each of these opens what is called in the Simulator a *workshop*. See Figure B.20.

Figure B.20 Selecting the Memory Windows

A workshop is just a collection of windows in the simulator, for each project. The contents of a workshop is entirely configurable.

18. If you wanted to include this window as part of the Src workshop for this project, right-click on the program space window and select the **Occupy Workshop...** option. See Figure B.21.

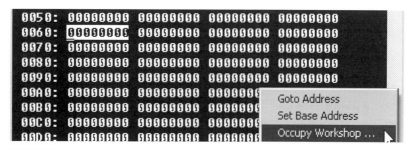

Figure B.21 Putting a Window in a Workshop

The Workshop window will open.

19. Select which workshops you want the window in question to occupy, and click **OK**. See Figure B.22.

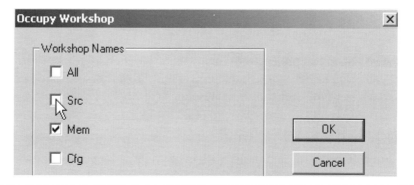

Figure B.22 Occupy Workshops Window

As you can see, you can configure up to 15 workshops.

20. To see the contents of WS5, for instance, use the **Activate/Workshop/** submenu. See Figure B.23.

Figure B.23 Viewing Additional Workshops

Once you have your windows the way you want them, you will want to save the entire configuration as a project so that the window configuration remains available to you.

21. To save a project, click on **Files/Project, Save As**... and then save the project in the desired location with the desired name. See Figure B.24.

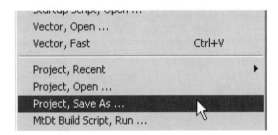

Figure B.24 Creating a Project

The next time you open that project, the window configuration as you last had it will be available for you. You needn't re-save the project once it has been created; the current configuration will be saved each time you close the project.

Other Features

Using the on-line help, ensure familiarity with the Simulator by performing the following actions:

* Change the selected waveform

- Snap the cursors to a pin transition
- Measure a pulse width
- Grab a cursor that is off the side of the Logic Analyzer
- Go to a point in time by grabbing and dropping a cursor
- Use the Trace window in conjunction with Logic Analyzer and source code … "context time"
- Enable/disable logging
- Use vector file to name pins, and select these named nodes for viewing
- Use Auto-Scroll
- Enable/disable logging of pin-transitions
- View thread activity
- Zooming
- Edit the script command file
- Change "reload on reset" setting
- Step, goto, breakpoints
- Show difference between loading script file and viewing script file (why isn't file visible when you load it?)
- Generate a waveform with the vector file
- Fast load a vector file

Installing and Running the Labs

Installing the Code Examples, Labs, and Lab Answers

1. From the installation CD, copy the **Code Examples and Labs** folder to a convenient location in your hard drive.

The code examples, labs, and lab answers will be installed in the target directory, as shown in Figure C.1.

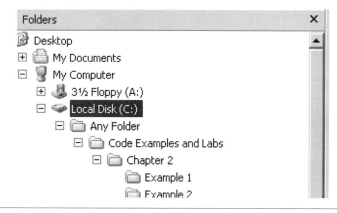

Figure C.1 Location of Lab sand Code Snippets

Code examples are displayed throughout the book. They are provided here for reference. Labs are run at the end of most chapter.

Opening Lab2 in the Compiler

1. Launch the Byte Craft eTPU_C Compiler (the IDE rather than the command line).

2. In the Compiler IDE, go into the File menu and select Open.

The dialog box in Figure C.2 appears.

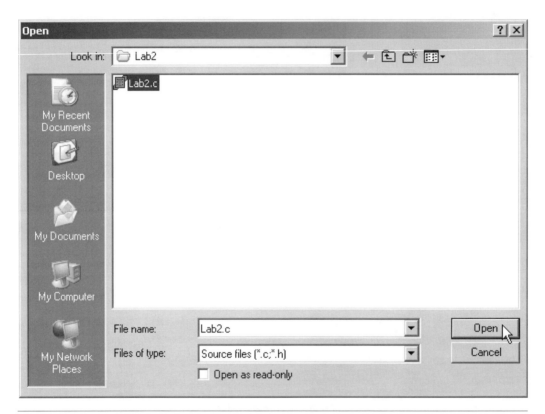

Figure C.2 Opening Lab1

3. Navigate to the Lab2 folder, and open the Lab2.c file (ensure that you're looking a files of type .c).

The window in Figure C.3 appears.

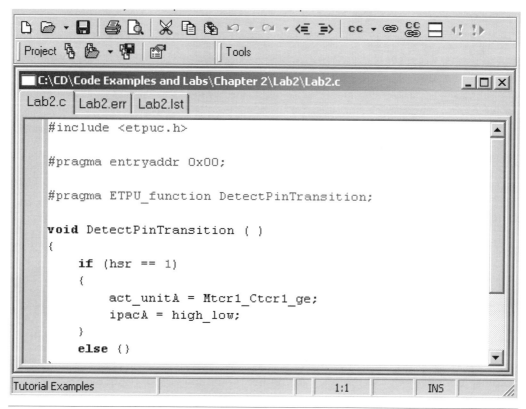

Figure C.3 Lab2 Open in the Compiler IDE

Opening Lab2 Answer in the Simulator

1. Navigate to the Lab2_Answer folder and double click the Lab2.ETpu-SimProject file.

The Simulator launches with various windows shown.

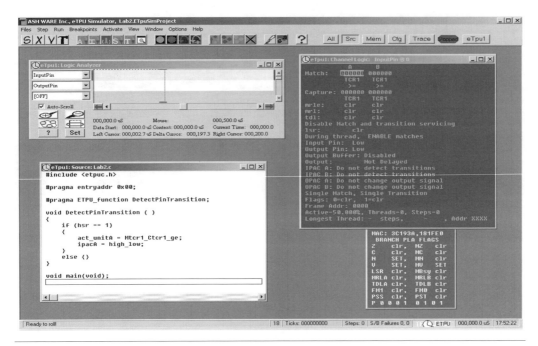

Figure C.4 Lab2 Answer in the Simulator

See chapters 2 through 6 in this book for further information about using the Simulator.

Appendix C. Installing and Running the Labs

Freescale Semiconductor's RAppID

Introduction to RAppID

RAppID, which stands for *Rapid Application Initialization & Documentation*, is a Windows-based tool that enables users of the MPC5554 to rapidly configure the many registers on the part and generate initialization "C" code as well as corresponding documentation (something engineers, by nature, find abhorrent).

Features and Benefits of RAppID

RAppID has the following features:

- Windows-based stand-alone tool that runs on NT, 2000 and XP;
- GUI based for speed and ease of use;
- Generates initialization code for the MPC5554;
- Generates documentation of all the peripheral settings;
- "C" code can be configured for any of the following compilers: MW, GH or Diab;
- Provides for revision control;
- Has on-line documentation;
- Built-in Tool Tips;

- Performs consistency checks;
- "C" code and documentation templates can be customized for a fee;
- A provision for user-specified software attributes;
- Wizards are planned for next release.

These features result in the following benefits:

- Reduced cycle time;
- Rapid creation of initialization code for the processor:
    - Off loads from the engineer the tedious task of scanning through hundreds of pages in the manual and writing the code to initialize the hundreds of registers in the part.
    - Built-in consistency checks reduce errors;
    - Enables quick reconfiguration of the processor;
    - Engineer has more time to spend on application code;
    - GUI-based application is easy to use and navigate;
- Automatically creates the following documentation:
    - Easy-to-read documentation on how the processor was configured. This is useful to hardware and software engineers during debug. This is also useful for communication among multiple departments. The documentation can be part of the review process before code is generated and can be easily integrated into system design documentation;
    - A listing of all the registers and highlights changes;
- Provides for version/revision control;
- With its built-in tutorials, RAppID can be used as a training tool.

The tool allows for easy navigation to all the peripherals, the CPU, and memory areas on the target device. Tool tips are provided on all screens of the product.

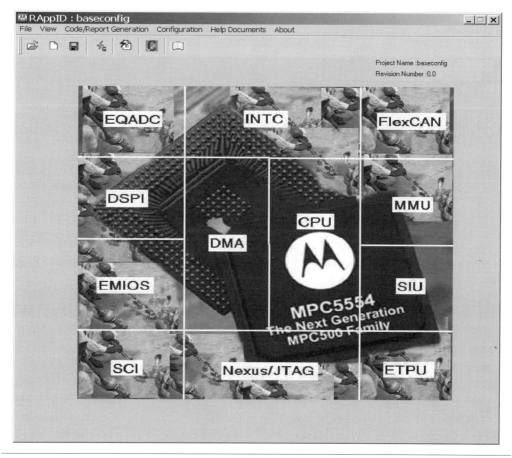

Figure D.1 RAppID Main Window

The top level pull-down menu buttons shown in Figure D.1 enable the user to do such operations as load files, direct the output into the user specified directories, generate code or documentation for all or specific peripheral blocks, etc.

The row of icons below the pull down menu perform the following functions.

	Load project files
0	Load a default or base configuration to start a new project

💾	Save project file
⚡G	Generate "C" code
R	Generate a report/documentation
C	Run consistency checks
📖	Help files

Table D.1 RAppID's Pull-Down Menu Icons

RAppID can generate "C" code that is compatible with the following MPC5554 compilers: Metrowerks, Green Hills, and Wind River (Diab). The user can select the compiler of choice via the pull-down menus.

There are some built-in consistency checks that are performed at the time of data entry in the peripheral GUIs. However it is recommended that a final chip-level consistency check be performed by clicking on the icon prior to code generation.

RAppID Uses

Training Aide
RAppID may be used as a hands-on training tool for an engineer to become more familiar with the MPC5554. With just some basic functional knowledge of the microcontroller, the engineer can use RAppID to learn how each peripheral works and the implications of different register settings. This can be accomplished by using RAppID to configure a peripheral, and generate code and documentation. The engineer can then examine the code and read the report that describes in plain English what the register settings mean. An engineer with access to an evaluation board and the accompanying tools can download the code, execute it on the evaluation board, and observe the operation of the peripheral in hardware.

There are several tutorials provided with RAppID that will assist the engineer through this process.

Testing Target Hardware Board

Typically, hardware design engineers rely on the software group to provide them with test code to prove or debug their hardware. With RAppID, the hardware engineer can easily generate initialization code and with very little effort have "C" code that will toggle most of the I/O pins of the processor. The RAppID tool does more than just initialization; it gives you a framework of "C" code with trigger functions, automatic queue setups for the eQADC, wizards for setting up the eMIOS channel functions, automatic setup of the DMA transfers, etc. As a result, testing the hardware is not only made easier but the report generation feature of RAppID now also enables the hardware engineer to document the test setup.

Software Development

Finally, software development is another use case for RAppID. If the user without a particular format or style guide to follow can easily adopt the format and style guide of RAppID and build his or her application software on top of the initialization code that RAppID generates. However, most large companies have well-documented and mandated guidelines they must follow. In this case, the modular nature of the "C" code generated by RAppID will allow the user to take code snippets or follow some of the code sequences that are in the RAppID generated C code. In this case the report generation feature can be used to specify initialization requirements or for review purposes before code is written.

eTPU Programming Application Note

This is one part of a series of Freescale Semiconductor application notes intended to help the microcontroller systems engineer design and implement code for the eTPU.[1] This note[2] provides an overview of the programming project and contains suggestions for partitioning and other top-level design decisions that will avoid common pitfalls.

Hardware Considerations in eTPU Function Design

The first step in applying the eTPU to a timing and control problem is to determine if the application fits within the capabilities of the eTPU. To do this requires a working understanding of the architecture of the timing channels. A detailed treatment of this will be covered in another application note, but here is a summary of the general capabilities and limitations of the channel hardware.

- **Resolution**
  The channel hardware can set a pin high or low or toggle it, either immediately or at some time in the future. The latter occurs when a free running counter/timer, called the timer count register (**TCR**), matches a particular value. The **TCR** is a 24-

---

1. Freescale Semiconductor's application notes, in general, will suggest design strategies, describe techniques for common classes of problems, and steer the user away from difficult operations and algorithms. Additional notes are in progress and can be obtained by contacting Freescale Semiconductor directly.

2. This application note was written by Mike Pauwels from Freescale Semiconductor Inc. It has been adapted for inclusion in this book.

bit register that can be incremented as fast as half the frequency of the MCU system clock.

- **Maximum Time**

  TCR can be slowed by prescaling, and the **TCR** range is 24 bits. If the **TCR** resolution is 100 nanoseconds, then the counter range is about 1.67 seconds. More significantly, signal timing can incorporate software counters, enabling virtually any maximum time length.

- **Minimum Time**

  The channel has two match comparators, and a pulse can be set to start at one time and end at another after only a single tick of the selected counter/timer. Thus the minimum time pulse that can be produced is two times the system clock.

- **Input Limits**

  The above limits are virtually the same for input transition measurements.

- **Interaction of Events**

  The channel hardware can be configured into a number of operating modes, in which, for example, output pulses can be timed by two different time bases, input pulses can be windowed by timers, or outputs can be used to enable timers. All this can be accomplished without direct software intervention.

- **Synchronization**

  Since all channels operate with respect to the same timer/counters, software can be used to synchronize inputs and outputs with quite complicated algorithms. For example, a spark pulse can be made to start at a projected time before the firing angle and fire exactly on the angle, tracking as closely as possible the variation in speed in an engine.

- **Latency**

  Since the channels have only two action units for each pin, the eTPU requires software intervention before a third transition can be acted upon. This means that while it is possible to accurately produce or measure a narrow single pulse, a third transition can be produced or detected only after the eTPU engine has begun to service the channel. The minimum time required to service one of the edges and reset the channel for the third edge is highly dependent on the configuration of and activity in the rest of the eTPU system. However, even with no other eTPU activity, this time cannot be reduced to less than 10 CPU clock cycles.

Software Considerations in eTPU Function Design

Simple functions like the PWM do not require an eTPU. By simply reloading a down counter, the hardware can sustain a PWM without service by a programmed engine. Suppose however that the user wants not just a PWM, but a PWM implemented sine wave modulated by a feedback signal. For example, the channel could produce a 40 kHz PWM waveform that is modulated by a 400 Hz sine wave whose amplitude is driven by a control loop parameter. A low-pass filter and amplifier would be all that was required to reproduce the desired 400 Hz signal. This means that the duty cycle of each period would be determined by a sine value multiplied by an externally determined amplitude.

While a special piece of hardware could be designed to implement this function, the eTPU can handle it quite well in software. The complete details of such a system are beyond the scope of this application note, but it is instructive to look at the optimal design strategy. The engine in the eTPU could be given the following equation:

```
HighTime = (Amp * sin(2π*PulseNumber/(PWM_frequency/
Modulation_frequency)))/MaxAmp
```

This works on a spreadsheet, and, given a floating point and trig library, the compiler could produce code for it. However, no sensible designer would write the algorithm in this way. The correct design approach is to look through the requirement to the CPU executing the code and then to design an optimal algorithm within the constraints of the system.

There are three hard limits on the eTPU execution engine: program space, data store, and time. Various methods can be used to trade off among these three, and the strategy adopted for this must be dictated by the particular system design. However, there is nothing to be gained from unused program or data memory, while every cycle wasted will affect the performance of all of the eTPU functions. Execution time then should be the primary focus for algorithm optimization. If the sine function in the above example could be provided in a lookup table and there is room for the table in the memory, the savings in code space and execution time will be significant.

The strategy used to husband these resources must be dictated by the application, but a few guidelines will help to plan a successful design.

- Make conservative decisions in partitioning the function between the host and the eTPU. If an operation can be placed in either machine, put it in the host. For example, if the requirement is to return the frequency of an input waveform, the eTPU can simply measure the period and make that value available to the host. Since the frequency is a scaled reciprocal of the period and since it is trivial to do the math using the more powerful processor, the host should perform the calculation. Partitioning the calculation into the eTPU would increase the execution time in the eTPU and would require a parameter to store the value.

- Design the applications programmers interface (API) as part of the eTPU function. An eTPU function cannot be considered complete without the means to initialize and exchange data with the host. Remember that the eTPU is a 24-bit processor while the host and memory system is organized around 32 bits.

- Use 24-bit data types if possible, particularly when indirectly referenced. The eTPU does not have a byte-size addressing mode. Significant code is generated by the compiler to de-reference byte pointers. An array of (int24) words will take up more data memory but save significant program space and execution time. Note, however, that the machine can handle arrays of bits quite efficiently.

- Remember that the eTPU data memory can be read by the host in two locations. One of these locations returns the 24-bit data automatically sign extended. Accesses by the host to these addresses will not affect the upper eight bits of the parameter. Using this alternate address space can simplify parameter passing between eTPU and host.

- Reconsider the use of nested subroutines. The eTPU has a single return address register and must store off the value the when a second call is made.

- Use the library functions where possible. They have been designed to balance proper operation with minimum code size. But note that source code changes in a library, particularly those that reduce the code size, may have undesirable side effects. Proceed only if you understand the consequences.

- Reconsider parameter-driven channel configurations. The TPU had a convenient instruction: *config := p*. The eTPU does not an equivalent instruction, mainly because the channel configuration options are much more numerous than in the TPU. If you need the option to invert your pulse from high going to low going, implement that option. However replicating the original *config* subinstruction in the eTPU has been found to be expensive.

- Be careful when using dynamic local variables (at least in the current version of the compiler, which is 1.3). A problem arises when the function is instantiated on both eTPU engines. The compiler will allocate an absolute address for these variables, and if one instance of the function is running on each engine simultaneously, there is a possible collision in accessing the variable and consequent corruption of the data. At this time the only work-around for such functions is to declare all local variables as *static*. A compiler extension that will correct this problem is currently being reviewed.

- Note that another compiler extension—one that will allow variables to be scoped by groups of functions—is under construction. When a user groups several channels in order to perform one coordinated function on several pins, for example an H-driver, and then instantiates a number of these groups, the "C" language does not provide a convenient scoping for the variables local to a group. The Byte Craft eTPU_C Compiler will provide an extension to handle this situation. Details of the extension will be provided in a later note.

- Remember that whenever a thread is entered or the **CHAN** register is written by the eTPU code, the **ERT_A** and **ERT_B** registers are updated from the channel capture registers. Since these registers are also used to read and write the match registers, the user should take care in all accesses of the channel's match and capture registers.

- Optimize your source. The compiler has a sophisticated system of optimizers, but it cannot always rewrite inefficiently written code. We will try to provide specific examples of this in a separate application note.

Third-Party Tools for eTPU Function Development

A "C" compiler for the eTPU, eTPU_C, is available from Byte Craft Limited of Waterloo, Ontario. Byte Craft Limited has posted and maintains a web page with frequently asked questions (FAQ) which can be a valuable resource for eTPU users. The URL for the FAQ is: www.bytecraft.com/public/etpuc/downloads/etpuc_faq.chm

The "C" compiler is designed to be compliant with a proposed *ISO Standard for "C" for Embedded Systems*. This new "C" language introduces significant new features that have been found to be vital in programming the eTPU. The new language, as well as the eTPU itself, have inspired a number of important compiler advances found in the Byte Craft Limited product.

- The Compiler passes information to the host processor, thereby allowing a one-step make process that effectively links the eTPU functions to the host code. The information passing is enabled through a number of post-processing macros available in the Compiler. Details of these macros will be described in a future application note.

- The host compiler and linker do not require special features to use the eTPU information. Information is provided in "C"-compatible files, and the subsequent compilation of the host project can provide all the information for code passing and reference resolution.

- The compiler compiles directly to eTPU microcode, often producing one microcode instruction for multiple source instructions.

- The mapping of entry addresses for service requests from the host or the channel hardware is compiled from "C" statements in the eTPU source.

- The new coding standard allows direct access to registers and other resources in the eTPU engine, enabling the user to write "assembly C," which provides the data flow analysis of a compiler in a low level, assembly-like language.

Further information on the eTPU_C Compiler can be obtained from Byte Craft Limited at www.bytecraft.com.

A simulator for the eTPU is available from ASH WARE Inc. of Beaverton, Oregon. ASH WARE has extensive experience with simulation for the TPU and cooperated during the development of the silicon by co-validating the Simulator. Most experienced users find that the ASH WARE eTPU Stand-alone Simulator is the best way to develop their initial eTPU software. When systems require tight coupling of the eTPU and the CPU, a full-system Simulator is also available for later stages of the project.

When a function under development is simulated on ASH WARE's eTPU Stand-Alone Simulator, the Simulator script files take the place of the host CPU. The Simulator is a powerful development tool that is seldom used to its fullest capacity. However, after an hour or two in an eTPU programming class, most users become sufficiently proficient to analyze and debug common designs. Some of the more useful features of the Simulator are listed below.

- Setting up one or more channels using commands similar to your host code. This includes interconnecting channels of the eTPU to test more complex systems.
- Providing external input pin stimuli through a script file. The pin transition can be timed to simulate a number of external inputs and can be interleaved with "host" operations in the script file.
- Displaying output pin action against time in a logic analyzer window. Hint: if you are having trouble finding your output signal, try checking the "Auto Scroll" button.
- Reading and modifying memory and watching source symbolic values.
- Breakpointing the script or the code of any function.
- Reading or modifying the contents of internal registers.
- Stepping through the code by instruction, source line, or thread.
- Tracing through recent history cycle by cycle.
- Post processing performance analysis.
- Automated testing.

For further information about this tool or the eTPU programming class, please contact ASH WARE at www.ashware.com.

Summary

The eTPU is a very powerful device, more complicated and with many more dimensions than a CPU. Its unique channel design allows the processing engine to meet the drive requirements of practically any physical control system. However, with this power comes a complexity that can be daunting to the new user. This note was intended to suggest some steps for a successful design approach and to point out possible traps and pitfalls in eTPU systems design. The advice is drawn from experience with real systems.[3]

Host Interface Application Note

This application note[1] shows how to build the host interface to access eTPU functions. The eTPU PWM driver is used as an example to illustrate what the host need to do to configure the eTPU module and channel and initialize the function. This note also describes how to export eTPU software information to the host compiler. Both the host and the eTPU code are provided in this appendix.

Introduction

The eTPU is the new generation of Time Processing Unit (TPU) by Freescale Semiconductor. Besides hardware enhancements, significant improvements have been made to the accompanying software development tools. These tools make the eTPU much easier to program. First, the eTPU_C Compiler from Byte Craft Limited allows the user to program the eTPU in "C" rather than microcode. Although the programmer will always need to have a clear understanding of how the eTPU hardware works in order to program effectively, nevertheless with the eTPU_C Compiler the programmer can focus more on application logic, leaving the mechanics (such as register usage and tracking, parameter packing, microinstruction packing) to the compiler. Second, ASH WARE Inc.'s eTPU Stand-Alone Simulator and eTPU Debugger allow eTPU code to be developed much like the software for the host CPU. Productivity is significantly increased.

---

1. This application note was written by Ming Li from Freescale Semiconductor Inc. It has been adapted for inclusion in this book.

The eTPU_C Compiler changes the way the host interfaces to the eTPU functions. With the help of the compiler, the same symbol can be referenced by both eTPU and host software. The host software can interface with eTPU functions via API functions instead of accessing physical memory locations and registers. For each eTPU function, a host interface API function can now be developed as a part of the eTPU "C" program. The host application can call these API functions to interface with the eTPU. The references to these API functions and symbols for parameters are resolved at compile time. The implementation details of the eTPU functions are hidden from the host application. This design improves the flexibility of the eTPU functions' implementation and the portability of the host application code. This application note discusses how to build the host interface for eTPU functions.

Overview

Host interface software adds another layer of abstraction between the host CPU and eTPU. The host interface API functions hide the complexity of the interaction between the host CPU and eTPU, providing a simple interface for host applications. Ideally, every eTPU function will have one or more host interface API functions.

The interface software between host and eTPU facilitates three major tasks:

1. eTPU hardware initialization, which configures eTPU peripheral hardware

2. eTPU function initialization, which passes initial parameters and initiates function execution

3. eTPU function run-time interactive control, which updates function parameters and handles hand shaking

Once the eTPU peripheral hardware and the eTPU functions are initialized, each eTPU function can start to execute with initial function parameters. The host interface API functions need to be provided for interactive control (i.e., parameters updating and control mode changing, etc.). To update the parameter or change the control mode, the host is responsible for passing updated parameters to the eTPU functions, and then informing the eTPU that the function parameters have changed. If a coherent change of function parameters is required, the logic has to be built into the eTPU functions in order to ensure coherency. For some eTPU functions, the interaction between host and eTPU is an essential part of the operation. In both host and eTPU software, the logic is needed to handle the handshaking between host and eTPU. The interaction between the eTPU and host can be encapsulated in the host interface API functions.

The host code and eTPU code are compiled by different compilers. The host compiler is normally used to build a single code image for both host and eTPU. In order to build eTPU code and host code together, the eTPU software building information (i.e., the eTPU code image) has to be exported to the host compiler. The symbol information has to be exported from eTPU compiler to the host compiler as well. In the eTPU_C Compiler, the mechanism is implemented as a set of host interface macros. These macros are inserted in the eTPU code to generate proper executable and symbol information for the host compiler. Further, several types of information are exported from eTPU_C through host interface files, generated from `#pragma write` statements during compilation. For detailed information on `#pragma write`, see the eTPU_C documentation.

The host interface design process will be illustrated in the eTPU PWM driver example in the Appendices.

eTPU and Host Interface Hardware

The host interface hardware for the eTPU is shown in Table F.1. The host and eTPU can communicate to each other via event or data.

The host has access to all eTPU host interface registers. When the host wants the eTPU's services, it can issue the host service request (HSR) by writing to a eTPU channel control registers (**eTPUCxCR**). Once the host service request is acknowledged, a thread of eTPU code associated with this HSR is activated for execution. The eTPU code in the thread implements the functions requested by the host. When eTPU needs the host service, it can issue an interrupt request or DMA data transfer request or generate a global exception. Event handling logic is needed in the host software to provide services to the eTPU corresponding to these requests.

The eTPU code memory (SCM) and data memory (SPRAM) are accessible by both host and eTPU. eTPU code memory stores the eTPU executable binary image. At power-up initialization, following the defined sequences, the host transfers the eTPU code that is stored in flash memory to the SCM. During execution, the eTPU microengine fetches the microinstructions from SCM.

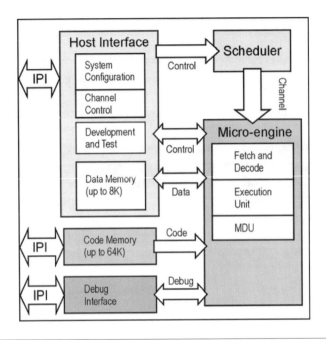

Figure F.1 eTPU Host Interface Hardware

The eTPU data memory is implemented by using tri-port RAM. It provides for data sharing between the host and eTPU engine (or among the host and eTPU engines in the case of a dual-engine implementation). Both host and eTPU can read and write the eTPU data memory in any data size (8 bit, 16 bit, 24 bit, and 32 bit). Since the eTPU data bus is 24 bits wide, it is best to pack a data word with an 8-bit value and a 24-bit value together to reduce data memory utilization. To reduce the overhead of packing and unpacking the data, a virtual mirror memory space of the normal eTPU data memory has been created. The virtual memory space is referred as *parameter sign extension* (PSE) memory space. When the host reads the 32-bit data from the PSE memory space, it will return the sign-extended 24-bit data. The conversion is needed if the 24-bit data is unsigned. Similarly, when the host writes the 32 bit data to the PSE memory space, only the 3 least-significant bytes will be written to the eTPU data memory. The most significant byte is untouched.

Host Interface Software

The function partition between the application software and low-level driver is defined during the software architecture design. To make the software portable, the application software is normally designed to interface with the low-level driver via abstracted interface APIs. The host interface of eTPU functions should be designed so that the implementation of the low level-driver is hidden from the application software.

Once the application software interface to the low-level driver is defined, the functionality of the low-level driver can be partitioned between host CPU and eTPU. The eTPU interface software running on the host CPU is an integral part of the low-level driver. It handles the details of the interaction between host and eTPU.

An example of application software and low-level driver partition is shown in Code Example 1.

Initialization

eTPU initialization process is accomplished by both host CPU and eTPU. During the initialization, the functional partition between host CPU and eTPU is as follows:

- Host responsibility
    a. Initializing the eTPU module
    b. Configuring the eTPU channels
    c. Providing initial eTPU function parameters
    d. Initiating the eTPU function execution
- eTPU responsibility
    a. Responding to the HSR
    b. Transitioning into the initialization state

The eTPU initialization can be broken down into three steps: eTPU module initialization, eTPU channel initialization and eTPU function initialization. The following sections discuss the interface design and the data exchange between host CPU and eTPU for each step of initialization.

eTPU Module Initialization

At the power up, the eTPU peripheral hardware is configured by the host. The eTPU peripheral hardware properly before the eTPU function can be executed. The eTPU module initialization include following steps:

1. 1.Initialize eTPU global registers
   - eTPU MISC Compare Register (**ETPUMISCCMPR**)
   - eTPU Module Configuration Register (**ETPUMCR**)
   - eTPU Time Base Configuration Register (**ETPUTBCR**)
   - eTPU STAC Bus Configuration Register (**ETPUSTACR**)
   - eTPU Engine Configuration Register (**ETPUECR**)
2. Load eTPU code from flash memory to eTPU code RAM
3. Copy initial values of eTPU code global variables to eTPU data memory

Most of the information required to configure the eTPU global registers are not dependent on the eTPU software implementation (i.e., time base, clock frequency, entry table address etc.). The configuration information is determined during the host peripheral configuration and resource allocation. Only the **MISC** value depends on the actual eTPU software implementation: it has to be exported to the host program after the eTPU code is compiled. The eTPU_C Compiler provides a macro (`::ETPUmisc`) to calculate the MISC value of the eTPU code image (see Code Example 3).

The eTPU code image is generated when the eTPU C program is compiled. To use this code in the host program, the eTPU code image can be exported as an array of constant values. The eTPU_C Compiler provides a macro (`::ETPUcode`) to generate and export the eTPU code image (refer to Code Example 3). The eTPU code image constant array is suitable to be included in the host source code. The host compiler locates the eTPU code image array in the flash memory at host source code compile time. Since the eTPU microengine can fetch microinstructions only out of eTPU code memory (SCM), the eTPU code image has to be loaded to SCM at during power-up initialization.

As it is in the standard "C" syntax, when the eTPU code is compiled, the global variables are allocated to the eTPU data memory and the initial values are assigned to the corresponding memory locations. The standard "C" syntax requires that all global variables are declared outside of any function. For the eTPU, this means that all global variables have to be declared outside of any execution thread. Since only the code in a thread can be executed by the eTPU microengine, the global variable cannot be initialized in the eTPU code. They have to be initialized by the host. Software statements have to be added to the host code to initialize the eTPU global variables. The initialization values have to be exported from the eTPU compiler to host compiler. The eTPU_C Compiler provides a macro (`::ETPUglobalimage`) to capture initial values for all global variables and export them as a constant array (see Code Example 4). At power up initialization, the global variables' initial values are loaded into SPRAM.

Host interface macros have to be added to the eTPU code in `#pragma write` statements to export the eTPU software information to the host compiler (see Code Example 3). These statements will generate header files that contain the **MISC** value, eTPU code image, and global variable memory image (Code Example 4).

The software for the eTPU module initialization can be encapsulated in an API function. An example of the eTPU module initialization function implementation is provided in Code Example 6 *(mc_etpu_init())*.

eTPU Channel Initialization

After the eTPU module is configured, each channel on the eTPU module can be configured. eTPU channel initialization includes the following tasks:

1. eTPU channel configuration registers initialization
   a. Assign eTPU function to a channel
   b. Set up channel priority
   c. Configure interrupt/DMA/output enable
   d. Select eTPU function entry table encoding
   e. Assign the function frame to a channel
2. eTPU channel status control register initialization
   a. Set up eTPU function mode

The eTPU channel assignment and the channel priority determination is a part of the host software architecture design. They are independent of the eTPU functions implementation. The information for the configuration is provided by the host software design.

During the channel initialization, a section of SPRAM is assigned to each channel. This memory section is called the *function frame*. The function frame contains all the function parameters and static local variables used by the eTPU function. The starting address of the function frame is assigned to the channel at initialization. The function frame assignment can be static or dynamic. Dynamic allocation assigns the function frame to the channel based on the next available memory space. The availability of the eTPU data memory depends on the number of functions that have been assigned and the number of parameters the function is using. Dynamic allocation can reduce the eTPU data memory consumption by minimizing unused memory "holes." To allocate the function frame dynamically, the host needs to know (`::ETPUram`) to report the number of parameters and static local variables used by a function at compile time (see Code Example 3).

The eTPU function table entry encoding, interrupt enable, DMA enable, output enable, output polarity, and function mode are constants specific to the eTPU function software implementation. It is a good practice to define them only once in the eTPU code and export the configuration information at compile time.

Once the host interface macros are added to the eTPU code (see Code Example 3), the #pragma write statements will generate a header file that contains all the eTPU function configuration and software symbol information at compile time (see Code Example 5). The header file can be included in the host interface code to resolve symbol references.

eTPU Function Initialization
The eTPU function initialization is the last step of the eTPU initialization process. During the eTPU function initialization, the host is responsible for passing the parameters to the eTPU functions and initiating the eTPU function execution by issuing a host service request. Once the host service request for initialization is recognized, the eTPU will transition to the initialization state.

Unlike in the host CPU, the eTPU function parameters passed from host are not placed on the stack. Instead, memory in the *function frame* is allocated to accommodate every function parameter. The host passes the eTPU function parameters by writing directly to the eTPU function frame. The host needs to know the function frame for each channel, as well as the data type and address offset for every parameter. The function frame can be obtained by reading the eTPU channel base address register. The eTPU_C compiler provides the host interface macros to export the offset of each function parameter; use them in `#pragma write` directives to export this information.

The function parameters can be 8 bit, 16 bit or 32 bit. The eTPU compiler can allocate function parameters at 8, 16, 24 or 32 bit boundaries. To pass 8 bit or 16 bit parameters, the host can directly write to eTPU data memory.

Most eTPU data registers and timers are 24 bits wide. To pass 24-bit eTPU function parameters, the host needs to pass a 32-bit parameter to the eTPU. Since the host cannot access eTPU data memory on the 24-bit boundary, the host code needs to realign the parameter to the 32-bit address boundary before writing it to the *function frame*. It is the responsibility of the host to ensure that the function parameters are within proper range. It is also responsibility of the host to ensure, when writing the 24-bit parameter, that the upper byte on the *function frame* is not corrupted. Similarly, when reading a 24-bit return value from the function frame, the host code has to mask of the upper byte before returning the correct 24-bit value. To simplify the interface code, it is recommended to access the 24-bit function parameter by using PSE memory space. An example of the eTPU function initialization is listed in Code Example 7 *(etpu_pwm_init())*.

eTPU and Host Interactive Control

Once the eTPU function is initialized, it will start execution based on the initial parameters and input/output conditions. The eTPU function can provide the API for the host application code to update the function parameter or change the control mode. Similarly, the host software has to provide proper logic to handle the eTPU interrupt or DMA requests.

The software to handle the host and eTPU interaction has to cross between two different compilers. When the host initiates the eTPU function, the data flows from host to eTPU. This behavior is the same as the call by value protocol in the standard C syntax. Sometimes call by reference is desired to access eTPU function internal variables. Since the data flow for call by reference has to cross both compilers, it is not directly supported by the compilers. However, the behavior of the call by reference can be implemented in the host interface software. The host interface software can pass a reference to the API function to access the eTPU function internal variables. An example of the call by reference implementation is shown in both Code Example 1 and Code Example 7 *(etpu_pwm_getStartTime())*.

Some eTPU functions require host or DMA service. The eTPU software can write the **CIRC** bits in the channel interrupt and data transfer request register to send the request to the host or DMA. The interrupt service routine has to be added, and the DMA channel to has to be configured in the host code to respond to the eTPU request.

The host interface software has to provide functions to update eTPU function parameters or change the control mode during the normal operation. Similar to the function initialization API, the interface API function needs to check the validity of the parameters, write them to the eTPU data memory, and then issue the host service request to inform eTPU that the parameters are newly updated. An example of the update PWM function parameter is shown in Code Example 7 *(etpu_pwm_update())*.

Software Integration

The eTPU code and host CPU code are compiled and linked separately. The eTPU code needs to be built first in order to generate and export the eTPU code image and parameter symbol information, as shown in Code Example 4 and Code Example 5. The host code needs to include these files properly to resolve all the symbol reference between eTPU and host code. This software build dependency can be easily added to the makefile to ensure the proper sequence.

Conclusion

The benefit of the host interface design is to isolate any hardware dependency from the application software by means of the host interface API functions. In the eTPU host interface design, all the interactions between host and eTPU are encapsulated in the interface API functions. With this interface design, the implementation of the low-level driver can be hidden from the host application. In the PWM example, the application software interfaces to a generic PWM driver with two control parameters, period and duty cycle. When the eTPU implementation of the PWM is changed, the host application software does not need to change. For the host application software, it does not make any difference if the low-level PWM driver is implemented by using a general purpose discrete output, eMIOS timer channel or eTPU channel.[2]

Code Example 1: main.c

```
#include "etpu_image.h"
#include "etpu_PWMControl.h"


/*******************************************************************************
* FUNCTION: main                                                              *
* PURPOSE:  This function is the entry point of the host PWM application. The   *
*           main function initializes the eTPU to execute PWM function. Once the *
*     eTPU PWM function is initialized, the main function calls the API   *
*           function periodically to update the PWM function parameters.      *
*******************************************************************************/
void main(void)
```

```
{
    unsigned long DutyCycle_host = 0x200000;
    uint16_t delay_counter;
    uint32_t pulseStartTime;

    /* init device */
    init_error = etpu_init();

    /* main user code goes here */
    while(1)
    {
        for (delay_counter=0; delay_counter <= 0x0FEE; delay_counter++)
        {}

        if (DutyCycle_Host == 0x800000)
            DutyCycle_Host = 0x400000;
```

```
        else
            DutyCycle_Host = 0x800000;

        etpu_pwm_update(PWM0, 4000, DutyCycle_Host);

        etpu_pwm_getPulseTime(PWM0, &pulseStartTime);
    }
}
/*******************************************************************************
* FUNCTION: etpu_init                                                          *
* PURPOSE:  This host function initializes eTPU module and configures each eTPU *
*           channel. The eTPU PWM functions initialization APIs are called to   *
*           initiate eTPU function execution.                                   *
*******************************************************************************/
int16_t etpu_init ()
{
    int16_t error_code;
    uint32_t chanConfigParam = 0;

    /* initialize eTPU hardware */
    mc_etpu_init(etpu_config_A, (uint32_t *)etpu_code,(uint8_t)ETPU_CODE_RAM_SIZE,
            (uint32_t *)etpu_globals);

    /* initialize eTPU channels */
    chanConfigParam = (ETPU_PWM_INT_REQ | ETPU_PWM_DMA_REQ | ETPU_PWM_OUT_DISABLE |
\
            (ETPU_PWM_TABLE_SELECT << 24) | (PWM0_CHAN_PRIORITY << 28));

    mc_etpu_chan_init(PWM0, ETPU_PWM_FUNCTION_NUMBER, ETPU_PWM_FUNC_MODE, \
                    ETPU_PWM_NUM_PARMS, chanConfigParam, AUTO_FUNC_FRAME);

    /* initialize eTPU functions */
    etpu_pwm_init(PWM0, 4000, DutyCycle_Host);
```

```
    /* enable all timebases */
    mc_mpc5500_timer_start();


    return (0);
```

Code Example 2: etpu_PWMControl.h

```
/*------------------------------------------------------------------+
|                      Include Header Files                         |
+------------------------------------------------------------------*/
#include "mpc5554.h"        //mpc5554 register definitions.
#include "mpc5500_util.h"   //useful utility routines.
#include "etpu_image.h"


/*------------------------------------------------------------------+
|                      Constants Definition                         |
+------------------------------------------------------------------*/
/* define functions to channels */
#define PWM0   0
#define PWM0_CHAN_PRIORITY3

#define ETPU_ENTRY_TABLE 0x0      // eTPU entry table address

struct etpu_config_t etpu_config_A = {
    ETPU_MISC_ENABLE,    //MCR register
    ETPU_MISC_VAL,             //MISC value from eTPU compiler link file

    //Configure eTPU engine A
    ETPU_FILTER_CLOCK_DIV8 +
    ETPU_CHAN_FILTER_3SAMPLE +
    ETPU_ENTRY_TABLE,

    //Configure eTPU engine A timebases
    ETPU_TCR2CTL_DIV8 + ( 7 << 16) +     //TCR2 prescaler of 8 (7+1)
```

```
    ETPU_TCR1CTL_DIV2 + 3,                  //TCR1 prescaler of 4 (3+1)
    0,


    //Configure eTPU engine b
    ETPU_FILTER_CLOCK_DIV4 +
    ETPU_CHAN_FILTER_3SAMPLE +
    ETPU_ENTRY_TABLE,


    //Configure eTPU engine B timebases
    ETPU_TCR2CTL_DIV8 + ( 7 << 16) +       //TCR2 prescaler of 8 (7+1)
    ETPU_TCR1CTL_DIV2 + 3,
    0

};
```

Code Example 3: etpuc_pwm.c

```c
#include <etpuc_PWM.h>

/*-------------------------------------------------------------------+
|                   Global Variable Definitions                      |
+-------------------------------------------------------------------*/
int DutyCycle = 500;


/*******************************************************************************
* FUNCTION: PWM                                                               *
* PURPOSE:  This is the eTPU function that modulate an eTPU output pin as PWM  *
*           signal based on the host service request and the parameters passed *
*           from the host.                                                    *
*                                                                             *
* INPUTS NOTES: This function has 2 parameters                                *
* RETURNS NOTES: N/A                                                          *
*                                                                             *
* WARNING:                                                                    *
```

```
    ****************************************************************************/

void PWM(int Period, unsigned fract24 Duty)
{
    static int StartTimeHi;

    int HighTime;

    if (hsr == hsrInitPWM)    // Init PWM HSR -- Required to initialize the signal.
    {
    InitPWM:
        SetChannelMode(em_nb_dt);
        SetupMatch_B(tcr1, Mtcr1_Ctcr1_ge, low_high); //set output high
immediately
    }
    else if (matchA_transB)   // Here on Match1 (falling edge)
    {
    FallingMatch:
        ClearMatchALatch();
        SetupMatch_B((StartTimeHi + Period), Mtcr1_Ctcr1_ge, low_high); //set up
for rising match

    }
    else if (matchB_transA)    // Here on Match2 (rising edge)
    {
    RisingMatch:
        ClearMatchBLatch();

        StartTimeHi = GetCapRegB();    // Store the time the pulse transition to
high

        if (Duty == 0xffffff) // Special case for 100% modulation
        {
            HighTime = 32 ;   // arbitrary value having no efect on the output
```

```
signal
            SetupMatch_A(HighTime, Mtcr1_Ctcr1_ge, match_no_change);
        }
        else
        {
            HighTime = Period * Duty + StartTimeHi;
            SetupMatch_A(HighTime, Mtcr1_Ctcr1_ge, high_low);     //setup for
falling match
        }
    }
    else
    {
        //This else statement is used to catch all unspecified entery table
conditions
    }
}


#pragma endlibrary;
```

/* Information exported to Host CPU program */

```
#pragma write h, (::ETPUfilename (etpu_pwm_auto.h));
#pragma write h, (/* WARNING this file is automatically generated DO NOT EDIT IT!
*/);
#pragma write h, ( );
#pragma write h, (::ETPUliteral(#ifndef __ETPU_PWM_AUTO_H));
#pragma write h, (::ETPUliteral(#define __ETPU_PWM_AUTO_H));
#pragma write h, ( );

#pragma write h, (/* Function Configuration Information */);
#pragma write h, (::ETPUliteral(#define ETPU_PWM_FUNCTION_NUMBER)
PWM_FUNCTION_NUMBER );
#pragma write h, (::ETPUliteral(#define ETPU_PWM_TABLE_SELECT) ::ETPUentrytype(PWM)
```

```
);
#pragma write h, (::ETPUliteral(#define ETPU_PWM_NUM_PARMS) ::ETPUram(PWM) );
#pragma write h, ( );
#pragma write h, (::ETPUliteral(#define ETPU_PWM_INT_ENABLE) PWM_INT_ENABLE );
#pragma write h, (::ETPUliteral(#define ETPU_PWM_DMA_ENABLE) PWM_DMA_ENABLE );
#pragma write h, ( );

#pragma write h, (::ETPUliteral(#define ETPU_PWM_OUT_DIS) PWM_OUT_DISABLE );
#pragma write h, (::ETPUliteral(#define ETPU_PWM_FUNC_MODE) PWM_FUNCTION_MODE );
#pragma write h, ( );

#pragma write h, (/* Host Service Request Definitions */);
#pragma write h, (::ETPUliteral(#define ETPU_PWM_INIT) hsrInitPWM );
#pragma write h, (::ETPUliteral(#define ETPU_PWM_UPDATE) hsrUpdtPWM );
#pragma write h, ( );

#pragma write h, (/* Parameter Definitions */);
#pragma write h, (::ETPUliteral(#define ETPU_PWM_PERIOD_OFFSET)
((::ETPUlocation(PWM,Period)-
                1)/4));
#pragma write h, (::ETPUliteral(#define ETPU_PWM_DUTY_OFFSET) (::ETPUlocation(PWM,
Duty)-1)/4 );
#pragma write h, ( );

#pragma write h, (::ETPUliteral(#endif /*__ETPU_PWM_AUTO_H */ ));

/* Information exported to Host CPU program */
#pragma write m, (::ETPUfilename (etpu_image.h));
#pragma write m, (/* WARNING this file is automatically generated DO NOT EDIT IT!
*/);
#pragma write m, ( );

#pragma write m, (::ETPUliteral(#ifndef __ETPU_IMAGE_H));
#pragma write m, (::ETPUliteral(#define __ETPU_IMAGE_H));
```

```
#pragma write m, ( );

#pragma write m, (/* eTPU Code RAM Constants Definitions */);
#pragma write m, (::ETPUliteral(#define ETPU_CODE_RAM_SIZE) ETPU_CODE_IMAGE_SIZE);
#pragma write m, (::ETPUliteral(#define ETPU_MISC_VAL) ::ETPUmisc);
#pragma write m, ( );

/* Global const initialization array */
#pragma write m, ( const uint32_t etpu_globals[]= { ::ETPUglobalimage32 };);
#pragma write m, ( );

/* This is an example of a code as a constant array */
#pragma write m, ( const uint32_t etpu_code[]= { ::ETPUcode32 };);
#pragma write m, ( );



#pragma write m, (/* End of eTPU Code Image */);

#pragma write m, (::ETPUliteral(#endif /*__ETPU_IMAGE_H */ ));
```

Code Example 4: etpuc_image.h

```
/* WARNING this file is automatically generated DO NOT EDIT IT! */

#ifndef __ETPU_IMAGE_H
#define __ETPU_IMAGE_H

/* eTPU Code RAM Constants Definitions */
#define ETPU_CODE_RAM_SIZE 2
#define ETPU_MISC 0x0EF38A79

const uint32_t etpu_globals[]= { 0x000001F4,0x00000000 };

const uint32_t etpu_code[]= { 0x4FFFFFE7,0x3BFC3FF4,0x4F3F0F9F,0xF73FFCFB,
```

0xDFEF7A80,0xBFE80A82,0x3B193FF4,0x4F3F0F9F,
0xF73FFCFB,0x7FF37FBB,0xBFFFFB82,0xBFEFFB81,
0x1FFFFFEC,0x3838FFF4,0xF0C0029F,0x1C8F5F96,
0x3BF42FF4,0x48F0FE7F,0xFF3FFCFB,0xF7C003DF,
0xBFEFFB80,0xBFE80A81,0x3B190FE9,0xF34802FF,
0x3BF70FB4,0xBFEFFB82,0x3B195FD4,0x3BF42FF4,
0x4AF0FE7F,0xFF3FFCFB,0x6FFFFFFF,0x6FFFFFFF,
0x00000000,0x00000000,0x00000000,0x00000000,
0x00000000,0x00000000,0x00000000,0x00000000,
0x00000000,0x00000000,0x00000000,0x00000000,
0x00000000,0x00000000,0x00000000,0x00000000,
0x00000000,0x00000000,0x00000000,0x00000000,
0x00000000,0x00000000,0x00000000,0x00000000,
0x00000000,0x00000000,0x00000000,0x00000000,
0x00000000,0x00000000,0x00000000,0x00000000,
0x00000000,0x00000000,0x00000000,0x00000000,
0x00000000,0x00000000,0x00000000,0x00000000,
0x00000000,0x00000000,0x00000000,0x00000000,
0x00000000,0x00000000,0x00000000,0x00000000,
0x40004000,0x40004000,0xC01FC01F,0xC01FC01F,
0xC01FC01F,0x40044004,0x40094009,0x40094009,
0x40044004,0x40044004,0x40044004,0x40044004,
0xC01FC01F,0xC01FC01F,0x40094009,0x40044004,
0x00000000,0x00000000,0x00000000,0x00000000,
0x00000000,0x00000000,0x00000000,0x00000000,
0x00000000,0x00000000,0x00000000,0x00000000,
0x00000000,0x00000000,0x00000000,0x00000000,
0x00000000,0x00000000,0x00000000,0x00000000,
0x00000000,0x00000000,0x00000000,0x00000000,
0x00000000,0x00000000,0x00000000,0x00000000,
0x00000000,0x00000000,0x00000000,0x00000000,
0x00000000,0x00000000,0x00000000,0x00000000,

......

0x00000000,0x00000000,0x00000000,0x00000000,

```
                           0x00000000,0x00000000,0x00000000,0x00000000,
                           0x00000000
                             };
```

#endif /*__ETPU_IMAGE_H */

Code Example 5: etpu_pwm_auto.h

/* WARNING this file is automatically generated DO NOT EDIT IT! */

#ifndef __ETPU_PWM_AUTO_H
#define __ETPU_PWM_AUTO_H

/* Function Configuration Information */
#define ETPU_PWM_FUNCTION_NUMBER 5
#define ETPU_PWM_TABLE_SELECT 0
#define ETPU_PWM_NUM_PARMS 0x0010

#define ETPU_PWM_INT_ENABLE 0
#define ETPU_PWM_DMA_ENABLE 0

#define ETPU_PWM_OUT_DIS 0
#define ETPU_PWM_FUNC_MODE 0

/* Host Service Request Definitions */
#define ETPU_PWM_INIT 1
#define ETPU_PWM_UPDATE 3

/* Parameter Definitions */
#define ETPU_PWM_PERIOD_OFFSET ((0x0001 - 1)/4)
#define ETPU_PWM_DUTY_OFFSET (0x0005 - 1)/4

/* Global variables image for etpuc_pwm.c*/

```
#endif /*__ETPU_PWM_AUTO_H */
```

Code Example 6: utility.c

```
/*******************************************************************************
* FUNCTION: mc_etpu_init                                                       *
* PURPOSE:   This function initialize the eTPU module including                *
*            1. Initialize global registers                                    *
*            2. Load eTPU code into memory                                     *
*            3. Copy initial values of global variables to data RAM            *
*******************************************************************************/
uint32_t mc_etpu_init(struct etpu_config_t p_etpu_config, uint32_t *code,uint8_t
codesize, uint32_t *globals)
{
    uint32_t *code_end;
    uint32_t unused_code_ram;

    unused_code_ram = (((ETPU.MCR.B.SCMSIZE - 1 ) * 1024) -
(uint32_t)codesize*1024);
    if ( unused_code_ram < 0 )
        return((uint32_t)ETPU_ERROR_CODESIZE);

    /* 1. Initialize global registers */
    ETPU.MISCCMPR.R = p_etpu_config.misc;          //write MISC value before it is
enable in MCR
    ETPU.MCR.R = p_etpu_config.mcr;

    /* Configure Engine 1 */
    ETPU.TBCR_1.R = p_etpu_config.tbcr_1;
    ETPU.STACR_1.R = p_etpu_config.stacr_1;
    ETPU.ECR_1.R = p_etpu_config.ecr_1;

    /* Configure Engine 2 */
    ETPU.TBCR_2.R = p_etpu_config.tbcr_2;
```

```
ETPU.STACR_2.R = p_etpu_config.stacr_2;
ETPU.ECR_2.R = p_etpu_config.ecr_2;


/* load eTPU code */
/* In order to write the eTPU code ram, both eTPU engine has to be stopped. */
/* Stopping eTPU engine can be achieved by set low power stop bit.          */


ETPU.ECR_1.B.MDIS = 1;
ETPU.ECR_2.B.MDIS = 1;


/* enable writing to SCM */
ETPU.MCR.B.VIS = 1;


/* 2. Copy eTPU code */
mc_memcpy32( &CODE_RAM, code, (uint32_t)codesize*1024);


/* disable writing to SCM */
ETPU.MCR.B.VIS = 0;


/* 3. Copy initial global values to parameter RAM. */
mc_memcpy32 ( &DATA_RAM, globals, ETPU_GLOBAL_MEM_SIZE);


/* After writing the eTPU code ram, both eTPU engine has to be re-started.  */
/* Restart eTPU engine can be achieved by clear low power stop bit.         */
ETPU.ECR_1.B.MDIS = 0;
ETPU.ECR_2.B.MDIS = 0;


    return((uint32_t) 0);
}


/***************************************************************************
* FUNCTION: mc_etpu_chan_init                                              *
* PURPOSE:  This function initialize the eTPU channel including            *
*           1. Assign the eTPU function to channel                         *
```

```
*              2. Configure the channel                            *
*              3. Calculate and auto assign function frame         *

**********************************************************************
********/

uint16_t mc_etpu_chan_init(uint8_t channel, uint8_t function, uint8_t mode, \
              uint8_t num_param, uint32_t config, uint16_t func_frame)
{
    if (func_frame == 0)
    {
        func_frame = mc_etpu_malloc(num_param);

        if (func_frame == 0)
        return((uint16_t)ETPU_ERROR_MALLOC);
    }

    ETPU.CHAN[channel].CR.R = config + (function<<16) + (func_frame>>3);

    ETPU.CHAN[channel].SCR.R = mode;

    return(func_frame);
}


/*****************************************************************************
* FUNCTION: mc_etpu_malloc                                                   *
* PURPOSE:  This function calculates the memory space for a eTPU function based *
*           the number and size of the parameter as well as the static local   *
*           variable for a eTPU function. The function returns the address at   *
*           which the next function frame can be assigned.                      *
*****************************************************************************/
uint16_t mc_etpu_malloc(uint16_t num_params)
{
    static uint16_t etpu_pram_used = ETPU_PRAM_START_ADDR;
```

```
    uint16_t next_function_frame = etpu_pram_used;


    //each parameter takes 4 bytes, check if there is enough space available
    if ((etpu_pram_used + num_params<<2) > ETPU_PRAM_SIZE)
    return(0);
    else
    etpu_pram_used += (num_params<<2);


    //Scale the pointer for the function frame
return (next_function_frame);
```

Code Example 7: etpu_pwm.c

```
#include "etpu_constants.h"
#include "etpu_pwm_auto.h"


#define ETPU_PSE_RAM_OFFSET 0x1000


/*******************************************************************************
* FUNCTION: etpu_pwm_init                                                      *
* PURPOSE:  This function executes on the host CPU.                            *
*           The function checks validity for parameters then pass them to      *
*           the eTPU functions. The function issue the host service request to *
*           eTPU PWM function to initiate the execution.                       *
*******************************************************************************/
int etpu_pwm_init(unsigned char channel, unsigned long period, unsigned long duty)
{
  int errorCode = 0;
  unsigned long functFrame = ETPU.CHAN[channel].CR.B.CPBA;
  unsigned long *pba_32 = &DATA_RAM + (functFrame << 1) + ETPU_PSE_RAM_OFFSET;

  // function parameter validity check
  if (period > 0xFFFFFF)
  {
```

```
      errorCode = PARAM_OUT_RANGE;

      period = 0xFFFFFF;

    }


    if (duty > 0xFFFFFF)

    {

      errorCode = PARAM_OUT_RANGE;

      duty = 0xFFFFFF;

    }


// passing function parameter to eTPU function frame

    *(pba_32 + ETPU_PWM_PERIOD_OFFSET) = period;

    *(pba_32 + ETPU_PWM_DUTY_OFFSET) = duty;


//write hsr

    ETPU.CHAN[channel].HSRR.R = ETPU_PWM_INIT;


    return (errorCode);

}


/******************************************************************************
* FUNCTION: etpu_pwm_update                                                  *
* PURPOSE:  This function executes on the host CPU.                          *
*           This function checks validity for parameters then pass them to   *
*           the eTPU functions. The function issue the host service request to *
*           eTPU PWM function to update the function parameters.             *
******************************************************************************/
int etpu_pwm_update(unsigned char channel, unsigned long period, unsigned long
duty)
{
  int errorCode = 0;
  unsigned long functFrame = ETPU.CHAN[channel].CR.B.CPBA;
  unsigned long *pba_32 = &DATA_RAM + (functFrame << 1) + ETPU_PSE_RAM_OFFSET;
```

```
  // function parameter validity check
  if (period > 0xFFFFFF)
  {
    errorCode = PARAM_OUT_RANGE;
    period = 0xFFFFFF;
  }


  if (duty > 0xFFFFFF)
  {
    errorCode = PARAM_OUT_RANGE;

  duty = 0xFFFFFF;
 }

// passing function parameter to eTPU function frame
    *(pba_32 + ETPU_PWM_PERIOD_OFFSET) = period;
    *(pba_32 + ETPU_PWM_DUTY_OFFSET) = duty;


//write hsr
    ETPU.CHAN[channel].HSRR.R = ETPU_PWM_UPDATE;
    return (errorCode);
}


/*******************************************************************************
* FUNCTION  : etpu_pwm_getPulseTime                                           *
* PURPOSE:  This function executes on the host CPU.                           *
*           This function is an application API to read the time stamp of the *
*           begining of the last peroid of the PWM output on the ePTU channel.*
*******************************************************************************/
int16_t etpu_pwm_getPulseTime(uint8_t channel, uint32_t * startTime)
{
  int16_t errorCode = 0;
  uint32_t functFrame = ETPU.CHAN[channel].CR.B.CPBA;
  uint32_t *pba_32 = &DATA_RAM + (functFrame << 1) + ETPU_PSE_RAM_OFFSET;
```

```
    // passing function parameter to eTPU function frame
        *startTime = *(pba_32 + ETPU_PWM_PULSE_TIME_OFFSET);


        return (errorCode);


    }
```

Microinstruction Formats

Figure G.1 shows the set of instruction formats utilized by the eTPU microengine. Recall that there are four types of instructions:

- SPRAM
- Channel configuration and control
- ALU/MDU
- Flow control

The SPRAM and channel configuration and control fields in this figure are described in detail in *Chapter 8. Engine Architecture and Programming Model*. The ALU/MDU and flow control instruction fields, which are arguably less important to know for eTPU programming itself (even debugging), are provided in this appendix, for reference. Descriptions of ALU and MDU flags, on the other hand, are described in *Chapter 8. Engine Architecture and Programming Model*.

Figure G.1 Microinstruction Formats — bit field layout table

format (new)	format (old)	31	30	29	28	27	26	25	24	23	22	21	20	19	18	17	16	15	14	13	12	11	10	9	8	7	6	5	4	3	2	1	0
A1	5C	0 0 0			IMM[15:13]					IMM[23:16]												IMM[12]	RTN/CCS		IMM[11:9]				T2D				IMM[8]	0 0
A2	5B																											ABSE	ABDE		0 1
A3	5D			ALUOPI[4]	CCSV	IMM[7:2]													ALUOPI[3:2]		AS/CE		IMM[1:0]			ALUOPI[1:0]		0	1 0				
A4	5A			FLC[2]																CCS		FLC[1:0]				ABSE	ABDE	1					
B1	1A	1 0	0	SHF						T4ABS				T2ABD							SRC	rsv		CCS	ZRO	AID[7:0] (global param)							
B2	1C		1	END																						AID[6:0] (channel param)							
B3	1D	0 0 0							RW									P/D		CCS	ZRO	STC		ABSE	ABDE	rsv	1 1					
B4	1E	0 0 1	0	CCSV	CIN	BINV	T4BBS												1			SMPR		ABSE	ABDE	ALUOP					
B5	1F								FL									0	SEXT	AS/CE												
B6	1G		1						rsv									SRC													
B7	2	0 1 1	END	SHF					TDL									PSC	MRLA	ERW_A	MRL_B	ERW_B	ABSE	ABDE	CCS	MRLE	PSCS					
C1	3H	0 1 0	0	OPAC_A		OPAC_B				TBS1				TBS2				LSR								PDCM						
C2	3I		1	IPAC_A		IPAC_B																										
D1	3A	1 1 0	0	END	MRLE	rsv		PSC	FLS	RW	PSCS				CIRC	R/D		0	P/D	RSIZ	ZRO	AID[7:0] (global param)							
D2	3C																	1				AID[6:0] (channel param)							
D3	3DE	1 1 1	rsv										FLC				1		STC		1 1	0	0	rsv				
D4	3F								FL								0		rsv	SMPR								
D5	4A	1 1 0	1	END	MRLE	rsv		MTD	rsv	RW	TDL				MRLA	ERW_A	MRL_B	ERW_B	0	P/D	RSIZ	ZRO	AID[7:0] (global param)						
D6	4C																	1				AID[6:0] (channel param)							
D7	4DE	1 1 1	rsv														1		STC		1 1	0	1	rsv				
D8	4F								FL								0		rsv	SMPR								
E1	3G1	1 1 1	rsv	J/C	BCC				RW	BCF			BAF[13:0]									00	P/D	STC				
E2	3G2								FLS												01	AID[2:0]						
E3	3G3								FL												10	rsv	SMPR					
E4	3G4								0												11	1	rsv					
F1	HALT	rsv							1						rsv									111	rsv				

All *rsv* fields are reserved, and must be coded as 1.

Legend:
- Execution Unit Operations
- RAM Input/Output Operations
- Channel Control Operations
- Microengine/Sequence Operations

Figure G.1 Microinstruction Formats

ALU/MDU Instruction Fields

ALU/MDU operations are generally indicated through the ALU operation (**ALUOP**), ALU operation immediate (**ALUOPI**), or shift (**SHF**) instruction fields. In formats that don't contain any of these three fields, the operation performed is always addition (if the B-inversion (**BINV**) field is 0) or subtraction (if **BINV** = 1). Except for some **ALUOPI** operations (see description of the T2 destination (**T2D**) field, below), all ALU and MDU operations require two sources (AS and BS) and one destination (AD). Each source and destination field value has a size associated with it; this size is used to select the flag sample position. Registers that are not 8, 16, or 24 bits are promoted to the next size up (for example, **CHAN[4:0]** is promoted to an 8-bit source.

Note: All microinstructions execute in two system clocks; the microinstruction's execution time of two system clocks is called a *microcycle*. A microcycle is further divided into four timing states: T1, T2, T3, and T4, where T1 and T2 constitute one system clock and T3 and T4 constitute another system clock. The *T2* in **T2D** and **T2ABD** indicates that the destination result of the AU will be driven during T2 of the microcycle. The *T4* in **T4ABS** and **T4BBS** indicates that the A and B buses will be sourced during T4 of the microcycle.

- **ALU Operation (ALUOP)**

  ALUOP is a 5-bit field that indicates the operation to be performed, as shown in Table G.1 (where *AS* refers to the A-bus source and *BS* refers to the B-bus source).

ALUOP	*Operation*	*Comment*
00000	AS mults BS[7:0]	Signed multiplication.
00001	AS multu BS[7:0]	Unsigned multiplication.
00010	AS fmults BS[7:0]	Signed fractional multiplication.
00011	AS fmultu BS[7:0]	Unsigned fractional multiplication.
00100	AS mults BS[15:0]	Singed multiplication.
00101	AS multu BS[15:0]	Unsigned multiplication.
00110	AS fmults BS[15:0]	Signed fractional multiplication.
00111	AS fmultu BS[15:0]	Unsigned fractional multiplication.
01000	AS mults BS[23:0]	Signed multiplication.
01001	AS multu BS[23:0]	Unsigned multiplication.
01010	AS macs BS[23:0]	Signed multiply-accumulate.
01011	AS macu BS[23:0]	Unsigned multiply-accumulate.
01100	AS div BS[7:0]	Unsigned division.
01101	AS div BS[15:0]	Unsigned division.

ALUOP	*Operation*	*Comment*
01110	AS div BS23:0]	Unsigned division.
01111	N/A	Reserved.
10000	AS[23:0] | BS[23:0]	24-bit bitwise OR. When **BINV** = 0, result is AS | (~BS).
10001	AS[23:0] ^ BS[23:0]	24-bit bitwise XOR. When **BINV** = 0, result is AS ^ (~BS).
10010	AS[23:0] & BS[23:0]	24-bit bitwise AND. When **BINV** = 0, result is AS & (~BS).
10011	abs(AS)	Absolute value of AS.
10100	AS + BS	Arithmetic addition.
10101	(AS + BS) shl 1	Arithmetic addition with 1-bit post-ALU shift left (depends on **SHF** value).
10110	(AS + BS) shr 1	Arithmetic addition with 1-bit post-ALU shift right (depends on **SHF** value).
10111	(AS + BS) ror 1	Arithmetic addition with 1-bit post-ALU rotate right (depends on **SHF** value).
11000	AS adc/sbc BS	When **BINV** = 1, addition with **C** flag as carry-in; when **BINV** = 0, subtraction with inverted **C** flag as carry-in.
11001	AS shl (2^(BS[1:0]+1))	AS shifted left: 2 bits for BS=0; 4 for BS=1; 8 for BS=2; 16 for BS=3.
11010	AS shr (2^(BS[1:0]+1))	AS shifted right: 2 bits for BS=0; 4 for BS=1; 8 for BS=2; 16 for BS=3.
11011	AS ror (2^(BS[1:0]+1))	AS shifted rotate right: 2 bits for BS=0; 4 for BS=1; 8 for BS=2; 16 for BS=3.
11100	AS EXCH BS[4:0]	Exchange **C** flag and AS bit as determined by **BS[4:0]**. BS is overridden to 8 bits; that is, the size of BS is considered to be 8 bits regardless of its actual size (BS is not truncated). If **BS[4:0]** resolves to a value greater than 23, no exchange is performed. When an exchange is performed, **CIN** is ignored, **BINV** inverts BS, and the **V** flag is *not* updated.
11101	AS SETB BS[4:0]	Set bit in AS as determined by BS[4:0]. The register that drives AS is not changed unless it is selected as the destination of the operation.
11110	AS CLRB BS[4:0]	Clear bit in AS as determined by BS[4:0]. The register that drives AS is not changed unless it is selected as the destination of the operation.
11111	N/A	Reserved.

Table G.1 ALUOP Instruction Field Settings

- **ALU Operation Immediate (ALUOPI)**

  ALUOPI is a 5-bit field that indicates the operation to be performed with immediate data, as shown in Table G.2 (where *AS* refers to the A-bus source and *BS* refers to the B-bus source).

ALUOPI	*Operation*	*Comment*
00000	AS mults #imm8	Signed multiplication.
00001	AS multu #imm8	Unsigned multiplication.
00010	AS fmults #imm8	Signed fractional multiplication.
00011	AS fmultu #imm8	Unsigned fractional multiplication.
00100	AS div #imm8	Unsigned division.
00101	N/A	Reserved.
00110	N/A	Reserved.
00111	N/A	Reserved.
01000	AD[7:0] = AS[7:0] | #imm8, AD[23:8] = AS[23:8]	Bitwise OR.
01001	AD[7:0] = AS[7:0] ^ #imm8, AD[23:8] = AS[23:8]	Bitwise XOR.
01010	AD[7:0] = AS[7:0] & #imm8, AD[23:8] = AS[23:8]	Bitwise AND.
01011	AD[7:0] = AS[7:0] & #imm8, AD[23:8] = 0x0	Bitwise AND with clear.
01100	AD[15:8] = AS[15:8] | #imm8, AD[23:16] = AS[23:16], AD[7:0] = AS[7:0]	Bitwise OR.
01101	AD[15:8] = AS[15:8] ^ #imm8, AD[23:16] = AS[23:16], AD[7:0] = AS[7:0]	Bitwise XOR.
01110	AD[15:8] = AS[15:8] & #imm8, AD[23:16] = AS[23:16], AD[7:0] = AS[7:0]	Bitwise AND.
01111	AD[15:8] = AS[15:8] & #imm8, AD[23:16] = 0x0, AD[7:0] = 0x0	Bitwise AND with clear.
10000	AD[23:16] = AS[23:16] | #imm8, AD[15:0] = AS[15:0]	Bitwise OR.
10001	AD[23:16] = AS[23:16] ^ #imm8, AD[15:0] = AS[15:0]	Bitwise XOR.

ALUOPI	Operation	Comment
10010	AD[23:16] = AS[23:16] & #imm8, AD[15:0] = AS[15:0]	Bitwise AND.
10011	AD[23:16] = AS[23:16] & #imm8, AD[15:0] = 0x0.	Bitwise AND with clear.
10100	AS + #imm8	Arithmetic addition.
10101	(AS + #imm8) shl 1	Arithmetic addition with 1-bit post-ALU shift left (depends on **SHF** value).
10110	(AS + #imm8) shr 1	Arithmetic addition with 1-bit post-ALU shift right (depends on **SHF** value).
10111	(AS + #imm8) ror 1	Arithmetic addition with 1-bit post-ALU rotate right (depends on **SHF** value).
11000	N/A	Reserved
11001	AS shl $(2^{(\#imm8[1:0]+1)})$	AS shifted left: 2 bits for #imm8=0; 4 for #imm8=1; 8 for #imm8=2; 16 for #imm8=3.
11010	AS shr $(2^{(\#imm8[1:0]+1)})$	AS shifted right: 2 bits for #imm8=0; 4 for #imm8=1; 8 for #imm8=2; 16 for #imm8=3.
11011	AS ror $(2^{(\#imm8[1:0]+1)})$	AS shifted rotate right: 2 bits for #imm8=0; 4 for #imm8=1; 8 for #imm8=2; 16 for #imm8=3.
11100	AS EXCH #imm8[4:0]	Exchange **C** flag and AS bit as determined by #imm8[4:0]. If #imm8[4:0] resolves to a value greater than 23, no exchange is performed. When an exchange is performed, **CIN** is ignored, **BINV** inverts #imm8, and the **V** flag is *not* updated.
11101	N/A	Reserved
11110	N/A	Reserved
11111	N/A	Reserved.

Table G.2 ALUOPI Instruction Field Settings

- **T4 A-Bus Source (T4ABS)**
  T4ABS indicates two possible register sets to be used for the AS. Which of the two is actually used is specified by **ABSE** (or, if **ABSE** is absent, by **T4BBS**).

T4ABS	First Register Set			Second Register Set		
	Register	Size		Register	Size	
0000	AS[7:0] = **P[7:0]**	8		AS[7:0] = 0	8	
0001	AS[7:0] = **P[15:8]**	8		AS[23:0] = **C[23:0]**	24	
0010	AS[7:0] = **P[31:24]**	8		AS[15:0] = **TPR[15:0]**	16	
0011	AS[23:0] = **ERT_B[23:0]**	24		AS[23:0] = **B[23:0]**	24	
0100	AS[23:0] = **D[23:0]**	24		AS[23:0] = **TRR[23:0]**	24	
0101	AS[15:0] = **P[15:0]**	16		AS[7:0] = 0, read_match[a]	8	
0110	AS[15:0] = **P[31:16]**	16		AS[13:0] = **RAR[13:0]**	16	
0111	AS[7:0] = **P[23:16]**	8		AS[23:0] = **MACH[23:0]**	24	
1000	AS[23:0] = **P[23:0]**	24		AS[23:0] = **MACL[23:0]**	24	
1001	AS[23:0] = **A[23:0]**	24		AS[4:0] = **CHAN[4:0]**	8	
1010	AS[23:0] = **SR[23:0]**	24		AS[14:2] = CHAN_BASE[b]	16	
1011	AS[23:0] = **DIOB[23:0]**	24		Reserved.	-	
1100	AS[23:0] = **TCR1[23:0]**	24		Reserved.	-	
1101	AS[23:0] = **TCR2[23:0]**	24		Reserved.	-	
1110	AS[23:0] = **ERT_A[23:0]**	24		Reserved.	-	
1111	AS[23:0] = 0	24		Reserved.	-	

a. In this case the constant 0x00 is used as AS (8-bit size) and the **MatchA** and **MatchB** registers of the selected channel (specified by **CHAN**) are copied to **ERT_A** and **ERT_B**, respectively. Note that an ALU destination can still be chosen by **T2ABD** in which case the ALU destination value overwrites the read value from the match registers.

b. CHAN_BASE is the channel's **CPBA** field *2. For instance, in indirect addressing mode, where the destination register is **DIOB**, CHAN_BASE is loaded into **DIOB[14:2]**, which is the parameter address, and **DIOB[14:0]** represents the byte address.

Table G.3 T4ABS Instruction Field Settings

- **T4 B-Bus Source (T4BBS)**

  This field indicates the B-bus source. When **ABSE** and **ABDE** are not present in an instruction format, **T4BBS** is used to indicate the A-bus source and A-bus destination.

T4BBS	B Source Selection	Register Set for T4ABS (When ABSE/ABDE is Absent)	Register Set for T2ABD (When ABSE/ABDE is Absent)
000	BS[23:0] = **P[23:0]**	First	First
001	BS[23:0] = **A[23:0]**		
010	BS[23:0] = **SR[23:0]**		
011	BS[23:0] = **DIOB[23:0]**		
100	When **ABSE/ABDE** is present this is reserved; otherwise BS = 0	Second	Second
101		First	Second
110		Second	First
111	If **CIN**=0 and **BINV**=0, BS = 0x800000; otherwise BS = 0.[b]	First	First
None[a]		First	First

a. Refers to operations with immediate data as B source, without **ABSE** or **ABDE**.

b. The "max constant" 0x800000 is the value which, added to a time base value minus 1, gives the farthest wrapped time base value that satisfied a "greater-than-or-equal-to" comparison.

Table G.4 T4BBS Instruction Field Settings

- **T2 A-Bus Destination (T2ABD)**

  T2ABD indicates two possible register sets to be used for the AD. Which of the two is actually used is specified by **ABDE** (or, if **ABDE** is absent, by **T4BBS**).

T2ABD	First Register Set		Second Register Set	
	Register	Size	Register	Size
0000	**A[23:0]** = AD[23:0]	24	**C[23:0]** = AD[23:0]	24
0001	**SR[23:0]** = AD[23:0]	24	**LINK[4:0]** = AD[4:0]	8
0010	**ERT_A[23:0]** = AD[23:0], write **ERT_A** to **MatchA**	24	**TPR[15:0]** = AD[15:0]	16
0011	**ERT_B[23:0]** = AD[23:0], write **ERT_B** to **MatchB**	24	**B[23:0]** = AD[23:0]	24
0100	**DIOB[23:0]** = AD[23:0]	24	**CHAN[4:0]** = AD[4:0]	8

T2ABD	First Register Set			Second Register Set		
	Register	Size		Register	Size	
0101	**P[15:0]** = AD[15:0]	16		**D[23:0]** = AD[23:0]	24	
0110	**P[31:16]** = AD[15:0]	16		**RAR[12:0]** = AD[12:0]	16	
0111	**P[23:0]** = AD[23:0]	24		**MACH[23:0]** = AD[23:0]	24	
1000	**TCR1[23:0]** = AD[23:0]	24		**MACL[23:0]** = AD[23:0]	24	
1001	**TCR2[23:0]** = AD[23:0]	24		Reserved.	-	
1010	**P[31:24]** = AD[7:0]	8		Reserved.	-	
1011	**P[23:16]** = AD[7:0]	8		Reserved.	-	
1100	**P[15:8]** = AD[7:0]	8		Reserved.	-	
1101	**P[7:0]** = AD[7:0]	8		Reserved.	-	
1110	**TRR[23:0]** = AD[23:0]	24		Reserved.	-	
1111	No destination selected. (ALU flags are updated, although the result is lost.)	24		Reserved.	-	

Table G.5 T2ABD Instruction Field Settings

- **T2 Immediate Destination (T2D) Fields**
  When using 24-bit immediate data (**ALUOPI** operations), the destination register is indicated by the **T2D** field, as shown in Example G.6.

T2D	Target Register
00	**P[23:0]**
01	**A[23:0]**
10	**SR[23:0]**
11	**DIOB[23:0]**

Table G.6 T2D Field Settings

- **A Bus Source and Destination (ABSE and ABDE) Fields**

  Note: What the *E* in **ABSE** and **ABDE** stands for has been lost in TPU lore.

  These fields are always present, or absent, together in microinstructions.

  ABSE controls the register set selected for **T4ABS** (source) while **ABDE** controls the register set selected for **T2ABD** (destination).

ABSE or ABDE	Register Set Selected
0	Second
1	First

Table G.7 ABSE and ABDE Field Settings

- **B Inverse (BINV) and Carry-In (CIN)**

   These two fields work together to change the ALU addition operation as well as the signed and unsigned MDU operations.

BINV	CIN	Operation (adder output)	Operation (signed output)	Operation (signed output)
1	1	AS + BS	AS *mdu_op* BS	AS *mdu_op* (BS + 1)
1	0	AS + BS + 1	Reserved	AS + BS + 1
0	0	AS - BS	AS *mdu_op* -BS	Reserved
0	1	AS - BS - 1	Reserved	Reserved

Table G.8 BINV and CIN Field Settings Affecting Addition

- **Shift Register Control (SRC)**

   This is one of three fields (along with **SHF** and **ALUOP**) that affects the contents of the shift register (**SR**).

SRC	Meaning
0	Shift **SR** right by 1 bit
1	Do not shift **SR**.

Table G.9 SRC Instruction Field Settings

- **Shift (SHF) Field**

   Post-ALU shifting is affected by the **SHF** field as well as some specific **ALUOP** values. Note that **SHF** and **ALUOP** fields never occur together in the same microinstruction. For all **SHF** values, ALU performs AS + BS before any shifting or rotating.

SHF	Post ALU Operation
00	Shift left 1 bit.
01	Shift right 1 bit.
10	Rotate right 1 bit.
11	No shift or rotate.

Table G.10 SHF Instruction Field Settings

- **A-Source/Condition Execution (AS/ CE) Field**

This field has multiple purposes. Values 000 and 001 are used for A-source size overriding; the remaining values provide conditional logic for ALU/ MDU operation execution, depending on the value of various ALU flags. Value 110 is used to indicate that the operation should execute unconditionally, and with no size override.

Note: When a conditional ALU/ MDU operation is not executed, the destination register is not updated; the ALU and MDU flags are not updated; MDU does not start any operation (so **MACH** and **MACL** are not updated); and SR does not shift.

AS/CE	Meaning
000	A-source size override to 8 bits
001	A-source size override to 16 bits.
010	ALU/MDU execution if C = 1.
011	ALU/MDU execution if C = 0.
100	ALU/MDU execution if Z = 1.
101	ALU/MDU execution if Z = 0.
110	ALU/MDU execution if N = 1.
111	Execute unconditionally/no size override.

Table G.11 AS/CE Field Meanings

- **A-source Sign Extension (SEXT) Field**

This field forces sign extension of AS according to the following table.

SEXT	Meaning
0	Extends signs of AS to 24 bits.
1	Does not extend sign of AS.

Table G.12 SEXT Instruction Field Settings

Flow Control Instruction Fields

The eTPU flow control operations are used to perform a jump, call, dispatch jump, dispatch call, end, halt, and repeat instruction.

- **END**
  The **END** bit field finishes the current thread (**END** = 0). **END** = 1 has no effect. When **END** = 0, any pending MDU operation is abandoned, and locked semaphores are released.

- **Jump/Call Selection (J/C)**
  This 1-bit indicated whether a jump (**J/C** = 0) or a call (**J/C**= 1) is executed. The only difference between these two flow control operations is that in the latter the return address is saved in the return address register (**RAR**). Nested sub-routine calls require that the return addresses be saved in a stack. All of these are provided as microinstruction fields, with the exception of halt, which is itself a microinstruction format.

- **Branch Condition Selection (BCC) and Branch Condition Inversion (BCF) Fields**

  Note: When the branching condition is a channel flag, the channel context is indicated by **CHAN**.

  The 5-bit **BCC** field indicates whether branching (jumps and calls) is to be unconditional (**BCC** = 11111) or conditional (any other value). If branching is to be conditional, the **BCC** indicates what the branching condition is. When branching is conditional, the 1-bit **BCF** field indicates whether branching is to occur when the branching condition specified by **BCC** is false (**BCF** = 0) or true (**BCF** = 1).

BCC	Branch Condition	BCC	Branch Condition
00000	**V**	10000	**PSS**
00001	**N**	10001	Reserved
00010	**C**	10010	**V** XOR **N** (signed)
00011	**Z**	10011	**Z** OR **~C** (unsigned)
00100	**MV**	10100	**P[24]**
00101	**MN**	10101	**P[25]**
00110	**MC**	10110	**P[26]**
00111	**MZ**	10111	**P[27]**
01000	**TDL_A**	11000	**P[28]**
01001	**TDL_B**	11001	**P[29]**
01010	**MRL_A**	11010	**P[30]**
01011	**MRL_B**	11011	**P[31]**
01100	**LSR**	11100	**PSTO**
01101	**MB**	11101	**PSTI**
01110	**FM[1]**	11110	**SMLCK**
01111	**FM[0]**	11111	False

Table G.13 BCC Instruction Field Settings

- **Return and Dispatch (R/D) Field**
  The dispatch microoperation specified a return from subroutine or an unconditional branch where the target address is always PC + **P[31:24]** (unsigned).

R/D	Meaning
00	Return from subroutine.
01	Dispatch jump.
10	Dispatch call.
11	Don't change instruction flow.

Table G.14 R/D Instruction Field Settings

- **Return from Subroutine (RTN) Field**
  When a call or dispatch call is executed, the return address is saved in

RAR. To return from a call, a microoperation loads the contents of **RAR** back to the PC. Fields **R/D** or **RTN** can be used to return from the subroutine. Using the RTN field (**RTN** = 0) to return from a call will always flush the pipeline (see below). **RTN**= 0 means do not return.

- **Flush Pipeline (FLS) Field**
  When a branch, dispatch, or subroutine return microoperation is executed, the next microinstruction can be executed unconditionally before the flow change takes effect since the microengine has two-stage pipeline. Executing the next microinstruction after a branch maximizes execution performance. When **FLS** = 0, the pipeline is flushed and the next microinstruction placed after a branch is a no operation (NOP) if the branch is taken. If **FLS** = 1, the microinstruction placed after the branch is executed, whether the branch is taken or not.

- **HALT Microinstruction**
  HALT is a microinstruction provided to implement software breakpoints. Note that HALT is a microinstruction format, not a field. The execution of this instruction puts the microengine in halt state. HALT is valid only if the debug mode is enabled at the debug interface. If debug is not enabled, HALT executes as NOP and is treated as an illegal instruction.

- **NOP Instruction**
  A NOP can be achieved through any of the microinstruction formats, namely when the programmer assigns to each individual field the value for "no operation." However, to prevent possible future untoward effects of future changes to instructions, the instruction value 0x4FFFFFFF should always be used for NOP.

- **Illegal Instructions**
  An instruction is considered illegal if any reserved field value is used, including zero bits at the fields marks rsv in the instruction formats. A global exception may be issued up to two microcycles after instruction fetch. The execution results of an illegal instruction on the microengine, the channel logic, or the host interface are unpredictable. If the microengine decodes an illegal instruction, a global execution is issued and, in order to indicate the illegal instruction to the host, the illegal instruction flag (**ILF_A** or **ILF_B**, depending on the engine in question) on the eTPU module configuration register (**EPTUMCR**) is set.

Registers Glossary

Term	Stands for	In Register	Type	Description	Length
A	A Register	--	Engine register	General-purpose register.	24 bits
ABDE	A Bus Destination	--	Field in instruction	Indicates whether first (1) or second (0) register set is to be used for **T2ABD** (destination). Always coupled with **ABSE**.	1 bit
ABSE	A Bus Source	--	Field in instruction	Indicates whether first (1) or second (0) register set is to be used for **T4ABS** (source). Always coupled with **ABDE**.	1 bit
AID	Absolute Immediate Data	--	Field in addressing mode	Used in absolute (8-bit) or channel-relative (3- or 7-bit) SPRAM addressing mode to indicate a SPRAM address.	3, 7, or 8
ALUOP	ALU Operation	--	Field in instruction	Indicates an enhanced ALU operation to be performed. Options are OR (|), XOR (^), and AND (&), without or without BS inversion (specified by BINV microinstruction field), set/clear bit, exchange bit, multi-bit shift/rotate, absolute value.	5 bits
ALUOPI	ALU Operation Immediate	--	Field in instruction	Indicates an enhanced ALU operation (of the types available in ALUOP), but with immediate data, to be performed.	5 bits
AM	Angle Mode Selection	**ETPUBCR_A/B**	Field in engine register	When this bit is set and neither **TCR1** nor **TCR2** are STAC interface clients, the EAC hardware provides angle information to the channels using the **TCR2** bus. When the **AM** is reset (i.e., non-angle mode), EAC operation is disabled and its internal registers can be used as general purpose registers.	1 bit
AS/CE	A-Source Override/ Conditional Execution	--	Field in instruction	Allows conditional execution of arithmetic operations. Can also be used for overriding the size of A-Source.	3 bits

Term	Stands for	In Register	Type	Description	Length
B	B Register	--	Engine register	General-purpose register.	24 bits
BAF	Branch Address Field	--	Field in instruction	Indicates the absolute address of a jump/call target.	14 bits
BCC	Branch Condition Selection	--	Field in instruction	Specifies a flag (e.g., **N**) or other bit (e.g., **P[24]**) to be used for branching purposes. See **BCF**.	5 bits
BCF	Branch Condition Inversion	--	Field in instruction	Determines branching depending on the true/false condition of the flag indicated in the **BCC** field.	1 bit
BINV	B-Source Inversion	--	Field in instruction	Inverts (bitwise Boolean NOT) the B-Source before the ALU operation. Allows for subtraction, increment, or decrement. (BINV does not invert C flag in fixed-carry operations).	1 bit
C	C Register	--	Engine register	General-purpose register.	24 bits
C	Carry Flag	--	ALU Flag	In an unsigned addition without shifting, C is the ALU carry from bit 7 to 8, 15 to 16, or 23 to 24 (on 8-, 16-, and 24-bit operations respectively). In an unsigned subtraction without shifting, C represents the sign of ALU's result considering operation size (C=0 indicates a negative result). Can be used as branch condition.	1 bit
CaptureA	--	--	Event Register	Captures the contents of **TCR1** or **TCR2** (depending on value of **TBS1[1]**) when **MRL_A** or **TDL_A** is set on a channel's action logic A. Cannot be directly written to or read by eTPU code; instead, during TST or **CHAN** assignment, contents of this register is copied into **ERT_A**. The capturing scheme is specified by **PDCM**.	24 bits

Term	Stands for	In Register	Type	Description	Length
CaptureB	--	--	Event Register	See **CaptureA**, which applies here with respect to **TBS2[1]**, action logic B, **MRL_B**, **TDL_B**, and **ERT_B**.	
CBPA	Channel Parameter Base Address	**ETPUCxCR_A/B**	Channel register field	Indicates base address of the parameters for the channel in question.	11 bits
CCS	Condition Code Set	--	Field in instruction.	Indicates whether ALU flags **C**, **N**, **V**, and **Z** will be updated or not. Flags are sampled, when they are, according to operation size.	1 bit
CCSV	Condition Code Set Valid	--	Field in instruction.	Indicates whether ALU flags **C**, **N**, **V**, and **Z** will be updated or not. Also indicates size of **C**, **N**, **V**, and **Z** flag sampling operation. Options are 8 bits, 16 bits, or as defined by operation size.	2 bits
CDFC	Channel Digital Filter Control	**ETPUECR_A/B**	Field in engine register	Selects a digital filtering mode for the channels when configured as inputs for improved noise immunity. These modes offer a trade-off between noise immunity and signal latency. The options are two-sample, three-sample, and continuous modes.	2 bits
CFS	Channel Function Select	**ETPUCxCR_A/B**	Field in channel register	Defines the function to be performed by the channel. This function must be compatible with the channel condition encoding scheme indicated by the **ETCS** field in the same register.	5 bits

Term	Stands for	In Register	Type	Description	Length
CHAN	Channel Register	--	Engine register	Indicates the channel being serviced. During a TST, **CHAN** is automatically updated with the channel to be serviced. The serviced channel is constant during the succeeding thread, but the value in **CHAN** can be changed at any time by eTPU code. Certain micro-instructions (condition branching using LSR and negate channel flag LSR) utilize the serviced channel rather than **CHAN**. Other than these, when the **CHAN** register is written to, accesses are qualified by the new **CHAN** register value from the instruction following the **CHAN** assignment on, except **CaptureA/B** samples into **ERT_A/B** and match register writing from **ERT_A/B**. Writing **CHAN** (including with the same value) updates **ERT_A/B** with the new capture values and update the branch logic with updated **MRL_A/B** and **TDL_A/B** flags. Can also be used as source or destination (but not for temporary values) in ALU operations.	5 bits
CIC	Channel Interrupt Clear	**ETPUCxSCR_A/B**	Field in channel register	Allows host to clear (or not) the **CIS** bit. **CIC** is the write name for the read **CIS** bit.	1 bit
CICx	Channel x Interrupt Clear	**ETPUCISR_A/B**	Field in engine register	Allows host to clear (or not) the CISx bit. **CICx** is the write name for the read CISx bit.	1 bit
CIE	Channel Interrupt Enable	**ETPUCxCR_A/B**	Field in channel register	Indicates whether or not interrupts are enabled for this channel.	1 bit
CIEx	Channel x Interrupt Enable	**ETPUCIER_A/B**	Field in engine register	Indicates whether or not interrupts are enabled for channel x.	1 bit

Term	Stands for	In Register	Type	Description	Length
CIN	Carry-In	--	Field in instruction	Controls the carry-in for addition/subtraction operations. Its functionality depends on the arithmetic operation selected by ALUOP (when ALUOP is not present the operation is ADD).	1 bit
CIOC	Channel Interrupt Overflow Clear	**ETPUCxS CR_A/B**	Field in channel register	Allows host to clear (or not) the **CIOS** bit. **CIOC** is the write name for the read **CIOS** bit.	1 bit
CIOCx	Channel x Interrupt Overflow Clear	**ETPUCIO SR_A/B**	Field in engine register	Allows host to clear (or not) the **CIOSx** bit. **CIOCx** is the write name for the read **CIOSx** bit.	1 bit
CIOS	Channel Interrupt Overflow Status	**ETPUCxS CR_A/B**	Field in channel register	Indicates whether or not this channel has an interrupt overflow. **CIOS** is the read name for the write **CIOC** bit.	1 bit
CIOSx	Channel x Interrupt Overflow Status	**ETPUCIO SR_A/B**	Field in engine register	Indicates whether or not channel x has an interrupt overflow. **CIOSx** is the read name for the write **CIOCx** bit.	1 bit
CIRC	Channel Interrupt and Data Transfer Requests	--	Field in instruction	Issues interrupt requests, data transfer requests, and a global exception for the serviced channel.	2 bits
CIS	Channel Interrupt Status	**ETPUCxS CR_A/B**	Field in channel register	Indicates whether or not this channel has a pending interrupt to the host CPU. **CIS** is the read name for the write **CIC** bit.	1 bit
CISx	Channel x Interrupt Status	**ETPUCIS R_A/B**	Field in engine register	Indicates whether or not channel x has a pending interrupt to the host CPU. **CISx** is the read name for the write **CICx** bit.	1 bit
CPBA	Channel Parameter Base Address	**ETPUCxC RR_A/B**	Field in channel register	The value of this field multiplied by 8 specifies the SPRAM parameter base host (byte) address for this channel (2-parameter granularity).	1 bit

Term	Stands for	In Register	Type	Description	Length
CPR	Channel Priority	ETPUCxCR_A/B	Field in channel register	Indicates that channel's priority (high, medium, or low), which is used by the scheduler to help determine the next channel to be serviced. A "null" value in this field indicates that the channel is disabled, in which case the scheduler does not grant any of its service requests.	2 bits
CTS-BASE	Channel Transfer Base	ETPUCDCR	Field in global engine	This field concatenates with fields **PARM0/1** to determine the absolute word offset (from the SPRAM base) of the parameters to be transferred.	5 bits
D	D Register	--	Engine register	General-purpose register.	24 bits
DIOB	Data Input/Output Register	--	Engine register	Can be used as a source of destination for ALU operations, SPRAM data, or SPRAM addressing (using the **DIOB** contents as an absolute 14-bit wide SPRAM address). When used as a SPRAM address, **DIOB** can be pre-decremented or post-incremented. Can be pre-loaded with one SPRAM parameter during TST. Also may be used as a general-purpose register.	24 bits
DTRC	Channel Data Transfer Request Clear	ETPUCxSCR_A/B	Field in channel register	Allows host to clear (or not) the **DTRS** bit. **DTRC** is the write name for the read **DTRS** bit.	1 bit
DTRCx	Channel x Data Transfer Request Clear	ETPUCDTRSR_A/B	Field in engine register	Allows host to clear (or not) the **DTRSx** bit. **DTRCx** is the write name for the read **DTRSx** bit.	1 bit
DTRE	Channel Data Transfer Enable	ETPUCxCRR_A/B	Field in channel register	Indicates whether or not data transfers are enabled for this channel.	1 bit

Term	Stands for	In Register	Type	Description	Length
DTREx	Channel x Data Transfer Enable	**ETPUCD TRER_A/B**	Field in engine register	Indicates whether or not data transfers are enabled for channel x.	1 bit
DTROC	Channel Data Transfer Request Overflow Clear	**ETPUCxS CR_A/B**	Field in channel register	Allows host to clear (or not) the **DTROS** bit. **DTROC** is the write name for the read **DTROS** bit.	1 bit
DTROC x	Channel x Data Transfer Request Overflow Clear	**ETPUCD TROSR_ A/B**	Field in engine register	Allows host to clear (or not) the **DTROSx** bit. **DTROCx** is the write name for the read **DTROSx** bit.	1 bit
DTROS	Channel x Data Transfer Request Overflow Status	**ETPUCxS CR_A/B**	Field in channel register	Indicates whether or not this channel has a data transfer request overflow. **DTROS** is the read name for the write **DTROC** bit.	1 bit
DTROSx	Channel x Data Transfer Request Overflow Status	**ETPUCD TROSR_ A/B**	Field in engine register	Indicates whether or not channel x has a data transfer request overflow. **DTROSx** is the read name for the write **DTROCx** bit.	1 bit
DTRS	Channel Data Transfer Request Status	**ETPUCxS CR_A/B**	Field in channel register	Indicates whether or not this channel has a pending data transfer request. **DTRS** is the read name for the write **DTRC** bit. Note that some channels are NOT connected to the DMA and so don't generate interrupt requests regardless of the value of this bit.	1 bit
DTRSx	Channel x Data Transfer Request Status	**ETPUCD TRSR_A/ B**	Field in engine register	Indicates whether or not channel x has a pending data transfer request. **DTRSx** is the read name for the write **DTRCx** bit.	1 bit
EAC	Angle Tick Counter	**ETPUTB2 R**	Field in engine register	Another name for **TCR2**, when the engine is in angle mode. Provides continuous count of the angle in units of angle ticks.	24 bits
END	--	--	Field in instruction	Finishes the current thread, allows other channels to be serviced, and releases and semaphore locked by the engine.	1 bit

Term	Stands for	In Register	Type	Description	Length
ERT_A	Event Register Temporary A	--	Engine register	Can be used as source or destination for ALU operations. Can also be written to by eTPU code, for instance to set up for a match (see **MatchA**). (In fact, it is s the only source for a write to a channel's **MatchA**.) Only valid destination of **MatchA** read operation. During TST, is loaded with the contents of the channel's **CaptureA** register (i.e., the capture register for action logic A). Also may be used as a general-purpose register.	24 bits
ERT_B	Event Register Temporary B	--	Engine register	See description of **ERT_A**, which applies analogously here with respect to **MatchB** and **CaptureB** (i.e., the capture register for action logic B).	24 bits
ERW_A	Write MatchA	--	Field in instruction.	Writes the value of **ERT_A** in **MatchA** and enables matches (i.e., sets **MRLE**) for **MatchA** register.	1 bit
ERW_B	Write MatchB	--	Field in instruction.	See description for **ERW_A** which applies analogously here with respect to **MatchB**.	1 bit
ETB	Entry Table Base	**ETPUEC R_A/B**	Field in engine register	Determines the location in the SCM of the entry table.	5 bits
ETCS	Entry Table Condition Select	**ETPUCxC RR_A/B**	Field in channel register	Determines the channel condition encoding scheme that selects, according to channel conditions, the entry point to be taken in an entry table. **ETCS** value has to be compatible for the function chosen for the channel, selected in field **CFS**. Two condition encoding schemes are available.	1 bit
ETPUC DCR	eTPU Coherent Dual-parameter Controller Register	--	Global register	Configures and controls dual-parameter coherent transfers.	32 bits

Term	Stands for	In Register	Type	Description	Length
ETPUC DTRER_ A/B	eTPU A/B Channel Data Transfer Request Enable Register	--	Engine register	Mirrors the **DTRE** field in each channel's **ETPUCxCR** register.	32 bits
ETPUC DTROS R_A/B	**eTPU A/B** Channel Data Transfer Request Overflow Status Register	--	Engine register	Mirrors the **DTROS/DTROC** field in each channel's **ETPUCxSCR** register.	32 bits
ETPUC DTRSR_ A/B	eTPU A/B Channel Data Transfer Request Status Register	--	Engine register	Mirrors the **DTRS/DTRC** field in each channel's **ETPUCxSCR** register. Note that some channels are NOT connected to the DMA and so don't generate interrupt requests regardless of the value of this bit.	32 bits
ETPUCI ER_A/B	eTPU A/B Channel Enable Register	--	Engine register	Mirrors the **CIE** field in each channel's **ETPUCxCR** register.	32 bits
ETPUCI OSR_A/ B	eTPU A/B Channel Interrupt Overflow Status Register	--	Engine register	Mirrors the **CIOS/CIOC** field in each channel's **ETPUCxSCR** register.	32 bits
ETPUCI SR_A/B	eTPU A/B Channel Interrupt Status Register	--	Engine register	Mirrors the **CIS/CIC** field in each channel's **ETPUCxSCR** register.	32 bits
ETPUCP SSR_A/ B	eTPU A/B Channel Pending Service Status Register	--	Engine register	Indicates for each channel whether it has a pending service request or not.	32 bits
ETPUCS SR_A/B	eTPU A/B Channel Service Status Register	--	Engine register	Indicates for each channel whether it is being serviced or not. At most one bit may be asserted in the register at a given time.	32 bits
ETPUCx CR_A/B	eTPU A/B Channel x Configuration Register	--	Channel register	Holds configuration information for a given channel.	32 bits

Term	Stands for	In Register	Type	Description	Length
ETPUCx HSRR_ A/B	eTPU A/B Channel x Host Service Request Register	--	Channel register	Allows the host to issue service requests to the channel.	32 bits
ETPUCx SCR_A/ B	eTPU A/B Channel Status Control Register	--	Channel register	Holds the interrupt and data transfer status and overflow information for the channel; the input and output pin states, and the channel function mode.	32 bits
ETPUEC R_A/B	eTPU A/B Engine Configuration Register	--	Engine register	Holds configuration and status fields that are programmed independently in each engine.	32 bits
ETPUM CR	eTPU Module Configuration Register	--	Global register	Holds global configuration and status information, including global exception. It is also used for configuring the SCM operation and test.	32 bits
ETPU-MISCC-MPR	eTPU MISC Compare Register	--	Global register	Holds the 32-bit signature expected from the whole SCM array.	32 bits
ETPUST ACR_A/ B	eTPU STAC Bus Configuration Register	--	Engine register	Registers and configures the eTPU STAC bus interface module and operations.	32 bits
ETPUTB 1R_A/B	eTPU A/B Time Base1	--	Engine register	Provides visibility of the **TCR1** time base for CPU host read access. This register is read-only.	32 bits
ETPUTB 2R_A/B	eTPU A/B Time Base2	--	Engine register	Provides visibility of the **TCR2** time base for CPU host read access. This register is read-only.	32 bits
ETPUTB CR_A/B	eTPU Time Base Configuration Register A/B	--	Engine register	Configures several time-base options.	32 bits

Term	Stands for	In Register	Type	Description	Length
FEND	Force END	**ETPUEC RA/B**	Field in engine register	Terminates any current running thread as if an END instruction has been executed. This bit is self-negating during the access—i.e., the host receives waitstates while the rest occurs and **FEND** always reads as 0. **FEND** assertion is ignored when the microengine is in TST, Halt, or Idle.	1 bit
FL	Free/Lock Semaphore	--	Field in instruction	Indicates whether semaphore is to be freed (0) or locked (1).	1 bit
Flag 1	Channel Flag 1	--	General channel register	See description for **Flag0**, which applies here.	1 bit
Flag0	Channel Flag 0	--	General channel register	Used to select channel service threads (i.e., entry point) based on channel software state. Cannot be tested by eTPU code. Set/reset by eTPU code through the microinstruction field **FLC**.	1 bit
FLC	Flush Control	--	Field in instruction	Allows for direct setting and clearing of **Flag0** and **Flag1**. Also allows **Flag0** and **Flag1** to be copied from selected bits of **P** register high byte, which is also used to hold application state.	3 bits
FLS	Flush Pipeline	--	Field in instruction	Indicates whether or not to flush the pipeline when a jump/call/dispatch jump/dispatch call/return is executed.	1 bit
FM	Channel Function Mode	**ETPUCxS CR_A/B**	Field in channel engine	Each function uses this field for specific configuration.	2 bits
FPSCK	Filter Prescaler Clock Controller	**ETPUEC R_A/B**	Field in engine register	Controls the prescaling of the clocks used in digital filters for the channel input signals and **TCRCLK** input. Filtering can be controlled independently by the engine, but all input digital filters in the same engine have the same clock prescaling.	3 bits

Term	Stands for	In Register	Type	Description	Length
FRAC-TION	Fraction Accumulator	**TRR**	Field in engine register	Holds 9-bit fractional part of **TCR1** clocks in one angle tick. The **FRACTION** value is accumulated in the EAC fraction accumulator, and whenever the result overflows (i.e., the accumulated fraction adds up to an integer), the tick prescaler is halted for one **TCR1** clock.	9 bits
GEC	Global Exception Clear	**ETPUMCR**	Field in global register	Write-only bit that negates global exception request and clears global exception status bits **MGE1**, **MGE2**, ILF1, **ILF2**, and **SAMMISF**. A read will always return 0.	1 bit
GTBE	Global Time Base Enable	**ETPUMCR**	Global register field	Enables time bases in both engines, allowing them to be started synchronously.	1 bit
HALT	Halt	--	Instruction format	Implements a software breakpoint. Is valid only if the debug mode is enabled at the debug interface (otherwise HALT executes as a NOP and is treated as an illegal instruction).	32 bits
HLTF	Halt Mode Flag	**ETPUECRA/B**	Field in engine register	Indicates that the engine has halted. This bit remains asserted while the engine is in halt state, even during a single-stop or forced instruction execution.	1 bit
HOLD	Force EAC Halt	**TPR**	Field in engine register	Forces the EAC to halt until a new physical tooth is detected.	1 bit
HSR	Host Service Request	**ETPUCxHSRR**	Field in channel register	Allows activation of a channel function by the host CPU.	3 bits
ILF1	Illegal Instruction Flag	**ETPUMCR**	Field in global register	Set when the microengine has decoded an illegal instruction in engine A.	1 bit

Term	Stands for	In Register	Type	Description	Length
ILF2	Illegal Instruction Flag	**ETPUMCR**	Field in global register	See description of **ILF1**, which applies analogously here with respect to engine B.	1 bit
INTE-GER	Integer	**TRR**	Field in engine register	Holds the integer part of **TCR1** clocks in one angle tick. This number, decremented by one, is a down-counter preload value. A value of INTEGER=0 represents and integer of 32768	15 bits
IPAC_A	Input Pin Action Control A	--	Field in instruction	Sets the **IPAC1** pin control register.	3 bits
IPAC_A	Input Pin Action Control A	--	Pin control register	Used to configure the transition detection sensitivity for a channel's input signal for action logic A. For **IPAC_A**=0xx, **MEF** must be asserted for the match to be enabled or recognized. For **IPAC_A**=1xx, **MatchA** is always enabled, regardless of state of **MEF**.	3 bits
IPAC_B	Input Pin Action Control B	--	Field in instruction	Sets the **IPAC_B** pin control register.	3 bits
IPAC_B	Input Pin Action Control B	--	Pin control register	See description for **IPAC_A**, which applies analogously here, with respect to action logic B.	3 bits
IPH	Insert Physical Tooth	**TPR**	Field in engine register	Used for exiting halt mode, which is caused by issuing a detection of a physical tooth. It generates a dummy physical tooth which has the same effect as a real physical tooth and resets itself subsequently. If EAC is in halt mode, it switches back to normal mode; if EAC is in normal mode, it switches to high-rate mode.	1 bit
IPS	Channel Input Pin State	**ETPUCxS CR_A/B**	Field in channel register	Indicates the current value of the filtered channel input signal state.	1 bit

Term	Stands for	In Register	Type	Description	Length
J/C	Jump/Call Selection	--	Field in instruction	Indicates whether a jump or a call is to be executed. When a call is executed the value of PC is saved in **RAR** register, whereas in a jump it is not.	1 bit
LAST	Last Tooth Indication	**TPR**	Field in engine register	Indicates the last tooth. When set, **TCR2** tooth counter will be re-set on the next physical tooth edge (or when **IPH**=1) when **MISSCNT**=0.	1 bit
LINK	Link Register	--	Engine register	Requests service to another channel by indicating an engine (2 bits) and the channel number (6 bits). This in turn causes the target channel's **LSR** flag to be set. The engine that receives the link cannot determine where the link comes from, except by some user-programmed protocol using SPRAM. Can also be used a s destination in arithmetic operations.	8 bits
LSR	Link Service Request Negation Control	--	Field in instruction	Clears the link service request flag of the serviced channel (which may not be the one selected by **CHAN**).	1 bit
LSR	Link Service Request	--	Channel flag	Indicates that a link service requests has been raised for the channel.	1 bit
MACH	Multiply Accumulate High Register	--	Engine Register	Part of the MDU. Can be used as source or destination in most ALU operations. When multiply or divide operations are used (including multiply-accumulate), serves a special purpose and some restrictions apply. Also may be used as a general-purpose register.	24 bits
MACL	Multiply Accumulate Low Register	--	Engine Register	See description of **MACH**, which applies analogously here.	24 bits

Term	Stands for	In Register	Type	Description	Length
MatchA	Match A	--	Action Logic Event Register	Holds the pending match value for action logic A which is compared against one of the two time bases by an equal-only/greater-equal comparator (see **TBS**). This is done every microcycle. This register may be written to only by eTPU code, through **ERT_A**. When a match occurs and/or is recognized depends upon a complex series of conditions related to **IPAC1_A, MEF, MRLE_A, MRL_A, MRL_B,** and **TDL_B**. Whether a recognized match is serviced depends on the value of **MTD**.	24 bits
MatchB	--	--	Action Logic Event Register	See description of **MatchA**, which applies analogously here, with respect to action logic 2, **ERT_B, IPAC_B, MEF, MRLE_B, MRL_B MRL_A,** and **TDL_A**.	24 bits
MB	MDU Busy	--	MDU flag	Indicates, when asserted, that the MDU is calculating. Otherwise it indicates that the MDU is idle. **MB** tests "true" at the next microinstruction after the MDU start operation, and "false" at the last microcycle of any MDU operation execution.	1 bit
MC	MDU Carry	--	MDU flag	In signed and unsigned MACs performed by the MDU, indicates if the result cannot be represented by a 48-bit number. It is reset in the other MDU operations.	1 bit
MCU					

Term	Stands for	In Register	Type	Description	Length
MDIS	Module Disable	**ETPUER**	Engine register field	When this bit is set, the engine shuts down its internal clocks. **TCR1** and **TCR2** cease to increment, and input sampling stops. The engine asserts **STF** to indicate that it has stopped. However, the **BIU** continues to run, and the host can access all registers except for the channel registers. After **MDIS** is set, even before **STF** asserts, data read from the channel register is not meaningful, a bus error is issued, and writes are unpredictable. When the **MDIS** bit is asserted while eTPU code is executing, the eTPU will stop when the thread is complete on the next clock. The **MDIS** bit is write-protected when **VIS** =1.	1 bit
ME	Match Enable	--	Field in Entry Point	Copied into **MEF** during TST. See **MEF**.	1 bit
MEF	Match Enable Flag	--	Engine (NOT channel) latch	Enables assertion of **MRL_A/B**, depending on the **IPAC_A/B** field. For **IPAC_A/B**=0xx, **MEF**=1 enables assertion of **MRL_A/B** for the scheduled channel during service. For **IPAC_A/B**=1xx, **MatchA/B** is always enabled. Matches of channels not being serviced are not disabled by **MEF**. **MEF** is negated at the beginning of TST for the channel being services. After two microcycles into the TST, regardless of TST wait-states, the **ME** bit in the entry point is copied to **MEF**.	1 bit
MGE1	Microcode Global Exception Engine A	**ETPUMCR**	Field in global register	Indicates that a global exception was asserted by eTPU code executed on engine A. The determination of the reason the global exception was asserted is application dependent: it can be coded in a SPRAM status parameter, for instance. This bit is cleared by writing 1 to the **GEC** field.	1 bit

Term	Stands for	In Register	Type	Description	Length
MGE2	Microcode Global Exception Engine B	**ETPUMCR**	Field in global register	See description for **MGE1**, which applies analogously here, with respect to engine B.	1 bit
MISS-CNT	Missing Tooth Counter	**TPR**	Field in engine register	Decremented on each estimated tooth; stops at 0. Used for generation of "dummy tooth" whenever it holds a non-zero value.	2 bits
MN	MDU Negative	--	MDU flag	Always a copy of the most significant bit of the MDU result, for both signed and unsigned operations.	1 bit
MRL_A	Match Recognition Latch A	--	Field in instruction	Used to clear a channel's **MRL_A** flag directly.	1 bit
MRL_A	Match Recognition Latch A	--	Event Register	Used to indicate a match has been recognized in the channel's action unit A. Asserted on T2. **MRL_A** assertion results in a capture of the specified time base to **CaptureA**. Match recognitions can cause, also depending on channel mode and current state, the channel to request service, configuring a match service request. A recognized match immediately forces a pin state as specified by **OPAC_A** and, in some cases by **IPAC_A** registers. Regardless of the channel mode, once **MRL_A** has been asserted, **MRLE_A** is negated, preventing future match recognitions until **MatchA** is rewritten by eTPU code. In some channel modes, assertion of **MRL_A** can block **MRL_B**.	1 bit
MRL_B	Match Recognition Latch B	--	Field in instruction	See description for **MRL_A** (instruction), which applies analogously here, with respect to **MRL_B**, **OPAC_B**, and **IPAC_B**.	1 bit
MRL_B	Match Recognition Latch B	--	Event Register	See description for **MRL_A** (state resolution flag), which applies analogously here, with respect to action logic B.	1 bit

Term	Stands for	In Register	Type	Description	Length
MRLE	Match Recognition Latch Enable	--	Field in instruction	Used to disable matches for a channel's **MatchA** and **MatchB** registers by setting or resetting the **MRLE_A** and **MRLE_B** registers.	1 bit
MRLE_A	Match Recognition Latch Enable A	--	Event Register	A match event recognition (for **MatchA**) may occur only if **MRLE_A** is set, which happens only upon a write to **MatchA** by eTPu code, copied from **ERT_A**. **MRLE_A** is negated when the match occurs on **MatchA**, by eTPU code, or, in some double match channel modes, when a match for the other match latch occurs. It ensures that the greater-equal comparison will not cause addition matches.	1 bit
MRLE2	Match Recognition Latch Enable 2	--	Event Register	See description for **MRLE_A**, which applies analogously here with respect to **MatchB** and **ERT_B**.	1 bit
MTD	Match and Transition Disable	--	Field in instruction	Disables match and transition service requests for the selected channel by controlling the **SRI** latch.	2 bits
MV	MDU Overflow	--	MDU flag	In MDU multiply operations, is and remains negated. In MDU MAC operations, is asserted if the result is wider than 48 bits.	1 bit
MZ	MDU Zero	--	MDU flag	In MDU multiply and MAC operations, is asserted if **MACH** and **MACL** are equal to 0 at the end of the operation. In MDU divide operations, is asserted if **MCL** (i.e., the result) is equal to 0.	
N	Negative Flag	--	ALU flag	Indicates the sign of result based on the operation size, regardless of the operation performed. Can be used as branch condition.	1 bit

Term	Stands for	In Register	Type	Description	Length
NOP	No Operation	--	--	There is no unique microinstruction with an assigned opcode for NOP; instead, NOP is achieved through any of the microinstruction formats where the user can assign to each individual field the corresponding value for NOP. However, to prevent future impacts of instruction changes on object code compatibility, the instruction value 0x4FFFFFFF should always be used for NOP	32 bits
OBE	Output Buffer Enable	--	Pin control register	Controlled by **TBS1**. Drives the Output Buffer Enable signal, which can be used (depending on MCU integration) to control the output signal pad driver. (However, note that the **OBE** signal on Copperhead is actually controlled by the CPU; the eTPU **OBE** signal is not used. This was a compromise to get everything else we wanted in the pads.)	
ODIS	Output Disable	**ETPUCxCRR_A/B**	Field in channel register	Enables the channel to have its output forced to the value opposite to **OPOL** when the output disable input signal corresponding to the channel group that it belongs to is active.	1 bit
OPAC_A	Output Pin Action Control A	--	Field in instruction	Used to set pin control register **OPAC_A**.	3 bits
OPAC_A	Output Pin Action Control A	--	Pin control register	Defines the action to be taken on the output signal (set high, set low, toggle, or do not change) when a match or input action occurs.	3 bits
OPAC_B	Output Pin Action Control B	--	Field in instruction	See description for instruction field **OPAC_A**, which applies analogously here.	3 bits
OPAC_B	Output Pin Action Control B	--	Pin control register	See description for pin control register **OPAC_A**, which applies analogously here.	3 bits

Term	Stands for	In Register	Type	Description	Length
OPOL	Output Polarity	**ETPUCxCR_A/B**	Field in channel engine	See the description for **ODIS**.	1 bit
OPS	Channel Output Pin State	**ETPUCxSCR_A/B**	Field in channel register	Indicates the current value of the channel output signal state, including the effect of the external output disable feature. If the channel's input and output signals are connected to the same pad, **OPS** reflects the value driven to the page (if **OBE**=1). This is not necessarily the actual pad value, which drives value in the **IPS** bit.	1 bit
P	P Flags	**P Register**	Fields in engine register.	Upper byte of the **P** register, which may be utilized as user-defined flags to indicate application state. **P[31:24]** is also used for a dispatch microoperation. Bit pairs **P[29:28]**, **P[27:26]**, and **P[25:24]** can be directly copied into **Flag0** and **Flag1** using the **FLC** field.	8 bits
P	Preload register	-	Engine register	As the only 32-bit register in the eTPU, this register can be used as source or destination for ALU operations or for SPRAM read/write operation source or destination. Is automatically loaded with one SPRAM parameter before a thread starts. Is able to access the upper byte, lower 24 bits or all 32 bits of a SPRAM parameter. Also, see **P Flags**. Also may be used as a general-purpose register.	32 bits
P/D	P or DIOB	--	Field in instruction	Indicates whether **P** or **DIOB** is the register to be used for the SPRAM access.	1 bit
PARM0	Channel Parameter0	**ETPUCDCR**	Field in global register	This in concatenation with **CTBASE** determines the word address (offset from the SPRAM base) of the parameter that is the destination or source (defined by **WR**) of the coherent transfer.	7 bits

Term	Stands for	In Register	Type	Description	Length
PARM1	Channel Parameter1	**ETPUCD CR**	Field in global register	This in concatenation with **CTBASE** determines the word address (offset from the SPRAM base) of the parameter that is the destination or source (defined by **WR**) of the coherent transfer.	7 bits
PBBASE	Parameter Buffer Base Address	**ETPUCD CR**	Field in global register	This field points to the base address of the parameter buffer location, with granularity of 2 parameters (8 bytes). The host (byte) address of the first parameter in the buffer is **PBBASE***8+ SPRAM Base Address. The microengine absolute (word) address of the first parameter in the buffer is **PBBASE***2.	10 bits
PDCM	Predefined Channel Mode	--	Field in instruction	Sets the **PDCM** register.	4 bits
PDCM	Predefined Channel Mode	--	General channel register	Defines the channel mode for a channel. See Channel Modes in dictionary.	4 bits
PP	Preload Parameter	--	Field in entry point	During each TST, up to two function variables are loaded from SPRAM into **P** and **DIOB**. **PP** indicates whether parameters 0 and 1 (0) or parameters 2 and 3 (1) parameters are loaded into **P** and **DIOB**, respectively.	1 bit
PSC	Pin State Control	--	Field in instruction	Forces **PSTO** high (01) or low (10) or (00) sets **PSTO** according to **OPAC_A** (if **PSCS**=1) or **OPAC_B** (if **PSCS**=0). If **PSC** is 11 then **PSTO** remained unchanged.	2 bits
PSCS	Pin State Control Setting	--	Field in instruction	Used with **PSC** to set **PSTO**. See **PSC**.	1 bit
PSS	Pin Sampled State	--	Pin control register	Sampled pin state, which is stable as long as **CHAN** does not change. **PSS** is **PSTI** or **PSTO** sampled on **CHAN** assignments and at thread start.	1 bit

Term	Stands for	In Register	Type	Description	Length
PSTI	Pin State Input	--	Pin control register	This is the channel's filtered input signal.	1 bit
PSTO	Pin State Output	--	Pin control register	This is the channel's filtered output signal.	1 bit
PWIDTH	Parameter Width Selection	**ETPUCDCR**	Field in global register	This bit selects the width (1 = 32 bits; 0 = 24 bits) of the parameters to be transferred between the **PB** and the target address.	1 bit
R/D	Return and Dispatch	--	Field in instruction	Causes an unconditional branch, where the target address is always **PC**+P[31:24] (unsigned).	2 bits
RAR	Return Address Register	--	Engine Register	Contains the return address in the case of a call or dispatch call. Also receives the contents of the **PC** register when a return from subroutine is executed. Is loaded with the value 0x3FFF during TST. Can also be used as source or destination in arithmetic operations. Can also be used as a general-purpose register.	14 bits
REN1	TCR1 Resource Client/Server Operation Enable Bit	**ETPUREDCR_A/B**	Field in engine register	Enables or disables client/server operation to eTPU STAC interface. **REN1** enables **TCR1**.	1 bit
REN2	TCR2 Resource Client/Server Operation Enable Bit	**ETPUREDCR_A/B**	Field in engine register	See description for **REN1**, which applies analogously here, with respect to **TCR2**.	1 bit
RSC1	**TCR1** Resource Server/Client Assignment Bit	**ETPUREDCR_A/B**	Field in engine register	Selects the eTPU data resource assignment to be used as a server or client. Selects the functionality of **TCR1**. For server mode, external plugging determines the unique server address assigned to each **TCR**. For client mode, this field determines the server address to which the client listens.	1 bit

Term	Stands for	In Register	Type	Description	Length
RSC2	**TCR2** Resource Server/Client Assignment Bit	**ETPURE DCR_A/B**	Field in engine register	See description for **RSC2**, which applies analogously here with respect to **TCR2**.	1 bit
RSIZ	Register Size	--	Field in instruction	Indicates the size of the operation when the **P** register is to be used for SPRAM access. Applicable sizes are most significant 8, lower 24 and all 32-bits.	2 bits
RTN	Return from Subroutine	--	Field in instruction	Used to return from subroutine. Pipeline will always be flushed when return occurs.	1 bit
RW	Read Write	--	Field in addressing mode	0 reads from SPRAM into **P** or **DIOB**; 1 writes to SPRAM from **P** or **DIOB**.	1 bit
SCMMISEN	SCM MISC Enable	**ETPUMCR**	Field in global register	Starts (1) or aborts (0) an **MISC** operation. When this bit is reset, the **MISC** address counter is set to the initial SCM address.	1 bit
SCMMISF	SCM MISC Flag	**ETPUMCR**	Field in global register	Set by the SCM **MISC** logic to indicate that an MISC mismatch has occurred. Automatically cleared when **SCMMISEM** changes from 0 to 1, or when the global exception is cleared by writing 1 to **GEC**.	1 bit
SCMSIZE	SCM Size	**ETPUMCR**	Field in global register	Read-only field that holds the number of 2Kbyte SCM blocks minus 1. This value is MCU dependent.	5 bits
SEXT	A-Source Sign Extension	--	Field in instruction.	Forces sign extension of A-Source.	1 bit

Term	Stands for	In Register	Type	Description	Length
SGR_A/B	Service Grant Register	--	Engine Register	Contains one bit for each channel. A bit is set when its corresponding channel has been serviced. Cleared as part of a priority group when a channel of that priority has just been serviced, and no other channel of that priority is requesting service (has a set **SRR**) and has not been granted service (has a clear **SGR**).	32 bit
SHF	Shift	--	Field in instruction	Indicates whether or not to do post-ALU shifting (left or right) or rotating (right). (Never appears with **ALUOP** in the same microinstruction format.)	2 bits
SMLCK	Semaphore Lock	--	Branch condition	Indicates if a semaphore is locked for the engine.	1 bit
SMPR	Semaphore Number	--	Field in instruction	Semaphore number selector	2 bits
SR	Shift Register	--	Engine register	Can be used as a source or destination for ALU operations. Is capable of a shift right by 1 bit. While shifting right, **SR** may receive in bit 23 the lost bit from a shift-right operation in the post-ALU shifter, thus allowing **SR** to be used to perform a 48-bit shift right. Also may be used as a general-purpose register.	24 bits
SRC	Shift Register Control	--	Field in instruction.	Indicates whether the contents of **SR** should be shifted right by 1 bit or not shifted at all.	1 bit
SRI	Match/Transition Service Request Inhibit Latch	--	General channel register	Blocks channel service requests due to the assertion of **MRL_A/B** or **TDL_A/B**. Does not affect recognition of LSRs, HSRs, **MRL_A/B**, or **TDL_A/B** eTPU code branch tests, or entry table selection. Asserted during rest and controlled by the instruction field **MTD**.	1 bit

Term	Stands for	In Register	Type	Description	Length
SRR_A/B	Service Request Register	--	Engine Register	Contains one bit for each channel. A bit is set when its corresponding channel requests service. Cleared when the channel has been serviced.	32 bits
SRx	Pending Service Request Pending x	**ETPUCP SSR_A/B**	Field in engine register	Indicates for that channel whether it has a pending service request or not. Pending service request is negated at the TST to the respective service thread.	1 bit
SSx	Service Status x	**ETPUCS SR_A/B**	Field in engine register.	Indicates for that channel whether it is currently being serviced or not. It is updated at the first microcyle of a TST.	1 bit
STC	Stack	--	Field in instruction	If this field is present indirect addressing mode is being used. This field indicates whether increment/decrement of **DIOB** register is to be performed.	2 bits
STF	Stop Flag	**ETPUEC R**	Engine register field	Indicates that the engine has stopped. The eTPU system is fully stopped when the **STF** bits of both eTPU engines are asserted.	1 bit
STS	Start Bit	**ETPUCC R**	Field in global register	This bit is set by the host in order to start the data transfer between the parameter buffer pointed by **PBBASE** and the target addresses selected by the concatenation of the fields **CTBASE** and **PARM0/1**. The host receives wait-states until the data transfer is complete, at which point this bit is reset by coherency logic.	1 bit
T2ABD	T2 A-Bus Destination	--	Field in instruction	Allows selection of an ALU destination from either one of two register sets. ABSE (or, if absent, T4ABS) controls which set T4ABS uses to select the source. Destination result is driven during T2 of the microcycle.	4 bits
T2D	T2 Destination	--	Field in instruction	Indicates destination register of 24-bit immediate data ALU/MDU operation. Destination result is driven during T2 of the microcycle.	2 bits

Appendix H. Registers Glossary

Term	Stands for	In Register	Type	Description	Length
T4ABS	T4 A-Bus Source	--	Field in instruction	Allows selection of an ALU/MDU source from either one of two register sets. **ABSE** (or, if absent, **T4BBS**) controls which set **T4ABS** uses to select the source. The A-bus is sourced during T4 of the microcycle.	4 bits
T4BBS	T4 B-Bus Source	--	Field in instruction	Specifies, when **ABSE** and **ABDE** are not available in a microinstruction format, the **register** sets for **T4ABS** and T2ABD. On instructions with immediate data, is used as B-Source. The B-bus is sourced during T4 of the microcycle.	3 bits
TBS_A	Time Base Selection A	--	Field in instruction	Writes to **TBS_A** event register (when **TBS_A[3]**=0) or the **OBE** (when **TBS_A[3]**=1).	4 bits
TBS_A	Time Base Selection A	--	Event Register	Used to configure the type of the comparator (greater or equal, or equal only) and the time base (**TCR1** or **TCR2**) used for match and capture for a channel's action logic A.	3 bits
TBS_B	Time Base Selection B	--	Field in instruction	See description for instruction field **TBS_A**, which applies analogously here with respect to action logic B.	4 bits
TBS_B	Time Base Selection B	--	Event Register	See description for event register **TBS1**, which applies analogously here with respect to action logic B.	3 bits
TCR_A/B	Time Base Clock Signal			See **TCRCLK**.	

Term	Stands for	In Register	Type	Description	Length
TCR1	Timer Count Register 1	ETPUTB1R	Field in engine register	Provides reference time bases for all match and input transition capture events. The clock for **TCR1** can be derived from the system clock or from an external input via the **TCRCLK** clock pin. **TCR1** value is updated in T2 and read in T4. The **TCR1** counters between the two engines are out of phase by 1 system clock, even when time bases are shared between them. However, all channels are in phase with respect to eTPU microcycles. Also can be read or written in ALU operations or used as general-purpose registers.	24 bits
TCR1CTL	**TCR1** Clock/Gate Control	ETPUBCR_A/B	Field in engine register	This field determines the clock source for **TCR1**. **TCR1** can count on detected rising edge of the **TCRCLK** signal or use it for gating system clock divided by 2.	2 bits
TCR1P	Timer Count Register 1 Prescaler Control	ETPUTBCR_A/B	Field in engine register	Provides the divisor used by the **TCR1** prescaler. The prescaler divides its input by **TCR1P**+1, allowing frequency divisions from 1 to 256. (The prescaler input is the system clock divided by 8 (in gated or non-gated clock mode) or **TCRCLK** filtered input.	8 bits
TCR2	Timer Count Register 2	ETPUTB2R	Field in engine register	See description for **TCR1**, which applies analogously here. The four modes available for **TCR2** are pin transition mode (count the rise, fall, or both transitions of **TCRCLK** signal), angle clock mode (count internal tooth angle in combination with the EAC hardware), gated mode (count with rate derived from the system clock divided by 8), or internally clocked modes (driven by internal clock, with count rate of system clock divided by 8).	24 bits

Term	Stands for	In Register	Type	Description	Length
TCR2CTL	**TCR2** Clock/Gate Control	**ETPUBCR_A/B**	Field in engine register	This field determines the clock source for **TCR2**. **TCR2** can count on any detected edge of the **TCRCLK** signal or use it for gating system clock divided by 8.	3 bits
TCR2P	Timer Count Register 2 Prescaler Control	**ETPUTBCR_A/B**	Field in engine register	See description for **TCR1P**, which applies analogously here. With just 6 bits instead of 8, **TCR2P** allows for division from 1 to 64 for the **TCR2** prescaler.	6 bits
TCRCF	TCRCLK Signal Filter Control	**ETPUBCR_A/B**	Field in engine register	Controls the **TCRCLK** digital filter, determining whether the **TCRCLK** signal input (after a synchronizer) is filtered with the same filter clock as the channel input signals or uses the system clock divided by 2. Also determines whether the **TCRCLK** digital filter works in integrator mode or two sample mode.	2 bits
TCRCLK	Time Base Clock Signal	--	Clock pin	Clock pin that controls the **TCR1** and **TCR2** time bases for eTPU_A and eTPU_B.	
TDL	Transition Detection latch	--	Field in instruction	Used to clear **TDL_A** and **TDL_B**. One bit is used to clear both flags.	1 bit
TDL	Transition Detection Latch	--	Field in instruction	Used to clear both of a channel's **TDL** flags directly.	1 bit

Term	Stands for	In Register	Type	Description	Length
TDL_A	Transition Detection Latch A	--	Event Register	Moving from 0 to 1 indicates that detection of specific transition occurrences on a channel's input signal. **TDL_A** assertion causes a capture of one or both selected **TCR** buses; assertion occurs on T2 and captures the time base value when **TDL_A** was asserted. Assertion of this latch causes a service request in single (but not double) transition mode, and depending on channel mode, previous events, and **SRI**. **IPAC_A** indicates the programmed edges of the first detected transition. The only methods of negating **TDL_A** are by reset and by eTPU code.	1 bit
TDL_B	Transition Detection Latch B	--	Event Register	See description of **TDL_A**, which applies analogously here with respect to action logic B. Assertion of this latch causes a service request in double (but not single) transition mode. In single transition mode **TDL_B** can be asserted on the second transition, but this assertion does not generate a service request. **TDL_B** is enabled only if **TDL_A** is asserted to detect an ordered input single double transition. **IPAC_B** indicates the programmed edges of the second detected transition.	1 bit
TICKS	Angle Ticks Number in the Current Tooth	**TPR**	Field in engine register	Defines the number of angle ticks in the current physical tooth. It partitions the tooth period to the required number of angle ticks. The actual number of angle tickets in a tooth is (**TICKS** + 1).	10 bits
TPR	Tooth Program Register	--	Engine Register	A counter register that provides configuration for the angle counter circuit. Also can be read or written in ALU operations or used as general-purpose registers.	16 bits

Term	Stands for	In Register	Type	Description	Length
TPR10	TPR Register Bit 10	**TPR**	Field in engine register	Reserved bit; must always be written 0 by the user but holds the value written.	1 bit
TRR	Tick Rate Register	--	Engine register	A counter register that holds the exact period of the angle tick, which is given in units of **TCR_A** clocks. Also can be read or written in ALU operations or used as general-purpose registers.	24 bits
V	Overflow Flag	--	ALU Flag	Updated on addition (with or without carry) and absolute value operations. In signed operations, **V** indicates that the result of the arithmetic operation (addition or subtraction) cannot be represented by a word of the size of the operation. V is calculated using ALU adder output (i.e., it is not affected by 10-bit shift/rotate operations). Can also be used as branch condition.	1 bit
VALID1	Server 1 Valid Bits	**ETPURE DCR_A/B**	Field in engine register	Provides the status of the internal valid state of the IP interface to **TCR1**. It can also be set by the host to 1 to force data transmission from the IP server on the next time slot that selects it. When set by the host, this bit automatically cleared when data is transmitted.	1 bit
VALID2	Server 2 Valid Bits	**ETPURE DCR_A/B**	Field in engine register	See description for **VALID1**, which applies analogously here, with respect to **TCR2**.	1 bit
VIS	SCM Visibility Flag	**ETPUMC R**	Field in global register	Makes SCM visible to the STAC bus. Also, it is necessary to turn **VIS** on to set software breakpoints.	1 bit

Term	Stands for	In Register	Type	Description	Length
WR	Read/Write	**ETPUCDCR**	Field in global register	Indicates whether the coherent data transfer is to be a write (1), which data is transferred from the **PB** to the selected parameter RAM address, or a read (0) in which data is transferred from the selected parameter RAM address to the **PB**.	1 bit
Z	Zero Flag	--	ALU Flag	Indicates that the result written in the destination register is zero, regardless of the operation performed. **Z** is operation-size dependent. Can also be used as branch condition.	1 bit
ZRO	Zero	--	Field in instruction	Indicates whether data written in to SPRAM or **P**/**DIOB** (a SPRAM read) will be 0x0.	1 bit

APPENDIX I   *General Glossary*

Term	Abbreviation	Description
Absolute Addressing Mode	--	Specifying an address in SPRAM with an actual value.
Addition	ADD	Selected by ALUOP or ALUOPI microinstruction fields when these fields are present in the microinstruction being executed. ADD is the default ALU operation when neither ALUOP or ALUOPI field is present. Result can optionally be shifted or rotated right by 1 bit (selected by SHF, ALUOP or ALUOPI fields). N and Z on shift are updated according to the result after shift. V with Post-ALU Shifter is updated according to the ADD operation; the Post-ALU Shifter does not affect the value of V.
Addition with Carry	ADC	Selected by the ALUOP microinstruction field. CIN field is ignored when ADC is selected. The ALU flags behave exactly the same way for ADC as for ADD without shift/rotate.
A-Destination	AD	A destination for ALU/MDU operations.
ALU_Cout	ALU Carry Out	Serves as the carry out for 24-bit operations.
ALU_OUT	ALU Output	Output result of arithmetic logic unit.
Angle Tick	--	A tooth period is partitioned into a programmable number of angle ticks.
Angle Tick Generator	--	Responsible for generating a programmed number of angle ticks in the tooth period (i.e., updated angle tick counter). It generates the ticks in an average rate, which ensures completion of the correct number of angle counts in the estimated period of the tooth, since the count of one tooth in angle ticks is independent on engine RPM.

Term	Abbreviation	Description
Arithmetic/Logic Unit	ALU	With the Post-ALU Shifter, performs basic arithmetic and logical operations within a microengine. The ALU's output goes directly to the Post-ALU Shifter, so it is possible, for example, to add and shift using only one microinstruction. In some microinstruction formats, it is not possible to specify the operation executed by the ALU; in these cases the ALU will always perform an addition operation. In formats that have the ALUOP field, all of the possible operations can be performed. These3 operations include add/subtract using C (carry) flag as ALU's carry-in, bitwise AND/OR/NOT/XOR, and shift/rotate of 2, 4, 8, and 16 bits. Subtraction, inversion, increment, and decrement can be performed by combinations of source inversion and setting ALU's carry-in to 1. The ALU always performs 24-bit operations on its inputs, called A-source and B-source, and outputs a 24-bit result. 8- and 16-bit inputs are zero-padded to 24 bits. Likewise, 24-bit ALU output is always truncated to the destination register size.
A-Source	AS	A source for ALU/MDU operations.
B-Source	BS	A source for ALU/MDU operations.
Bus Interface Unit	BIU	Allows the host to access eTPU registers and SPRAM.
Channel Base	CHAN_BASE	Represents a parameter address (**CPBS***2) and can be used as A-source using **T4ABS**=1010 when **T4ABS** selects a source from the second register set. In channel-relative address mode, represents the selected channel's base SPRAM address in channel-relative address mode.
Channel Modes		Various modes of operation combining Match1 and Match2 and tradition detection events that set MRL1/2 and TDL1/2. The order in which events occur, combined with the channel mode (PDCM), establish which of the following event detections are inhibited or enabled, as well as the actions taken: time base capture, flag setting (MRL1/2, TDL1/2), match disabling (MRLE1/2), output signal transition, and service request.
Channel-Relative Addressing Mode	--	Specifying an address in SPRAM based on a channel's base address offset by some value.
Coherent Dual-Parameter Controller	CDC	Used to ensure coherent access to eTPU data shared by both engines and the host CPU. Limited to two parameters only but has lower latency than transfer service thread or software semaphore mechanisms and wastes no microengine resources. During CDC operation, the host may suffer 4 to 11 system clock wait states while the microengine(s) may suffer up to 2 microcycle wait states. CDC may also suffer up to 3 system clock wait states from SPRAM arbiter, so that it does not break atomic back-to-back accesses from the microengine(s).

Term	Abbreviation	Description
Coherent Parameter Collision Rate	CPCR	The estimated percentage of SPRAM accesses in the system that will result in an engine stall due to coherent transfer multiplied with the average number of system clocks the engine is stalled for each transfer.
Communication Collision Rate	CCR	The estimated percentage of engine-to-engine coherent multiple parameter coherent communication multiplied with the average number of system clocks the engine is stalled for each such transfer.
Counter Control	--	Counter control is a hardware mode used by the eTPU angle counter. The angle counter can be in one of three states: normal, halt, and high-rate.
Cyclical Redundancy Check	CRC	Used as a signature calculator check to ensure data integrity of shared code memory.
Debug Interface	--	Used for eTPU debug and development.
Direct Memory Access Controller	DMA	eTPU channels assigned DMA channels can request a DMA transfer operation instead of interrupting the host CPU.
Enhanced Channel Filter	ECF	Digital input filter used to qualify the input signal on the channel.
Enhanced Digital Filter	EDF	Eliminates passing of signal transitions caused by noise. Its purpose is to eliminate false transition service requests caused by noise pulses, which are shorter than a programmed width. See CDFC.
enhanced Modular I/O Timer System	EMIOS	Some MPC5500 family derivatives have multiple timers: one or two eTPUs and a third timer system called eMIOS.
Enhanced Time Processor Unit	eTPU	A co-processor for the MPC5554 microcontroller. The eTPU contains two engines, each of which in turn contains 32 channels, each of which in turn contains two Action Logics, two match registers, two capture registers, one transition register, one input signal, and one output signal.
Entry Point	--	An address that points to the SCM of the first instruction of a thread. It also contains PP and ME.
Entry Table	--	A listing, located in the SCM, of each entry point for all channels in the eTPU. With 32 entry points per channel, 64 channels, and an entry point size of 2 bytes, the entry table will occupies 4096 bytes.

Term	Abbreviation	Description
ETPU Angle Counter	EAC	A piece of hardware that follows the flywheel angle, based on the tooth rate and, working in combination with the TCRCLK signal and the TCR2 counter, generated angle information. The EAC helps to implement a digital angle PLL. The EAC supports deceleration, acceleration, lost tooth, and missing tooth scenarios. In case of a missing tooth, the EAC can be configured to insert a dummy tooth or to simply measure a longer tooth.
Event	--	In eTPU processing, an event is an occurrence that produces a request for service. There are three types of events: a host service request, a match or transition, and a link service request.
Event Register Set	ER1/2	Each channel contains two identical event register sets, ER1 and ER2, corresponding to the two actions modes supported. ER1 and ER2 and associated with the first and second events in double action modes, always in that order for transition detections, but not necessarily for match recognitions. The order of match events associated with ER1 and ER2 depends on the programmed channel mode, the Match2 and Match2 values, and the time bases selected by TB1 and TBS2. ER1 contains: • Match1 • Capture1 • TBS1 • MRL1 • MRLE1 • TDL2 ER2 contains the analogous registers.
Execution Unit	EU	The eTPU microengine.
Field	--	One or more bits of a microinstructions, with a particular meaning.
Forced Microinstruction Execution	--	When the microengine is in halt state, it can run forced microinstructions through NDEDI. MDU stat commands and the microinstruction field END are ignored. FLS works, and except for branches, returns, and dispatches, the PC does not change. Previous pre-fetched instruction in the pipeline is bypassed but not discarded.

Term	Abbreviation	Description
Function	--	Or: *eTPU function*. A software entity consisting of a set of microengine routines that attend to eTPU service requests. A function, when assigned to a channel, defines the behavior for that channel. A function may be assigned to several channels, but only one function may be assigned to a given channel at a time. A function is made up of threads.
Halt	HALT	A microinstruction format that implements a software breakpoint. Is valid only if the debug mode is enabled at the debug interface; otherwise HALT executes as a NOP.
Halt Mode	--	Indicates, in angle mode, deceleration. During halt mode, the EAC holds the Angle Tick Counter at the end of the tooth with a "hold" command, waiting for the physical tooth to arrive. When the physical tooth is detected, the EAC switches back to Normal Mode and releases the Angle Tick Counter to count the angle ticks of the new tooth. At that point the Angle Tick Counter wraps to 09 and the tooth counter is incremented.
Hardware Breakpoint	--	Hardware breakpoints halt the microengine on specific conditions.
Hardware Watch-point	--	A watchpoint is similar to a breakpoint. However, when a watchpoint is reached, eTPU code continues execution.
High-Rate Mode	--	Indicates, in angle mode, acceleration. During high-rate mode, the tick is updated at the rate of system clock/8 until the system is set back to normal mode, at which point the new TRR value is used.
Host	--	The CPU.
Host Interface	--	Allows the hose CPU to control the operation of the eTPU.
Indirect Addressing Mode	--	Specifying an address in SPRAM based on the value in DIOB.

Term	Abbreviation	Description
MAC and Divide Unit	MDU	Autonomous resource in the microengine that performs multiply, multiply-accumulate (MAC), and divide operation length; signed and unsigned multiplication, MAC, and fraction multiplication; and unsigned divide operations. The MDU uses A-Source and B-Source as sources. As with the microengine, the operation performed is selected by the microinstruction fields ALUOP and ALUOPI. The MDU works in parallel with the microengine, though when an END command is issued, any operation in executing in the MDU terminates immediately and is left incomplete. Results of this MDU operation are always placed in the MACH and MACL registers (the register selected by the eTPU code is not written). MDU operations don't update C, N, V, or Z flags but instead update flags MC, MN, MV, MZ, and MB! CIN and BINV do, however, affect MDU operation.
Microcycle	--	Two system clocks.
Microengine	--	A RISC CPU within an eTPU engine. An eTPU has two engines and therefore two microengines.
Microengine Stall	--	Occurs when microengine is attending request from NDEDI and there is a temporary lack of resources. During a stall the microengine stops execution but all the other engine logic continues (time bases, angle logic, channel logic, input samples and filters. Unlike halt, stall does not enable any of the debug features, and it does not break and atomic microengine access.
Microinstruction	--	A 32-bit piece of code. A microinstruction can execute up to three microoperations in parallel. Microinstructions are grouped into formats.
Microinstruction Format	--	Each microinstruction format is defined by a set of microinstruction fields, which determine the operations that may be performed in that format.
Microoperation	--	There are four types of microoperations: ALU/MDU, SPRAM, channel configuration and control, and flow control.
Microprocessor	--	The EU within a microengine. An eTPU has two microprocessors, one for each of its microengines.
Multiple Input Signature Calculator	MISC	An SCM test feature accessible through registers ETPUMCR and ETPUMISCCMPR. Sequentially reads all SCM positions and calculates, in parallel, a 32-bit signature from a 32-input CRC signature calculator. Allows SCM test on the fly with no impact on eTPU functionality or performance.

Term	Abbreviation	Description
Nexus Debug Interface	NDEDI	A Nexus interface that provides access to various debug features.
No Operation	NOP	A microinstruction format that is used to perform no operation for a microcycle.
Normal Mode	--	Indicates, in angle mode, constant flywheel speed. In this mode, the Counter Control logic receives the angle ticks from the Angle Tick Generator in an average rate determined by TRR. When the Angel Counter in TCR2 reaches a multiple of the value stored in TPR field TICKS, the hardware detects the end of the estimated toot period and advances to the next estimated tooth. If the physical tooth and the estimated tooth arrive at the same time the EAC stays in Normal mode and the angle counter is incremented. If the physical tooth and the estimated tooth do not arrive at the same time, the EAC switches, appropriately to High-Rate Mode (acceleration) or Halt Mode (deceleration).
Output Flip-Flop	Output FF	Channel output signal is latched into the flip-flop.
Parameter Buffer	PB	A temporary storage location in SPRAM used for moving parameters coherently between the host and the eTPU.
Parameter Signal Extension	PSE	Allows the hose to access the SPRAM space mirrored in other areas; allows for data with fewer than 32 bits to be accessed as 32-bit sign-extended data without using the host's bandwidth to extend the data.
Permanent Parameter Area	PPA	SPRAM area from which channel parameters are normally accessed by function eTPU code. Related to TPA.
Phase-Locked Loop	PLL	eTPU angle counter is implemented as a phased-locked loop to adjust angle tick duration.
Post-ALU Shifter	--	With the ALU, performs basic arithmetic and logical operations within a microengine.
Priority	--	A level (high, middle, or low) assigned by eTPU code to each channel that assists the scheduler in choosing the next channel to be serviced.
Priority Inversion	--	The situation where a lower-priority channel is serviced before a higher-priority channel. This would occur when no channel is requesting service during a lower-priority time slot and then two channels (say of high and low priority) request service simultaneously, in which case the low-priority channel will be serviced before the high-priority channel. The eTPU avoids priority inversion by resetting any idle low- or medium-priority time slot to a time slot one (i.e., a high-priority time slot).

Term	Abbreviation	Description
Priority Passing	--	The mechanism by which the scheduler chooses another priority from which to obtain the next thread to be processed, when no channel of the priority associated with the current TST is requesting service. The order of passing always gives priority to the higher of the remaining requesting priority levels. Priority passing is implemented in hardware and so does not contribute to WCL.
RAM Collision Rate	RCR	The estimated percentage of SPRAM accesses in the system that will result in a microengine stall.
Reduced Instruction Set Computer	RISC	There are two basic engine architectures: reduced instruction set computing (RISC) and a complex instruction set computing (CISC). The eTPU is a RISC-like architecture.
Scheduler	--	Determines the order in which channels are serviced based on channel number and assigned priority. eTPU code then determines the next thread to be executed, based on the type of even that generated the service request, the function assigned to the target channel, the target channel pin state, and the state of the channel logic.
Semaphore	--	There are two types of semaphores: software and hardware. The former is a mailbox mechanism that is used to ensure coherent access to eTPU data shared by both engines and the host CPU. The latter is used for sharing parameters specifically between the engines. The eTPU has four semaphores. When an engine attempts to lock one semaphore (even if unsuccessfully), any other semaphores locked by that engine will be unlocked. An eTPU code END command, or the engine being idle, automatically releases any semaphores locked by that engine.
Service Request	--	A request made by an eTPU channel to the microengine to be serviced in response to a match, transition, link request, or host service request.
Shared Bus Interface Unit	Shared BIU	Allows the host to access eTPU registers and SPRAM.
Shared Code Memory	SCM	Holds the code to be executed by the eTPU's two engines. 64 Kbytes
Shared Parameter Random Access Memory	SPRAM	Holds application parameters and work data. It is accessed by host and both engines. 8Kbytes for each engine; each channel can have access to at least 256 32-bit wide parameters.
Single-Step Execution	--	When the microengine is in the halt state, it can run the next microinstruction in the normal program flow and get back to halt state.

Term	Abbreviation	Description
Software Breakpoint	--	To allow for debugging, the HALT microinstruction is used by the eTPU as a software breakpoint.
SPRAM Arbitration	--	Used to ensure coherent access to eTPU data shared by both engines and the host CPU.
SPRAM Parameter Sign Extension Mirror	SPRAM PSE Mirror	A mirrored location in SPRAM holding all data, sign extended.
STAC Interface	STAC	The shared timer and counter (STAC) bus is a time base that can be shared by all timers in the microcontroller system. For example, one eTPU engine may drive the STAC bus while the other timers, if applicable, can use it as their time base.
State	--	See *Thread*.
Thread	--	A sequence of microinstructions executed as a group, within a function, during a time slot. Typically a thread consists of the code necessary to calculate the next phase of waveform to be input to, or output from, a given channel. Once a thread begins, its execution cannot be interrupted by host or channel events.
Tick Prescaler	--	A value programmed in the tooth rate register (TRR) to select the angle tick resolution when in angle mode.
Time Slot	--	The period of time during which a thread is executed. The length of the time slot varies with the length of the thread.
Time Slot Latency	--	The amount of time between a service request and the beginning of service on that channel. It is affected by the number of active channels, the number of channels on a priority level, the number of available time slots on a priority level, the number of microcycles required to execute a thread of a function, the number of parameter RAM accesses during execution of a thread, and the system clock frequency. Also see WCL.
Time Slot Transition	TST	The period of time (minimally 6 system clocks) between two time slots, during which various pieces of information about the channel to be serviced (such as channel-specific registers, flags, and parameter base address) are loaded into global registers.

Term	Abbreviation	Description
Transfer Parameter Area	TPA	SPRAM area directly accessed by the host for reads and writes. Related to PPA.
Worst-Case Latency	WCL	The longest amount of time that can elapse between the execution of any two (non-initialization) threads on a channel; it includes the time to execute any intervening threads for other channels and any other delays. These delays include the clearing of SGLs (at 4 clocks per), the RCR (at 2 clocks per), the CPCR, and the CCR but not priority passing.

Index

Symbols

"C" programming language vi, vii, 5, 16, 46, 68, 204, 219–230

A

A, B, C, and D registers **106**, 303, 304, 305, 309
ABDE microinstruction field 303, 304, **305–306**
ABSE microinstruction field 302, 303, 304, **305–306**
Absolute addressing mode **109**
A-bus
    destination (AD) 299, 304, 305
    source (AS) 108, 299, 305
Action units **25**, 34
    dual *See eTPU dual-action hardware*
AID 109, 110
ALU/MDU
    conditional operations 307
    instruction fields **299–308**
ALUOP 112
ALUOP microinstruction field 299, **299–301**, 306
ALUOPI microinstruction field 299, **301–302**, 305
AM 99
Angle

clock 5
mode 9, 92–93, **150–157**
mode, application example 159–172
Angle-based engine control applications 90
Arithmetic/logic unit (ALU) **104**, 106, **110–112**, 297
    condition code flags 111–112
AS/CE microinstruction field **307**
ASH WARE Inc. iv, vii, x, xi, 9, 12
Automatic code generation 5

B

B-bus
    source (BS) 108, 299
BCC microinstruction field **308–309**
BCF microinstruction field **308**
BF **113**
BINV microinstruction field 299, 300, 304, **306**
BPBASE **203–204**
Branch conditions **119–120**
Bus interface unit (BIU) 86
Byte Craft Limited iv, vii, x, xi, 9, 12

C

C flag 68, **111**, 119
Calculating engine angular position 150
CAM 161, 162
    signal 150
Capture **55**, 129
    event 18, 29
    events 141
        overwriting 129
    registers 7, 8, **18**, 19, 21, 23, 24, 25, 31, 39, 53, 67, 106, 141, 191
CDFC **87**
CFS 65, 67, **95**, 95, 100, 177
CHAN 66, 67, **108**, 114, 119, 120, 191, 299, 303, 304, 308
CHAN_BASE **303**
Channel
    assigning priority to 100
    assigning time function to 95, 100
    conditions 45, 46, 47, 67, 75, 177, 180, 182
    configuration 83, **94–96**
        example 100
    configuration and control 114–119, 297
    context 65–68
    data transfer request status 97
    disabling 74–75, 94

N

N flag 68, **111**, 119, 309
NOP instruction 221, **310**

O

ODIS **95**
OPAC 14, 24, 28, 30, 55, 68, 116, 128, 131, 139
OPAC microinstruction fields **116**
OPOL **95**
OPS **98**
Output
  events 9
  pin 7, 8, 11, 20, 25, 66
  pin edge generation 27
  pin, state 67, 98

P

P 222
P register **105**, 108, 119, 120, 176, 303, 304, 305, 309
Parameter buffer (PB) 204
Parameter signed extended (PSE) 109
Parameter zero 109
PDCM 55, 55–56, 117, **128–131**, 139
PDCM microinstruction field **117**
PP **176**, 222
PRAM **203**, 204
Priority passing **185**, 187, 188, 190
Priority schemes 9, 187, 190
  primary **184**
  secondary **184**
Program counter (PC) 107, 119, 309
PSC 28
PSC microinstruction field **116**
PSCS 28, 128
PSCS microinstruction field **116**
PSS 119, 120, 309
PSTI 16, 120
PSTO 120
PWIDTH 204

R

R/D microinstruction field **309**, 310

RAM collision rate (RCR) **192**
RAppID x, xi
RAR **107**, 119, 303, 305, 308, 310
Return from subroutine 309
Return/dispatch 309
RS232 protocol 95
RSIZ microinstruction field 108
RTN microinstruction field **309–310**
RW **108**

S

Scheduler 6, 9, 49, 74, **183–204**
  SRR and SGR latches 186–187
Scheduling example 187–189
SCMMISF **85**
SCMSIZE **84**, 85
Semaphores 192, **204**
  lock state 68
  releasing 308
Service requests 57, 75
  caused by four types of events 41, 183
  scheduling 183–189
Servicing
  non-preemption 9
SEXT microinstruction field **307–308**
SGR **186**, 186, 187, 188
Shared code memory (SCM) vi, 5, **7**, 43, 84, 85, 86, 87, 95, 99, 104, 107, 174, 176
  and entry table 43–44, 175
  visibility to host 99
Shared parameter RAM (SPRAM) vi, 4, 6, 7, 20, 86, 96, 99, 100, 104, 105, 106, 108, **108–110**, 191, 192, 202, 203, 204, 297
  addressing modes 109–110
  and collisions 191–194
  microoperations 108–110
  normal and mirrored 109
Shared time and counter (STAC) 7, 99
SHF 299
SHF microinstruction field 300, 306, **306–307**
SMLCK 120, 309

Software breakpoints 310
SR **106**, 303, 304, 305, 306
SRC microinstruction field **306**
SRI latch 117
SRR **186**, 186, 187, 188
SS 75
STAC bus 92, 147, 148, 157–159
STF **86**, 86
STOP 99
STS 204
Switch statement 48
System clock 90, 91, 147, 202
System clocks 190, 299

T

T2ABD microinstruction field 303, **304–305**, 305
T2D microinstruction field 299, **305**
T4ABS microinstruction field **302–303**, 305
T4BBS microinstruction field 302, **303–304**
TBS 129
TBS microinstruction field **115**
TCR1CTL **90**, 90, 91, 147
TCR1P 90, 148
TCR2CTL **90–91**, 148
TCRCF 91, **91**
TCRCLK 7, 90, 91, 99, 147, 148, 150, 163
TDL 13, 25, 28, 29, 31, 37, 49, 53, 55, **55**, 57, 58, 120, 128, 129, 146, 183, 309
  clearing 30
TDL microinstruction field **117**
Teeth
  missing 164
Threads 42, 45, 46, 57, 59, 61, 63, 66, 67, 74, **173–174**, 183
Tick generator 150
TICKS 151
Time bases 28, 34, 85, 86
  clocking options 147
  enabling 100
Time slot 74, **183**
  duration 183
  priority 74
  priority of 184–186, 187–189
Timer count register